AMERICAN DRAMA CRITICISM

AMERICAN DRAMA CRITICISM

*Interpretations, 1890-1965 inclusive, of American Drama
Since the First Play Produced in America*

Compiled by

HELEN H. PALMER
and
JANE ANNE DYSON,

Louisiana State University Library

THE SHOE STRING PRESS, INC.
Hamden, Connecticut
1967

Dedicated to
Our Husbands,
Arthur and Harold

INTRODUCTION

This bibliography of criticisms of American drama, since the first play was produced, is designed to furnish a quick source of interpretations published between 1890-1965 in books, periodicals and monographs. All playwrights who have made a significant contribution to American drama, or who have gained renown as an important force in American theater, are included. An effort has been made to be as inclusive as possible for all playwrights listed; however, plays about which interpretations could not be found have been omitted. Entries are not limited to those in English, but only few foreign references were located.

Representative American playwrights listed in: Twenty-five Best Plays of the Modern American Theatre: Early Series, Second Series, Third Series; Pulitzer prize plays; New York Theatre Critics Awards playwrights and others were included. Although an exhaustive search cannot be claimed, as thorough a search as possible was made for criticism listed in the following indexes: PMLA bibliographies; International Index; Essay and General Literature Index; Readers' Guide to Periodical Literature; as well as in books and periodicals not listed in indexes.

The quality of the articles was not considered; the primary criterion was that critical material relating to a certain play could be located in a particular book or article. However, source material per se has been omitted, as have explications of just a sentence or word.

The arrangement of the book is alphabetical by playwright with the plays alphabetized under the author's name. Dates of first production of each play have been included in most cases. Interpretations of known authorship in both books and scholarly journals are then alphabetized by author. A listing of further criticisms in periodicals, alphabetized by title, follows with as complete entries as possible, including volume number, page or pages, month, if needed, and year.

There is one index, which is arranged in continuous alphabetical order. In general, author's dates have been included in the index. The title entries are italicized. Cross references for pseudonyms and joint authors are included in the text material.

The authors hope that this bibliography will serve as a useful research tool for students of both high schools and colleges, as well as anyone interested in checking criticisms of particular plays. Every effort has been made to prevent errors and omissions. Nevertheless, some mistakes may have escaped detection—we hope the number will be small. Both the authors and the publisher will be grateful if omissions and such errors as appear are drawn to their attention. Corrections will be incorporated in future supplements.

Our thanks are extended at this time to our husbands for all their patience and help; to Mr. T. N. McMullan, Director, Louisiana State University Libraries, and to Mr. George G. Guidry, Jr., Associate Director, Louisiana State University Libraries, for their sympathetic cooperation. We also wish to acknowledge our indebtedness to Mr. William Robert Lacey, English Department, Louisiana State University, for furnishing us with a list of the plays studied in the drama courses taught in the English Department of Louisiana State University.

October 1966   Helen H. Palmer and Anne Jane Dyson

See p. 229,
    for information regarding "List of Books
        indexed ...."

GEORGE ABBOTT

"The Boys from Syracuse" (adapted from Shakespeare's Comedy of Errors), 1938

>   Catholic World, 148:474-6, Jan., 1939
>   Commonweal, 29:190, Dec. 9, 1938
>   Nation, 147:638, Dec. 10, 1938
>   New Republic, 97:173, Dec. 14, 1938
>   North American Review, 247 no. 1:159-60, March, 1939
>   Theatre Arts Monthly, 23:10-11, Jan., 1939

"Dancer", 1946

>   New Yorker, 22:40, June 15, 1946

"Ladies' Money", 1934

>   Catholic World, 140:343, Dec., 1934
>   Newsweek, 4:27, Nov. 10, 1934
>   Theatre Arts Monthly, 18:904, Dec., 1934

"Sweet River" (adapted from Uncle Tom's Cabin by H. B. Stowe), 1936

>   New Republic, 89:78, Nov. 18, 1936
>   Theatre Arts, 20:935, Dec., 1936

GEORGE ABBOTT AND LEON ABRAHAMS

"Heat Lightning", 1933

>   Catholic World, 138:219, Nov., 1933
>   Literary Digest, 116:18, Oct. 14, 1933
>   Nation, 137:390-1, Oct. 4, 1933

GEORGE ABBOTT AND PHILIP DUNNING

"Lilly Turner", 1932

>   Theatre Arts Monthly, 16:868, Nov., 1932

GEORGE ABBOTT AND ANN PRESTON BRIDGERS

"Coquette", 1927

> Saturday Review, 147:763, June 8, 1929
> Theatre Arts Anthology; a record and a prophecy, ed. by
>   Rosamond Gildes and others, Theatre Arts Books, 1950,
>   p. 606-09

GEORGE ABBOTT AND JOHN CECIL HOLM

"Three Men on a Horse", 1935

> Nathan, George Jean, Theatre Book of the Year, 1945-1946,
>   Knopf, p. 96-98
>
> Catholic World, 140:723-4, March, 1935
> Commonweal, 21:458, Feb. 15, 1935
> Literary Digest, 119:20, Feb. 9, 1935
> Mercure de France, 268:137-8, May 15, 1936
> Spectator, 156:343, Feb. 28, 1936

GEORGE ABBOTT AND GEORGE MARION, JR.

"Beat the Band", 1942

> Catholic World, 156:337, Dec., 1942
> Theatre Arts Monthly, 26:742, Dec., 1942

GEORGE ABBOTT AND BETTY SMITH

"Tree Grows in Brooklyn", 1951

> Nathan, George Jean, Theatre Book of the Year, 1950-51,
>   Knopf, p. 274-79

SEE ALSO

PHILIP DUNNING AND GEORGE ABBOTT

LEON ABRAHAMS

SEE

GEORGE ABBOTT AND LEON ABRAHAMS

ZOE AKINS

"Daddy's Gone A-Hunting", 1921

Drama, 12:82, Dec., 1921
Nation, 113:324-5, Sept. 21, 1921

"Declassee", 1919

Current Opinion, 68:187-93, Feb., 1920
New Republic, 22:95, March 17, 1920

"Furies", 1928

New Republic, 54:155-6, March 21, 1928
Outlook, 148:545, April 4, 1928

"Magical City", 1916

Current Opinion, 60:331, May, 1916

"Moonflower", 1924

Canfield, Mary Cass, Grotesques and other Reflections,
Harper, 1927, p. 204-13

Independent, 112:231-2, April 26, 1924

"Mrs. January and Mr. Ex", 1944

Nathan, George Jean, Theatre Book of the Year, 1943-44,
Knopf, 1943-1947, p. 271-74

Catholic World, 159:170, May, 1944
Commonweal, 40:14-15, April 21, 1944
New Republic, 110:532, April 17, 1944
New Yorker, 20:44, April 8, 1944
Newsweek, 23:92, April 10, 1944
Theatre Arts, 28:328, 333, June, 1944
Time, 43:44, April 10, 1944

"O Evening Star", 1936

>   Commonweal, 23:356, Jan. 24, 1936
>   Literary Digest, 121:19, Jan. 18, 1936
>   Pictorial Review, 37:50, April, 1936

"Old Maid" (dramatization of novel by E. Wharton), 1935

>   Catholic World, 140:602, Feb., 1935
>   Commonweal, 21:375, Jan. 25, 1935
>   New Republic, 82:162, Mar. 20, 1935
>   Theatre Arts Mo., 19:176, March, 1935

"Royal Fandango", 1923

>   Independent, 111:257, Nov. 24, 1923

"Thou Desperate Pilot", 1927

>   Woollcott, Alexander, Portable Woollcott, selected by
>   Joseph Hennessey, Viking, 1946, p. 436-38

EDWARD ALBEE

"American Dream", 1961

>   Goodman, Henry, "The New Dramatists: Edward Albee",
>   Drama Survey, 2:72-79, Spring, 1962
>
>   Hamilton, Kenneth, "Mr. Albee's Dream", Queen's Quarterly,
>   70:393-99, 1963
>   Harris, Wendell V., "Morality, Absurdity, and Albee",
>   Southwest Review, 49:249-56, 1964
>   Lewis, Allan, "The Fun and Games of Edward Albee",
>   Educational Theatre Journal, 16:29-39, 1964
>   Kostelanetz, Richard, ed., "The New American Arts", New
>   York, Horizon Press, 1965, p. 55
>
>   America, 108:891-2, June 22, 1963
>   Catholic World, 193:335-6, Aug., 1961
>   Christian Century, 78:275, March 1, 1961
>   Horizon, 3:117, July, 1961
>   Nation, 192:125-6, Feb. 11, 1961
>   New Republic, 144:30, March 27, 1961
>   New Statesman, 62:668, Nov. 3, 1961
>   New Yorker, 36:62, Feb. 4, 1961

Saturday Review, 44:54, Feb. 11, 1961
Theatre Arts, 45:68, March, 1961
Time, 77:53, Feb. 3, 1961

"Ballad of the Sad Cafe", 1963

> Lewis, Allan, "The Fun and Games of Edward Albee",
> Educational Theatre Journal, 16:29-39, 1964

> America, 110:26, Jan. 4, 1964
> Catholic World, 198:264, Jan., 1964
> Commonweal, 79:256, Nov. 22, 1963
> Hudson Review, 17:81-3, Spring, 1964
> Nation, 197:333-4, Nov. 23, 1963
> National Review, 16:34-5, Jan. 14, 1964
> New Republic, 149:28-9, Nov. 16, 1963
> New Yorker, 39:95, Nov. 9, 1963
> Newsweek, 62:76, Nov. 11, 1963
> Partisan Review, 31:97-8, Winter, 1964
> Saturday Review, 46:54, Nov. 16, 1963
> Time, 82:67, Nov. 8, 1963
> Vogue, 143:20, Jan. 1, 1964

"Death of Bessie Smith", 1960

> Daniel, Walter C., "Absurdity in 'The Death of Bessie
> Smith'", College Language Assocation Journal, 8:76-80,
> 1964
> Lewis, Allan, "The Fun and Games of Edward Albee",
> Educational Theatre Journal, 16:29-39, 1964

> Catholic World, 193:335, Aug., 1961
> Horizon, 3:116, July, 1961
> Nation, 192:242, March 18, 1961
> New Republic, 144:29-30, March 27, 1961
> New Statesman, 62:667, Nov. 3, 1961
> New Yorker, 37:114, March 11, 1961
> Theatre Arts, 45:56, May, 1961

"Tiny Alice", 1965

> Franzblau, A. N., "A Psychiatrist Looks at 'Tiny Alice'",
> Saturday Review, 48:39, Jan. 30, 1965

> America, 112:336-7, March 6, 1965
> Catholic World, 200:384, March, 1965
> Commonweal, 81:543, Jan. 22, 1965

Esquire, 63:58, April, 1965
Life, 58:14, Jan. 29, 1965
Nation, 200: 65, Jan. 18, 1965
New Republic, 152:33-4, Jan. 23, 1965
New Yorker, 40:84, Jan. 9, 1965
Newsweek, 65:75, Jan. 11, 1965
Reporter, 32:53-4, Jan. 28, 1965
Saturday Review, 48:40, Jan. 16, 1965
Saturday Review, 48:38-9, Jan. 30, 1965
Saturday Review, 48:43, Sept. 4, 1965
Time, 85:32, Jan. 8, 1965
Time, 85:68, Jan. 15, 1965
Vogue, 145:50, Feb. 15, 1965

"Who's Afraid of Virginia Woolf?", 1962

Downer, Alan S. , ed. , American Drama and its Critics,
    University Chicago Pr. , 1965, p. 241-44.
Finkelstein, Sidney, "Norman Mailer and Edward Albee",
    American Dialog, V. 2, #1, Feb. - March, 1965,
    p. 26-28
Hankiss, Elemer, "Who's Afraid of Edward Albee ",
    New Hungarian Quarterly, V, XV:168-174, 1964
Harris, Wendell V. , "Morality, Absurdity and Albee",
    Southwest Review, 49:249-56, 1964
Kerr, Walter, The Theatre in Spite of Itself, Simon and
    Schuster, 1963, p. 122-26.
Kostelanetz, Richard, ed. , The New American Arts,
    New York, Horizon Press, 1965, p. 55-60
Lewis, Allan, "The Fun and Games of Edward Albee",
    Educational Theatre Journal, 16:29-39, 1964
McDonald, Daniel, "Truth and Illusion in 'Who's Afraid of
    Virginia Woolf ", Renascence, 17:63-69, 1964
Nagel, Ivan, "Requiem fur die Seele: Uber Albees 'Wer
    hat Angst vor Virginia Woolf ' ", Neue Rundschau,
    74:646-51, 1963
Schein, Harry, "Vem är rädd för Virginia Woolf "
    Bonniers Litterara Magasin, 30:706-710, 1961
Stroman, Ben, "Edward Albee's 'Who's Afraid of Virginia
    Woolf?" DeVlaamse Gids, 48:342-44, 1964
Trilling, Diana, Claremont essays, Harcourt, 1964,
    p. 203-27

America, 107:1105-6, Nov. 17, 1962
Atlantic Monthly, 213:122, April, 1964
Catholic World, 196:263-4, Jan., 1963
Commentary, 35:296-30, April, 1963
Commentary, 36:272, Oct., 1963
Commonweal, 77:175-6, Nov. 9, 1962
Educational Theatre Journal, 15:77-80, March, 1963
Esquire, 60:69, Dec., 1963
Hudson Review, 15:571-3, Winter, 1962-63
Illustrated London News, 244:288, Feb. 22, 1964
Life, 53:107-8, Dec. 14, 1962
Nation, 195:273-4, Oct. 27, 1962
National Review, 14:35-6, Jan. 15, 1963
New Republic, 147:29-30, Nov. 3, 1962
New Yorker, 38:85, Oct. 20, 1962
Newsweek, 60:52, Oct. 29, 1962
Newsweek, 60:75, Nov. 5, 1962
New Statesman, 67:262, Feb. 14, 1964
Reporter, 28:48, April 25, 1963
Saturday Review, 45:29, Oct. 27, 1962
Spectator, 212:213-14, Feb. 14, 1964
Theatre Arts, 46:10, Nov., 1962
Time, 80:84, Oct. 26, 1962

"The Zoo Story", 1959

Kostelanetz, Richard, ed., The New American Arts,
    N.Y., Horizon Press, 1965, p. 52-55
Lewis, Allan, "The Fun and Games of Edward Albee",
    Educational Theatre Journal, 16:29-39, 1964
Lyons, C.R., "Two Projections of the Isolation of the
    Soul: Brecht's 'Im dickicht der staedte' and Albee's
    'The Zoo Story'" Drama Survey, 4:121-38, Summer, 1965
Zimbardo, Rose A., "Symbolism and Naturalism in Edward
    Albee's 'The Zoo Story'", Twentieth Century Literature,
    8:10-17, 1962

America, 108:891-2, June 22, 1963
Esquire, 55:48-50, April, 1961
Nation, 190:153, Feb. 13, 1960
New Republic, 142:21, Feb. 22, 1960
New Yorker, 35:75-6, Jan. 23, 1960
Saturday Review, 43:32, Feb. 6, 1960

MAXWELL ANDERSON

"Anne of the Thousand Days", 1948

Brown, John Mason, Still Seeing Things, McGraw, 1950,
  p. 207-13
Nathan, George Jean, Theatre Book of the Year, 1948-49,
  Knopf, p. 197-205

Catholic World, 168:321-2, Jan., 1949
Commonweal, 49:281, Dec. 24, 1948
Forum, 111:92-3, Feb., 1949
Life, 26:74-6, Jan. 17, 1949
Nation, 168:24-5, Jan. 1, 1949
New Republic, 119:29, Dec. 27, 1948
New York Times Mag., p. 40-1, Nov. 28, 1948
New Yorker, 24:48, Dec. 18, 1948
Newsweek, 32:72, Dec. 20, 1948
Saturday Review of Literature, 31:24-6, Dec. 25, 1948
Theatre Arts, 32:11-12, Oct., 1948
Theatre Arts, 33:52, March, 1949
Time, 52:60, Dec. 20, 1948

"Bad Seed" (dramatization of novel by W. March), 1954

America, 92:346, Dec. 25, 1954
Catholic World, 180:387-8, Feb., 1955
Commonweal, 61:358-9, Dec. 31, 1954
Illustrated London News, 226:794, April 30, 1955
Life, 38:53-54, Jan. 10, 1955
Nation, 179:556-7, Dec. 25, 1954
New Republic, 131:21, Dec. 27, 1954
Saturday Review, 38:26, April 30, 1955
Spectator, 194:502, April 22, 1955
Theatre Arts, 39:26, April, 1955
Theatre Arts, 39:33-4, Dec., 1955

"Barefoot in Athens", 1951

Brown, John Mason, As They Appear, McGraw, 1952,
  p. 199-206
Nathan, George Jean, Theatre in the Fifties, Knopf, 1953,
  p. 40-42

Catholic World, 174:226-7, Dec. 1951
Commonweal, 55:142-3, Nov. 16, 1951
Nation, 173:430-1, Nov. 17, 1951
New Yorker, 27:66, Nov. 10, 1951
Newsweek, 38:92, Nov. 12, 1951
Saturday Review of Literature, 34:26-8, Nov. 24, 1951
Saturday Review of Literature, 35:28, Feb. 23, 1952
Theatre Arts, 35:3, Dec., 1951
Theatre Arts, 36:81, Jan., 1952
Time, 58:60, Nov. 12, 1951

"Both Your Houses", 1933

Brown, John Mason, Two on the Aisle, Norton, 1933,
p. 208-11
Downer, Alan S., ed. American Drama and its Critics,
Univ. Chicago Pr., 1965, p. 164-65

Catholic World, 137:80-1, April 1933
Commonweal, 17:582, March 22, 1933
Literary Digest, 115:15, March 25, 1933
Nation, 136:355, March 29, 1933
New Republic, 74:188, March 29, 1933
Newsweek, 1:29, March 18, 1933
Theatre Arts Mo., 17:333-40, May, 1933

"Candle in the Wind", 1941

Catholic World, 154:334-5, Dec., 1941
Commonweal, 35:71, Nov. 7, 1941
Current History n.s., 1:379-80, Dec., 1941
Nation, 153:462, Nov. 10, 1941
New Republic, 104:621, Nov. 10, 1941
New Yorker, 17:40, Nov. 1, 1941
Theatre Arts, 25:861-2, Dec., 1941
Theatre Arts, 26:80, Feb., 1942

"Elizabeth the Queen", 1930

Downer, Alan S., ed., American Drama and its Critics,
Univ. Chicago Pr., 1965, p. 151-54

Bookman, 72:628, Feb., 1931

Catholic World, 132:335, Dec., 1930
Collier's, 87:10, Feb. 7, 1931
Commonweal, 13:76, Nov. 19, 1930
Drama, 21:11-12, Dec., 1930
Literary Digest, 107:17-18, Nov. 22, 1930
Nation, 131:562, Nov. 19, 1930
New Republic, 65:17-19, Nov. 19, 1930
Theatre Magazine, 53:66, Jan., 1931
Woman's Journal n. s., 15:15, Dec., 1930

"Eve of St. Mark", 1942

Nathan, George Jean, Theatre Book of the Year, 1942-1943,
    Knopf, p. 89-93

Catholic World, 156:214-15, Nov., 1942
Commonweal, 37:15, Oct. 23, 1942
Current History n. s., 3:264-5, Nov., 1942
Independent Woman, 21:368, Dec., 1942
Life, 13:51-2, Oct. 19, 1942
New Republic, 107:546, Oct. 26, 1942
New Yorker, 18:36, Oct. 17, 1942
Newsweek, 20:76-8, Oct. 19, 1942
Scholastic, 41:20, Nov. 9, 1942
Sociology and Social Research, 27:250, Jan., 1943
Theatre Arts, 26:735-7, Dec., 1942
Time, 40:60, Oct. 19, 1942

"Golden Six", 1958

Commonweal, 69:175-6, Nov. 14, 1958
New Yorker, 34:91-3, Nov. 8, 1958
Theatre Arts, 43:66, Jan., 1959
Time, 72:50, Nov. 3, 1958

"Gypsy", 1929

Downer, Alan S., ed., American Drama and its Critics,
    Univ. Chicago Pr., 1965, p. 151

Catholic World, 128:724-5, March, 1929
Commonweal, 9:406, Feb. 6, 1929
Nation, 128:168, Feb. 6, 1929
Outlook, 151:171, Jan. 30, 1929

"High Tor", 1936

> Young, Stark, <u>Immortal Shadows, a Book of Dramatic Criticism</u>, Scribner, 1948, p. 185-88
>
> <u>Catholic World</u>, 144:728-9, March, 1937
> <u>Commonweal</u>, 25:388, Jan. 29, 1937
> <u>Commonweal</u>, 26:132, May 28, 1937
> <u>Forum</u>, 97:353, June, 1937
> <u>Literary Digest</u>, 123:21, Jan. 23, 1937
> <u>Nation</u>, 144:136, Jan. 30, 1937
> <u>New Republic</u>, 84:411-12, Feb. 3, 1937
> <u>New Republic</u>, 90:295, April 14, 1937
> <u>Newsweek</u>, 9:32, Jan. 16, 1937
> <u>Scribner's Magazine</u>, 101:65-6, June, 1937
> <u>Theatre Arts Monthly</u>, 21:175-9, March, 1937
> <u>Time</u>, 29:47, Jan. 18, 1937

"Joan of Larraine", 1946

> Nathan, George Jean, <u>Theatre Book of the Year, 1946-1947</u>, Knopf, p. 189-96
>
> <u>Catholic World</u>, 164:357-8, Jan., 1947
> <u>Commonweal</u>, 45:200, Dec. 6, 1946
> <u>Life</u>, 21:51-2, Dec. 2, 1946
> <u>Nation</u>, 163:671, Dec. 7, 1946
> <u>New Republic</u>, 115:726, Dec. 2, 1946
> <u>New York Times Mag.</u>, p. 22-3, Nov. 10, 1946
> <u>New Yorker</u>, 22:58, Nov. 30, 1946
> <u>Newsweek</u>, 28:94, Dec. 2, 1946
> <u>Saturday Review of Literature</u>, 29:24-5, Dec. 21, 1946
> <u>Theatre Arts Monthly</u>, 31:12-13, Jan., 1947
> <u>Time</u>, 48:54, Dec. 2, 1946

"Journey to Jerusalem", 1940

> <u>American Mercury</u>, 51:481-3, Dec., 1940
> <u>Arts & Decoration</u>, 52:40, Nov., 1940
> <u>Catholic World</u>, 152:216-17, Nov., 1940
> <u>Commonweal</u>, 32:530, Oct. 18, 1940
> <u>Nation</u>, 151:373, Oct. 19, 1940
> <u>New Republic</u>, 103:557, Oct. 21, 1940
> <u>New Yorker</u>, 16:46, Oct. 12, 1940
> <u>Theatre Arts</u>, 24:850, Dec., 1940
> <u>Time</u>, 36:62, Oct. 14, 1940

"Key Largo", 1939

Brown, John Mason, Broadway in Review, Norton, 1940,
   p. 67-71
Downer, Alan S., ed., American Drama and its Critics,
   Univ. Chicago Pr., 1965, p. 162-64

Catholic World, 150:467-8, Jan., 1940
Commonweal, 31:163, Dec. 8, 1939
Forum, 103:32, Jan., 1940
Nation, 149:656, Dec. 9, 1939
New Republic, 101:230, Dec. 13, 1939
New Statesman and Nation, 23:123, Feb. 21, 1942
Newsweek, 14:34, Dec. 11, 1939
Theatre Arts Monthly, 24:81-3, Feb., 1940
Time, 34:49, Dec. 11, 1939

"Knickerbocker Holiday", 1938

Catholic World, 148:343-4, Dec., 1938
Commonweal, 29:48, Nov. 4, 1938
Nation, 147:488-9, Nov. 5, 1938
New Republic, 97:18, Nov. 9, 1938
North American Review, 246 no. 2:374-6, Dec., 1938
Theatre Arts Monthly, 22:862, Dec., 1938
Time, 32:55, Oct. 31, 1938

"Mary of Scotland", 1933

Moses, Montrose Jonas and Brown, John Mason, eds.,
   American Theatre as seen by its Critics, 1752-1934,
   Norton, 1934, p. 315-18

Canadian Forum, 15:275, April, 1935
Catholic World, 138:473-5, Jan., 1934
Commonweal, 19:189-90, Dec. 15, 1933
Nation, 137:688, Dec. 13, 1933
New Republic, 77:130-1, Dec. 13, 1933
Newsweek, 2:32, Dec. 9, 1933
Review of Reviews, 89:39, Feb., 1934
Theatre Arts Monthly, 18:14-18, Jan., 1934

"Masque of Kings", 1936

Downer, Alan S., ed., American Drama and its Critics,
   Univ. Chicago Pr., 1965, p. 169-70

Catholic World, 144:731-2, March, 1937
Commonweal, 25:502, Feb. 26, 1937
Commonweal, 26:216, June 18, 1937
Literary Digest, 123:24, Feb. 20, 1937
Nation, 144:221-2, Feb. 20, 1937
New Republic, 90:111-12, March 3, 1937
Newsweek, 9:24, Feb. 20, 1937
Saturday Review of Literature, 15:23, March 13, 1937
Theatre Arts Monthly, 21:260-1, April, 1937
Time, 29:39, Feb. 15, 1937

"Night Over Taos", 1932

Avery, L. G., "Conclusion of 'Night Over Taos' ",
American Literature, 37:318-21, Nov., 1965

Arts & Decoration, 37:56, May, 1932
Catholic World, 135:76, April, 1932
New Republic, 70:181-2
Theatre Arts Monthly, 16:360-2, May, 1932

"Outside Looking In", 1925

Taylor, C. B. "Outside Looking In: criticism", World
Tomorrow, 8:310, Oct., 1925

"Saturday's Children", 1927

London Mercury, 17:91-3, Nov., 1927
Nation, 124:194, Feb. 16, 1927
New Republic, 49:357, Feb. 16, 1927

"Star Wagon", 1937

McCarthy, Mary Therese, Sights and Spectacles, 1937-1956,
Farrar, Straus, 1956, p. 3-8.

Catholic World, 146:215-16, Nov., 1937
Commonweal, 26:580, Oct. 15, 1937
Independent Woman, 16:351, Nov., 1937
Nation, 145:411, Oct. 16, 1937
New Republic, 92:302, Oct. 20, 1937
Newsweek, 10:27, Oct. 11, 1937
Scribner's Magazine, 102:53-4, Dec., 1937
Theatre Arts Monthly, 21:838, Nov., 1937
Time, 30:52-3, Oct. 11, 1937

"Storm Operation", 1944

> Nathan, George Jean, Theatre Book of the Year, 1943-1944, Knopf, p. 207-12.
>
> Catholic World, 158:489-90, Feb. , 1944
> Commonweal, 39:398-9, Feb. 4, 1944
> Nation, 158:105-7, Jan. 22, 1944
> New Republic, 110:148, Jan. 31, 1944
> New York Times Mag. , p. 10-11, Dec. 26, 1943
> New Yorker, 19:34, Jan. 22, 1944
> Theatre Arts, 28:133-6, March, 1944

"Truckline Cafe", 1946

> Nathan, George Jean, Theatre Book of the Year, 1945-1946, Knopf, p. 319-24
>
> Commonweal, 43:553-4, March 15, 1946
> Forum, 105:753-5, April, 1946
> Nation, 162:324, March 16, 1946
> New Republic, 114:349, March 11, 1946
> New Yorker, 22:43-4, March 9, 1946
> Newsweek, 27:82, March 11, 1946
> Theatre Arts Monthly, 30:260, May, 1946
> Time, 47:86, March 11, 1946

"Valley Forge", 1934

> Young, Stark, Immortal Shadows, a Book of Dramatic Criticism, Scribner, 1948, p. 165-68
>
> Catholic World, 140:596-7, Feb. , 1935
> Commonweal, 21:264, Dec. 28, 1934
> Golden Book, 21:30a, Feb. , 1935
> Literary Digest, 118:22, Dec. 22, 1934
> Nation, 139:750, Dec. 26, 1934
> New Republic, 81:196, Dec. 26, 1934
> Newsweek, 4:24, Dec. 22, 1934
> Theatre Arts Monthly, 19:94-6, Feb. , 1935

"Wingless Victory", 1936

> Downer, Alan S. , ed. , American Drama and its Critics, Univ. Chicago Pr. , 1965, p. 164.
>
> Young, Stark, Immortal Shadows, a Book of Dramatic Criticism, Scribner, 1948, p. 185-88

Catholic World, 144:598-9, Feb., 1937
Commonweal, 25:304, Jan. 8, 1937
Forum, 97:354, June, 1937
Nation, 144:53-4, Jan. 9, 1937
New Republic, 89:411, Feb. 3, 1937
Newsweek, 9:22, Jan. 2, 1937
Scholastic, 30:19, Feb. 13, 1937
Scribner's Magazine, 101:69-70, March, 1937
Theatre Arts Monthly, 21:89-95, Feb., 1937
Time, 29:29, Jan. 4, 1937
New Statesman and Nation, 26:184, Sept. 18, 1943
Spectator, 171:263, Sept., 17, 1943

"Winterset", 1935

Abernethy, Francis E., " 'Winterset': A Modern Revenge
Tragedy, "Modern Drama, 7:185-189, 1964

Brown, John Mason, Dramatis Personae; a Retrospective
Show, Viking, 1963, p. 73-76

Davenport, William H., "Anderson's 'Winterset' ",
Explicator, X, p. 41, 1952

Downer, Alan S., ed., American Drama and its Critics,
Univ. Chicago Pr., 1965, p. 156-157

Dusenbury, Winifred Loesch, The theme of Loneliness
in Modern American Drama, Univ. Florida Press, 1960,
p. 113-134

O'Hara, Frank Hurburt, Today in American drama, Univ.
Chicago Press, 1939, p. 1-52

Pearce, Howard D., "Job in Anderson's 'Winterset' ",
Modern Drama, 6:32-41, 1963

Roby, Robert C., "Two Worlds: Maxwell Anderson's
'Winterset' ", College English, 18:195-202, 1957

Theatre Arts Anthology, a Record and a Prophecy, ed. by
Rosamond Gilder and others, Theatre Arts Books, 1950,
p. 632-34.

Zabel, Morton Dauwen, ed., Literary Opinion in America,
Harper, 1951, p. 532-34

Zabel, Morton Dauwen, ed., Literary Opinion in America,
Harper, 1962, 2 vols., vol. 2:532-34

Catholic World, 142:211-12, Nov., 1935
Commonweal, 22:585, Oct. 11, 1935
Commonweal, 24:218, June 19, 1936
Forum, 95:345-6, June, 1936
Literary Digest, 120:20, Oct. 5, 1935
Nation, 141:420, Oct. 9, 1935
Nation, 142:484-5, April 15, 1936
New Republic, 84:274, 365, Oct. 16 and Nov. 6, 1935
New Republic, 85:257, Jan. 8, 1936
Newsweek, 6:32-3, Oct. 5, 1935
Saturday Review of Literature, 12:16, Oct. 12, 1935
Theatre Arts Monthly, 19:815-20, Nov., 1935
Theatre Arts Monthly, 20:465, June, 1936
Time, 26:38, Oct. 7, 1935

MAXWELL ANDERSON AND BRENDAN GILL

"Day the Money Stopped" (dramatization of the novel), 1956

New Yorker, 34:56, March 1, 1958
Time, 71:74, March 3, 1958

MAXWELL ANDERSON AND HAROLD HICKERSON

"Gods of the Lightning", 1928

Catholic World, 128:338-9, Dec., 1928
Dial, 86:80-2, Jan., 1929
Nation, 127:528, 593, Nov. 14 and Dec. 5, 1928
New Republic, 56:326-7, Nov. 7, 1928
Theatre Arts Monthly, 13:11-13, Jan., 1929

MAXWELL ANDERSON AND LAURENCE STALLINGS

"First Flight", 1925

Nation, 121:390-1, Oct. 7, 1925

"What Price Glory?", 1924

Block, Anita Cahn, Changing World in Plays and Theatre,
Little, 1939, p. 302-51

Brown, John Mason, Still Seeing Things, McGraw, 1950,
 p. 227-32

Downer, Alan S., ed., American Drama and its Critics,
 Univ. Chicago Pr., 1965, p. 149-150

Knight, G. C., ed., Readings from the American Mercury,
 Knopf, 1926, p. 138-42

Krutch, Joseph Wood, American Drama since 1918; an
 Informal History, Random House, 1939, p. 26-72

Littell, Robert, Read America First, Harcourt, 1926,
 p. 233-37

Moses, Montrose Jonas and Brown, John Mason, eds.,
 American Theatre as seen by its Critics, 1752-1934,
 Norton, 1934, p. 245-47

Nathan, George Jean, Theatre Book of the Year, 1949-1950,
 Knopf, 1950, p. 72-76

Woollcott, Alexander, Portable Woollcott, Viking, 1946,
 p. 441-43

American Review, 3:220, March, 1925
Canadian Monthly, 64:74, April, 1925
Current Opinion, 77:617-18, Nov., 1924
Drama, 15:4, Oct., 1924
Independent, 113:403, Nov. 15, 1924
Literary Digest, 83:30-1, Oct. 4, 1924; 84:30-1, Jan. 10,
 1925
Living Age, 324:68, Jan. 3, 1925
New Republic, 40:160-1, Oct. 15, 1924
Outlook, 138:439-41, Nov. 19, 1924
Saturday Review of Literature, 28:18, Dec. 8, 1945
Woman Citizen, n.s., 9:11, Oct. 18, 1924
World Tomorrow, 7:309-10, Oct., 1924

MAXWELL ANDERSON AND KURT WEILL

"Lost in the Stars"

Brown, John Mason, Still Seeing Things, McGraw, 1950,
 p. 227-32

Nathan, George J., Theatre Book of the Year, 1949-1950,
 Knopf, p. 72-76

ROBERT WOODRUFF ANDERSON

"All Summer Long" (dramatization of Wreath and a Curse by
D. Wetzel), 1954

>   Gassner, John, Theatre at the Crossroads; Plays and
>   Playwrights of the Mid-century American Stage, Holt,
>   1960, p. 288-93

>   America, 92:110, Oct. 23, 1954
>   Catholic World, 180:144-5, Nov., 1954
>   Commonweal, 61:60, Oct. 22, 1954
>   Nation, 179:314, Oct. 9, 1954
>   New Republic, 131:22, Oct. 4, 1954
>   New Yorker, 30:63, Oct. 2, 1954
>   Newsweek, 44:83, Oct. 4, 1954
>   Saturday Review, 37:26, Oct. 9, 1954
>   Theatre Arts, 38:20, Dec., 1954
>   Time, 64:56, Oct. 4, 1954

"Silent Night, Lonely Night", 1959

>   America, 102:428, Jan. 9, 1960
>   Christian Century, 77:16, Jan. 6, 1960
>   Commonweal, 71:395, Jan. 1, 1960
>   Nation, 189:476, Dec. 19, 1959
>   New Yorker, 35:102-3, Dec. 12, 1959
>   Saturday Review, 42:24, Dec. 19, 1959
>   Time, 74:77, Dec. 14, 1959

"Tea and Sympathy", 1953

>   Bentley, Eric, Dramatic Event; an American Chronicle,
>   Horizon Press, 1954, p. 149-53

>   Gassner, John, Theatre at the Crossroads; Plays and
>   Playwrights of the Mid-Century American Stage, Holt,
>   1960, p. 288-93

>   Tynan, Kenneth, Curtains; Selections from the Drama
>   Criticism and Related Writings, Atheneum, 1961, p. 172

>   Weales, Gerald Clifford, American Drama since World
>   War II, Harcourt, 1962, p. 40-56

America, 90:107, Oct. 24, 1953
Catholic World, 178:148-49, Nov., 1953
Commonweal, 59:90, Oct. 30, 1953
Life, 35:121-3, Oct. 19, 1953
Nation, 177:317-18, Oct. 17, 1953
New Republic, 129:20-1, Oct. 19, 1953
New Statesman, 53:570, May 4, 1957
New Yorker, 29:71, Oct. 10, 1953
Newsweek, 42:84, Oct. 12, 1953
Newsweek, 42:60, Dec. 21, 1953
Saturday Review, 36:35, Oct. 17, 1953
Saturday Review, 36:45, Dec. 12, 1953
Spectator, 198:587, May 3, 1957
Theatre Arts, 37:62-7, Nov., 1953
Theatre Arts, 37:18-19, Dec., 1953
Time, 62:49, Oct. 12, 1953

WILLIAM ARCHIBALD

"The Innocents" (dramatization of Turn of the Screw by Henry James), 1952

Catholic World, 170:469, March, 1950
Catholic World, 189:321, July, 1959
Commonweal, 51:509, Feb. 17, 1950
Life, 28:91-2, April 3, 1950
Nation, 170:141, Feb. 11, 1950
New Statesman, 44:39-40, July 12, 1952
New Yorker, 25:44, Feb. 11, 1950
New Yorker, 35:97-9, May 2, 1959
New Republic, 122:20, Feb. 27, 1950
Newsweek, 35:80, Feb. 13, 1950
Saturday Review of Literature, 33:32, Feb. 25, 1950
School and Society, 71:214-15, April 8, 1950
Theatre Arts, 34:16, April, 1950
Theatre Arts, 34:22-3, June, 1950
Time, 55:52-3, Feb. 13, 1950

"Portrait of a Lady" (dramatization of the novel by Henry James), 1954

Theatre Arts, 39:13, 91-2, March, 1955

ARTHUR ARENT

"One Third of a Nation", 1938

Catholic World, 146:728-9, March, 1938
Commonweal, 27:414, Feb. 4, 1938
Current History, 48:54, April, 1938
Literary Digest, 125:21, Feb. 12, 1938
Nation, 146:137-8, Jan. 29, 1938
New Republic, 94:46, Feb. 16, 1938
Theatre Arts Monthly, 22:173-4, March, 1938
Time, 31:40, Jan. 31, 1938

"Power", 1937

American Federationist, 44:632-43, June, 1937
Catholic World, 145:342, June, 1937
Commonweal, 25:556, March 10, 1937
Nation, 144:256, March 6, 1937
Newsweek, 9:30, March 6, 1937
Scribner's Magazine, 101:66, May, 1937
Time, 29:47, March 8, 1937

GEORGE AXELROD

"Goodbye, Charlie", 1959

Kerr, Walter, The Theatre in Spite of Itself, Simon and
    Schuster, 1963, p. 265-68

Commonweal, 71:630-1, March 4, 1960
New Yorker, 35:48, Dec. 26, 1959
Newsweek, 54:43, Dec. 28, 1959
Saturday Review, 43:30, Jan. 2, 1960

"Seven Year Itch", 1952

Nathan, George Jean, Theatre in the Fifties, Knopf, 1953,
    p. 76-78

Catholic World, 176:307, Jan., 1953
Commonweal, 57:259, Dec. 12, 1952
Life, 33:145-8, Dec. 8, 1952
Nation, 175:563, Dec. 13, 1952
New Yorker, 28:67, Dec. 6, 1952

Newsweek, 40:79, Dec. 1, 1952
Saturday Review, 35:25, Dec. 13, 1952
Theatre Arts, 37:27-8, Feb., 1953
Time, 60:78, Dec. 1, 1952

"Will Success Spoil Rock Hunter?", 1955

America, 94:138, Oct. 29, 1955
Catholic World, 182:226, Dec., 1955
Commonweal, 63:141, Nov. 11, 1955
Nation, 181:405, Nov. 5, 1955
New Republic, 134:20, Jan. 2, 1956
New Yorker, 31:88, Oct. 22, 1955
Newsweek, 46:54, Oct. 24, 1955
Saturday Review, 38:20, Oct. 29, 1955
Theatre Arts, 39:26, Dec., 1955
Time, 66:86, Oct. 24, 1955

JOHN LLOYD BALDERSTON

"Farewell Performance" (adapted from the novel by Lajos Zilahy),
1936

London Mercury, 34:534, Oct., 1936
Spectator, 157:455, Sept. 18, 1936

JOHN LLOYD BALDERSTON AND JOHN C. SQUIRE

"Berkeley Square", 1926

Catholic World, 130:464-6, Jan., 1930
Commonweal, 11:85, Nov. 20, 1929
English Review, 43:590-1, Nov., 1926
Literary Digest, 103:19, Nov. 30, 1929
Nation, (Lond), 40:84, Oct. 16, 1926
Nation, 129:604-5, Nov. 20, 1929
New Republic, 60:374-5, Nov. 20, 1929
New Statesman and Nation, 28:45-6, Oct. 23, 1926
New Statesman and Nation, 32:761, March 23, 1929
Outlook (Lond), 58:370, Oct. 16, 1926
Outlook, 153:470, Nov. 20, 1929
Saturday Review of Literature, 142:405-6, Oct. 9, 1926
Spectator, 137:673, Oct. 23, 1926

Spectator, 166:35, Jan. 10, 1941
Theatre Arts Monthly, 14:11-12, Jan., 1930

JOHN LLOYD BALDERSTON AND J. E. HOARE

"Red Planet", 1933

Commonweal, 17:271, Jan. 4, 1933
Nation, 136:27-8, Jan. 4, 1933
Theatre Arts Monthly, 17:105-6, Feb., 1933

JAMES BALDWIN

"Amen Corner", 1965

America, 112:690, May 8, 1965
Catholic World, 201:215-16, June, 1965
Commonweal, 82:221-2, May 7, 1965
Life, 58:16, May 14, 1965
Nation, 200:514-15, May 10, 1965
New Yorker, 41:85, April 24, 1965
Newsweek, 65:90, April 26, 1965
Saturday Review, 48:49, May 1, 1965
Time, 85:59, April 23, 1965
Vogue, 145:68, June, 1965

"Blues for Mr. Charlie", 1964

America, 110:776-7, May 30, 1964
Catholic World, 199:263-4, July, 1964
Commonweal, 80:299-300, May 29, 1964
Ebony, 19:188, June, 1964
Harper, 231:34, May, 1965
Hudson Review, 17:421-4, Autumn, 1964
Nation, 198:495-6, May 11, 1964
National Review, 16:780-1, Sept. 8, 1964
New Republic, 150:35-7, May 16, 1964
New Republic, 153:34-6, Nov. 27, 1965
New Statesman, 69:737-8, May 7, 1965
New Yorker, 40:143, May 9, 1964
Newsweek, 63:46, May 4, 1964
Partisan Review, 31:389-94, Summer, 1964
Saturday Review, 47:27-8, May 2, 1964

Saturday Review, 47:36, May 9, 1964
Time, 83:50, May 1, 1964
Time, 83:96, June 5, 1964
Vogue, 144:32, July, 1964

MARGARET AYER BARNES

SEE

EDWARD SHELDON AND MARGARET AYER BARNES

PHILIP BARRY

"Animal Kingdom", 1932

Arts & Decoration, 36:63-4, March, 1932
Bookman, 74:562-3, Jan., 1932
Catholic World, 134:714-15, March, 1932
Commonweal, 15:441-2, Feb. 17, 1932
Nation, 134:151, Feb. 3, 1932
New Republic, 69:293-4, Jan. 27, 1932
North American Review, 234:173, Aug., 1932
Outlook, 160:118, Jan. 27, 1932
Theatre Arts Monthly, 16:187-8, March, 1932

"Bright Star", 1935

Commonweal, 23:19, Nov. 1, 1935
Nation, 141:520, Oct. 30, 1935
Theatre Arts Monthly, 19:899-900, Dec., 1935
Time, 26:39, Oct. 28, 1935

"Foolish Notion", 1954

Nathan, George Jean, Theatre Book of the Year, 1944-45,
    Knopf, p. 294-98

Catholic World, 161:70, April 1945
Commonweal, 41:589, March 30, 1945
Nation, 160:340-1, May 24, 1945
N. Y. Times Magazine, p. 24-5, Feb. 25, 1945
New Republic, 112:421, March 26, 1945
New Yorker, 21:48, March 24, 1945

Newsweek, 25:88, March 26, 1945
Saturday Review of Literature, 28:18-19, March 24, 1945
Theatre Arts Monthly, 29:199, April 1945
Theatre Arts Monthly, 29:269-70, May, 1945
Time, 45:70, March 26, 1945

"Here Come the Clowns", 1938

Brown, John Mason, Broadway in Review, Norton, 1940,
p. 165-169

America, 104:100, Oct. 15, 1960
Catholic World, 148:473-4, Jan., 1930
Catholic World, 179:308, July, 1954
Commonweal, 29:244, Dec. 23, 1938
Commonweal, 29:552, March 10, 1939
Forum, 101:72, Feb., 1939
Nation, 147:700, Dec. 24, 1938
New Republic, 97:230, Dec. 28, 1938
New Yorker, 36:131-2, Oct. 1, 1960
Newsweek, 12:25, Dec. 19, 1938
North American Review, 247 no. 1:156-7, March, 1939
Theatre Arts Monthly, 23:89-91, Feb., 1939
Time, 32:43-4, Dec. 19, 1938

"Holiday", 1928

American Mercury, 16:245, Feb., 1929
Bookman, 68:684-5, Feb., 1929
Commonweal, 9:405, Feb. 6, 1929
New Republic, 57:96-7, Dec. 12, 1928
Outlook, 151:11, Jan. 2, 1929
Review of Reviews, 79:160, Feb., 1929

"Hotel Universe", 1930

Brown, John Mason, Two on the Aisle, Ten Years of the
American Theatre in Performance, Norton 1938, p. 159-63
Downer, Alan S., ed., American Drama and its Critics,
Univ. Chicago Pr., 1965, p. 121-26

Catholic World, 131:337-8, June, 1930
Commonweal, 11:741, April 30, 1930
Nation, 130:525-6, April 30, 1930
New Republic, 62:326-8, May 7, 1930
Review of Reviews, 81:130, June, 1930

"In a Garden", 1925

    Independent, 116:48, Jan. 9, 1926

"John", 1927

    Nation, 125:582-3, Nov. 23, 1927

"Joyous Season", 1934

    Catholic World, 138:729-30, March, 1934
    Commonweal, 19:413, 469, Feb., 1934
    Literary Digest, 117:23, Feb. 24, 1934
    Nation, 138:200-2, Feb. 14, 1934
    New Republic, 78:21, Feb. 14, 1934
    Newsweek, 3:39, Feb. 10, 1934
    Review of Reviews, 89:47, March, 1934
    Theatre Arts Monthly, 18:244, April, 1934

"Liberty Jones", 1941

    Catholic World, 152:725-6, March, 1941
    Commonweal, 33:447, Feb. 21, 1941
    Nation, 152:192, Feb. 15, 1941
    New Republic, 104:276, Feb. 24, 1941
    New Yorker, 17:30, Feb. 15, 1941
    Newsweek, 17:67, Feb. 17, 1941
    Theatre Arts Monthly, 25:261, April, 1941
    Time, 37:85, Feb. 17, 1941

"My Name is Aquilon", (adapted from the novel by Jean Pierre Aumont), 1949

    Nathan, George Jean, Theatre Book of the Year, 1948-49, Knopf, p. 275-78

    Nation, 168:256, Feb. 26, 1949
    New Yorker, 24:60, Feb. 19, 1949
    Newsweek, 33:79, Feb. 21, 1949

"Paris Bound", 1927

    Brown J. "'Paris bound'; criticism", Saturday Review, 147:640, May 11, 1929

    Nation, 126:75-6, Jan. 18, 1928
    New Republic, 53:273, Jan. 25, 1928

Outlook, 148:147, Jan. 25, 1928
Saturday Review of Literature, 4:515-16, Jan. 14, 1928

"Philadelphia Story", 1939

Brown, John Mason, Broadway in Review, Norton, 1940,
  p. 127-31

Catholic World, 149:216-17, May, 1939
Commonweal, 29:692, April 14, 1939
Nation, 148:410-11, April 8, 1939
Newsweek, 13:28-9, April 10, 1939
North American Review, 247 no. 2:366, June, 1939
Theatre Arts Monthly, 23:324-5, May, 1939
Time, 33:56, April 10, 1939

"Spring Dance", 1936

Commonweal, 24:487, Sept. 18, 1936
Literary Digest, 122:19, July 25, 1936
Literary Digest, 122:24, Sept. 5, 1936
Nation, 143:284, Sept. 5, 1936
Newsweek, 8:27, Sept. 5, 1936
Time, 28:53, Sept. 7, 1936

"Tomorrow and Tomorrow", 1931

Dusenbury, Winifred Loesch, The Theme of Loneliness in
  Modern American Drama, Univ. Florida Press, 1960,
  p. 86-112
Wilson, Edmund, Shores of light, Farrar, Straus, 1952,
  p. 504-508

Arts & Decoration, 34:84, March, 1931
Bookman, 73:72-3, March, 1931
Catholic World, 132:717-18, March, 1931
Commonweal, 13:357-8, Jan. 28, 1931
Drama, 21:10-11, March, 1931
New Republic, 65:322-3, Feb. 4, 1931
Outlook, 157:152, Jan. 28, 1931
Theatre Arts Monthly, 15:185-6, March, 1931
Theatre Magazine, 53:24, March, 1931

"Without Love", 1942

> Nathan, George Jean, Theatre Book of the Year, 1942-1943, Knopf, p. 121-26
>
> Catholic World, 156:336-7, Dec., 1942
> Commonweal, 37:144, Nov. 27, 1942
> Current History, n.s. 3:456, Jan., 1943
> Life, 12:78, May 11, 1942
> Nation, 155:553-4, Nov. 21, 1942
> New Republic, 107:679-80, Nov. 23, 1942
> New Yorker, 18:36, Nov. 21, 1942
> Newsweek, 20:73, Nov. 23, 1942
> Theatre Arts Monthly, 27:15, Jan., 1943
> Time, 39:61, April 27, 1942

PHILIP BARRY AND ELMER RICE

"Cock Robin", 1928

> Outlook, 148:423, March 14, 1928

PHILIP BARRY AND ROBERT EMMET SHERWOOD

"Second Threshold", 1951

> Gassner, John, Theatre at the Crossroads; Plays and Playwrights of the Mid-century American Stage, Holt, 1960, p. 130-132
> Nathan, George Jean, Theatre Book of the Year, 1950-1951, Knopf, p. 171-74
>
> Catholic World, 172:385, Feb., 1951
> Christian Science Monitor Magazine, p. 6, Jan. 6, 1951
> Life, 30:53-4, Jan. 29, 1951
> Nation, 172:44, Jan. 13, 1951
> New Republic, 124:22, Feb. 5, 1951
> New Statesman and Nation, 44:375, Oct. 4, 1952
> New Yorker, 26:42, Jan. 13, 1951
> Newsweek, 37:78, Jan. 15, 1951
> Saturday Review of Literature, 34:25-7, Jan. 27, 1951
> School and Society, 73:183, March 24, 1951
> Spectator, 189:424, Oct. 3, 1952
> Theatre Arts Monthly, 35:16, March, 1951
> Theatre Arts Monthly, 35:17, Sept., 1951

LEWIS BEACH

"Merry Andrew", 1929

    Commonweal, 9:431, Feb. 13, 1929

"Square Peg", 1923

    Nation, 116:224, Feb. 21, 1923

SAMUEL N. BEHRMAN

"Amphitryon 38" (adaptation of Amphitryon 38 by J. Giraudoux), 1937

    Catholic World, 146:338-9, Dec., 1937
    Commonweal, 27:78, Nov. 12, 1937
    Nation, 145:539, Nov. 13, 1937
    New Republic, 93:44, Nov. 17, 1937
    New Republic, 94:132, March 9, 1938
    Newsweek, 10:20-1, July 3, 1937
    Newsweek, 10:22, Nov. 8, 1937
    Scribner's Magazine, 102:66, Oct., 1937
    Theatre Arts Monthly, 21:924, Dec., 1937
    Time, 30:25, Nov. 8, 1937

"Biography", 1932

    Arts & Decoration, 38:56, Feb., 1933
    Catholic World, 136:590, Feb., 1933
    Commonweal, 17:245, Dec. 28, 1932
    Nation, 135:654, Dec. 28, 1932
    New Republic, 73:188-9, Dec. 28, 1932
    Saturday Review of Literature, 9:438, Feb. 18, 1933
    Theatre Arts Monthly, 17:103-5; 18:495-6, Feb., 1933,
      July, 1934

"Brief Moment", 1931

    Arts & Decoration, 36:78, Jan., 1932
    Catholic World, 134:469-70, Jan., 1932
    Commonweal, 15:134, Dec. 2, 1931
    Nation, 133:621-2, Dec. 2, 1931
    New Republic, 69:70, 136, Dec. 2 and 16, 1931

"But for Whom, Charlie", 1964

America, 110:657, May 9, 1964
Commonweal, 80:90, April 10, 1964
Educational Theatre Journal, 16:175-6, May, 1964
Hudson Review, 17:237, Summer, 1964
Nation, 198:335-6, March 30, 1964
New Yorker, 40:64, March 21, 1964
Newsweek, 63:70, March 23, 1964
Saturday Review, 47:21, March 28, 1964
Time, 83:55, March 20, 1964
Vogue, 143:62, May, 1964

"The Cold Wind and the Warm", 1958

Tynan, Kenneth, Curtains, Selections from the Drama
    Criticism and Related Writings, Atheneum, 1961, p. 290-94

America, 100:438, Jan. 10, 1959
Catholic World, 188:421, Feb., 1959
Commentary, 27:256-60, March, 1959
Commonweal, 69:496-7, Feb. 6, 1959
New Yorker, 34:69, Dec. 20, 1958
Newsweek, 52:46, Dec. 22, 1958
Theatre Arts Monthly, 43:20-1, Feb., 1959
Time, 72:54, Dec. 22, 1958

"Dunnigan's Daughter", 1946

Nathan, George Jean, Theatre Book of the Year, 1945-1946,
    Knopf, p. 246-52

Catholic World, 162:456, Feb., 1946
Nation, 162:81, Jan. 19, 1946
New Yorker, 21:43-4, Jan. 5, 1946
Theatre Arts Monthly, 30:138, March, 1946
Time, 47:86, Jan. 7, 1946

"End of Summer", 1936

Catholic World, 143:86-7, April, 1936
Commonweal, 23:497, Feb. 28, 1936
Literary Digest, 121:19, Feb. 29, 1936
Nation, 142:291-2, March 4, 1936
New Republic, 86:113, 141, March 4 and 11, 1936
Newsweek, 7:31-2, Feb. 29, 1936

Theatre Arts Monthly, 20:258-60, April, 1936
Time, 27:59, March 2, 1936

"I Know My Love" (adaptation of Aupres de ma blonde by
M. Achard), 1949

Brown, John Mason, Still Seeing Things, McGraw, 1959,
p. 127-31
Nathan, George Jean, Theatre Book of the Year, 1949-1950,
Knopf, p. 81-84

Catholic World, 170:229, Dec., 1949
Forum, 112:337-8, Dec., 1949
Nation, 169:498, Nov. 19, 1949
New Republic, 121:19, Nov. 21, 1949
New Yorker, 25:54, Nov. 12, 1949
Newsweek, 34:84, Nov. 14, 1949
Saturday Review of Literature, 32:54-5, Dec. 3, 1949
Theatre Arts Monthly, 34:13, Jan., 1950
Time, 53:58, March 7, 1949
Time, 54:49, Nov. 14, 1949

"Jacobowsky and the Colonel", 1944

Nathan, George Jean, Theatre Book of the Year, 1943-1944,
Knopf, p. 263-67

"Jane" (dramatization of the story by W. S. Maugham), 1952

Nathan, George Jean, Theatre in the Fifties, Knopf, 1953,
p. 57-59

Catholic World, 174:465, March, 1952
Commonweal, 55:496, Feb. 22, 1952
Nation, 174:162, Feb. 16, 1952
New Republic, 126:23, Feb. 18, 1952
New Yorker, 27:56-7, Feb. 9, 1952
Newsweek, 39:82, Feb. 11, 1952
Saturday Review of Literature, 35:34, Feb. 16, 1952
School and Society, 75:325, May 24, 1952
Theatre Arts, 31:59, April, 1947
Theatre Arts, 36:71, April, 1952
Time, 59:79, Feb. 11, 1952

"Lord Pengo", 1962

America, 108:52, Jan. 12, 1963
Hudson Review, 16:83-4, 1963
Life, 54:51-2, Feb. 22, 1963
Nation, 196:214, March 9, 1963
New Yorker, 38:118, Dec. 1, 1962
Newsweek, 60:63, Dec. 3, 1962
Theatre Arts, 47:11, Jan., 1963
Time, 80:53, Nov. 30, 1962

"Meteor", 1929

Catholic World, 130:724-5, March, 1930
Commonweal, 11:310, Jan. 15, 1930
Nation, 130:78-9, Jan. 15, 1930
New Republic, 61:250, Jan. 22, 1930
Outlook, 154:73, Jan. 8, 1930

"No Time for Comedy", 1939

Brown, John Mason, Broadway in Review, Norton, 1940,
  p. 83-87
O'Hara, Frank Hurburt, Today in American Drama, Univ.
  Chicago Pr., 1939, p. 53-141

Catholic World, 149:344-5, June, 1939
Commonweal, 30:48, May 5, 1939
Nation, 148:509-10, April 29, 1939
New Republic, 98:378, May 3, 1939
New Statesman and Nation, 21:364, April 5, 1941
Newsweek, 13:45, May 1, 1939
North American Review, 247 no. 2:367-8, June, 1939
Spectator, 166:395, April 11, 1941
Theatre Arts Monthly, 23:395-6, June, 1939
Time, 33:61, May 1, 1939

"Pirate" (adaptation of Der Seerauber by L. Fulda), 1942

Nathan, George Jean, Theatre Book of the Year, 1942-43,
  Knopf, p. 148-50

Catholic World, 156:475-6, Jan., 1943
Commonweal, 37:206, Dec. 11, 1942
Current History, n.s. 4:55, Jan., 1943

Independent Woman, 21:367, Dec., 1942
Life, 13:89-92, Oct. 5, 1942
Nation, 155:659, Dec. 12, 1942
New Republic, 107:792-3, Dec. 14, 1942
N. Y. Times Mag., p. 16-17, Oct. 4, 1942
Theatre Arts, 27:12, Jan., 1943
Time, 40:54-5, Dec. 7, 1942

"Rain from Heaven", 1934

Canadian Forum, 15:194-5, Feb., 1935
Catholic World, 140:599, Feb., 1935
Commonweal, 21:318, Jan. 11, 1935
Nation, 140:55-6, Jan. 9, 1935
New Republic, 81:308, Jan. 23, 1935
Theatre Arts Monthly, 19:96, Feb., 1935

"Second Man", 1927

American Mercury, 11:249-50, June, 1927
London Mercury, 17:91-3, Nov., 1927
Nation, 124:484, April 27, 1927
New Republic, 50:274, April 27, 1927
Outlook (Lond), 61:141, Feb. 4, 1928
Saturday Review, 145:98-9, Jan. 28, 1928
Spectator, 140:152-3, Feb. 4, 1928

"Serena Blandish", 1928

Catholic World, 128:722-3, March, 1929
Commonweal, 9:430-1, Feb. 13, 1929
Nation, 128:212-14, Feb. 13, 1929
New Republic, 57:346-7, Feb. 13, 1929
New Statesman and Nation, 16:457, Sept. 24, 1938
Outlook, 151:262, Feb. 13, 1929

"Talley Method", 1941

American Mercury, 52:355-6, March, 1941
Catholic World, 153:85-6, April, 1941
Commonweal, 33:519, March 14, 1941
Nation, 152:277, March 8, 1941
New Republic, 104:340, March 10, 1941
New Yorker, 17:34, March 8, 1941
Theatre Arts, 25:256, April, 1941
Time, 37:44, March 10, 1941

"Wine of Choice", 1938

>Catholic World, 147:85, April, 1938
>Commonweal, 27:554, March 11, 1938
>Nation, 146:280-1, March 5, 1938
>New Republic, 94:132, March 9, 1938
>Theatre Arts Monthly, 22:253-4, April, 1938
>Time, 31:52, March 7, 1938

DAVID BELASCO

"Darling of the Gods", 1903

>Critic, 42:70-2, Jan., 1903

"The Girl of the Golden West", 1905

>Theatre Arts, 42:25, Jan., 1958

"Heart of Maryland", 1895

>Atheneum, 111:511, April 16, 1898

"Madame Butterfly" (adaptation of story by John Luther Long), 1962

>Stedman, J. W., "Bee and the Butterfly", Opera News, 26:8-12, Feb. 3, 1962

"Naughty Anthony", 1899

>Bookman, 10:514-5, Feb., 1900

DAVID BELASCO AND HENRY CHURCHILL DE MILLE

"Men and Women", 1890

>Atheneum, 101:419-20, April 1, 1893
>Critic, 17 (ns14): 224, Nov. 1, 1890

J. HARRY BENRIMO
SEE

GEORGE C. HAZELTON, JR. AND J. HARRY BENRIMO

IRVING BERLIN

<u>SEE</u>

MOSS HART AND IRVING BERLIN

WILLIAM CLAIBOURNE BERNEY AND HOWARD RICHARDSON

"Dark of the Moon", 1945

<u>Catholic World</u>, 161:168-9, May, 1945
<u>Commonweal</u>, 42:71, May 4, 1945
<u>Life</u>, 17:55-7, Sept. 11, 1944
<u>Nation</u>, 160:370, March 31, 1945
<u>New Republic</u>, 112:447, April 2, 1945
<u>N.Y. Times Mag.</u>, p. 24-5, March 11, 1945
<u>New Yorker</u>, 21:48, March 24, 1945
<u>Newsweek</u>, 25:88, March 26, 1945
<u>Theatre Arts</u>, 29:262, 264-5, 267-8, May, 1945
<u>Time</u>, 45:70, March 26, 1945

"Design for a Stained Glass Window", 1950

Nathan, George Jean, <u>Theatre Book of the Year, 1949-1950</u>,
Knopf, p. 204-06

<u>New Yorker</u>, 25:51, Feb. 4, 1950
<u>Theatre Arts</u>, 34:11, April, 1950

"Protective Custody", 1956

<u>New Yorker</u>, 32:60, Jan. 12, 1957
<u>Theatre Arts</u>, 41:18, March, 1957

<u>SEE ALSO</u>

HOWARD RICHARDSON AND WILLIAM CLAIBOURNE BERNEY

LEONARD BERNSTEIN

"Candide", 1956

<u>Catholic World</u>, 184:384-5, Feb., 1957
<u>Christian Century</u>, 74:171, Feb. 6, 1957
<u>Commonweal</u>, 65:333-4, Dec. 28, 1956

Musical America, 76:26, Dec. 15, 1956
Nation, 183:527, Dec. 15, 1956
New Republic, 135:30-1, Dec. 17, 1956
New Yorker, 32:52, Dec. 15, 1956
Newsweek, 48:77, Dec. 10, 1956
Reporter, 16:35, Jan. 24, 1957
Saturday Review, 39:34, Dec. 22, 1956
Saturday Review, 40:49, Feb. 23, 1957
Theatre Arts, 41:17-18, Feb., 1957
Time, 68:70, Dec. 10, 1956

"Trouble in Tahiti", 1955
America, 93:192, May 14, 1955
Catholic World, 181:227, June, 1955
Commonweal, 62:255, June 10, 1955
Musical Quarterly, 39:94-8, Jan., 1953
Nation, 180:410, May 7, 1955
New Republic, 132:22, May 2, 1955
New Yorker, 31:69-71, April 30, 1955
New Yorker, 34:138, April 19, 1958
Saturday Review, 38:26, May 14, 1955
Theatre Arts, 39:17, 23, July, 1955
Time, 65:78, May 2, 1955

"West Side Story", 1958
Tynan, Kenneth, Curtains: Selections from the Drama
Criticism and Related Writings, Atheneum, 1961, p. 280-81

DONALD JOSEPH BEVAN AND EDMUND TRZCINSKI

"Stalag 17", 1951
Catholic World, 173:307-8, July, 1951
Commonweal, 54:165, May 25, 1951
Life, 20:110, May 28, 1951
Nation, 172:477, May 19, 1951
New Republic, 124:23, May 28, 1951
New Yorker, 27:64, May 19, 1951
Newsweek, 37:86, May 21, 1951
Saturday Review of Literature, 34:28-30, May 26, 1951
Theatre Arts, 35:5, Sept., 1951
Theatre Arts, 36:20, May, 1952
Time, 57:83, May 21, 1951

ROBERT MONTGOMERY BIRD

"Gladiator", 1831

> Moses, Montrose Jonas and Brown, John Mason, eds.,
> American Theatre as seen by its Critics, 1752-1934,
> Norton, 1934, p. 69-70

CLARE BOOTHE

SEE

CLARE BOOTHE LUCE

DION G. BOUCICAULT

"After Dark", 1929

> Nation, 128:54, Jan. 9, 1929

"London Assurance", 1841

> Harper's Weekly, 40:1215, Dec. 12, 1896

"Mary Barton", 1866

> Altick, Richard D., "Dion Boucicault Stages 'Mary Barton' ",
> Nineteenth Century Fiction, 14:129-141, 1959.

"Octoroon", 1859

> America, 104:714, Feb. 25, 1961
> Commonweal, 73:636, March 17, 1961
> Life, 50:39-40, Feb. 24, 1961
> Nation, 192:126, Feb. 11, 1961
> New Yorker, 36:75-6 Feb. 11, 1961
> Saturday Review, 44:41, Feb. 25, 1961

"Streets of London", n. d.

> Spectator, 149:914, Dec. 30, 1932

"Streets of New York", 1931

> Catholic World, 134:210, Nov., 1931
> Commonweal, 14:608, Oct. 21, 1931

Literary Digest, 111:19, Nov. 14, 1931
Nation, 133:467-8, Oct. 28, 1931
New Republic, 68:301, Oct. 28, 1931
Outlook, 159:248, Oct. 21, 1931
Theatre Arts Monthly, 15:984, Dec., 1931

LEO BRADY

SEE

WALTER FRANCIS KERR AND LEO BRADY

ANN PRESTON BRIDGERS

SEE

GEORGE ABBOTT AND ANN PRESTON BRIDGERS

TRUMAN CAPOTE

"The Grass Harp", 1952

Bentley, Eric Russell, Dramatic Event; an American
Chronicle, Horizon Press, 1954, p. 20-24
Gassner, John, Theatre at the Crossroads; Plays and
Playwrights of the Mid-century American Stage, Holt,
1960, p. 149-51
Nathan, George Jean, Theatre in the Fifties, Knopf, 1953,
p. 84-88

Catholic World, 175:147-8, May, 1952
Catholic World, 177:228, June, 1953
Commonweal, 56:68-9, April 25, 1952
Commonweal, 58:179, May 22, 1953
Life, 32:142, April 14, 1952
Nation, 174:353, April 12, 1952
Nation, 176:421, May 16, 1953
New Republic, 126:22-3, April 14, 1952
New Yorker, 28:70, April 5, 1952
Newsweek, 39:94, April 7, 1952

Saturday Review, 35:43-4, April 19, 1952
Saturday Review, 36:30, May 16, 1953
School and Society, 75:323-4, May 24, 1952
Theatre Arts, 36:17-18, June, 1952
Theatre Arts, 37:16, July, 1953
Time, 59:77, April 7, 1952

LEWIS JOHN CARLINO

"Cages", 1963

Theatre Arts, 47:13, Aug., 1963

"Double Talk", 1964

New Yorker, 40:165, May 16, 1964
Newsweek, 63:80, May 18, 1964

"Telemachus Clay", 1963

Commonweal, 79:543-4, Jan. 31, 1964
New Republic, 149:28, Dec. 21, 1963
New Yorker, 39:146-7, Nov. 23, 1963
Saturday Review, 46:35, Dec. 7, 1963

RANDOLPH CARTER

"Eugenia" (dramatization of Europeans by Henry James), 1957

Commonweal, 65:638, March 22, 1957
New Yorker, 32:74-5, Feb. 9, 1957
Newsweek, 49:67, Feb. 11, 1957
Theatre Arts, 41:16, April, 1957
Time, 69:70, Feb. 11, 1957

ROBERT HARRIS CHAPMAN

SEE

LOUIS OSBORNE COXE AND ROBERT HARRIS CHAPMAN

MARY COYLE CHASE

"Bernardine", 1952
> Catholic World, 176:227-8, Dec., 1952
> Commonweal, 57:119, Nov. 7, 1952
> Life, 175:414, Nov. 1, 1952
> New Yorker, 28:74, Oct. 25, 1952
> Newsweek, 40:78, Oct. 27, 1952
> Saturday Review, 35:26, Nov. 1, 1952
> School and Society, 76:403, Dec. 20, 1952
> Theatre Arts, 36:26-8, Dec., 1952
> Time, 60:75, Oct. 27, 1952

"Harvey", 1944
> Brown, John Mason, Seeing Things, McGraw, 1946, p. 212-16
> Nathan, George Jean, Theatre Book of the Year, 1944-45, Knopf, 1945, p. 133-35

> Catholic World, 160:260, Dec., 1944
> Commonweal, 41:124, Nov. 17, 1944
> France Illustration, 6:496-7, Nov. 4, 1950
> Illustrated London News, 214:152, Jan. 29, 1949
> Life, 17:96-8, Nov. 27, 1944
> Life, 18:55-8, Jan. 8, 1945
> Nation, 159:624, Nov. 18, 1944
> New Republic, 111:661, Nov. 20, 1944
> New Statesman and Nation, 37:55, Jan. 15, 1949
> New Yorker, 20:44, Nov. 11, 1944
> New Yorker, 23:40, July 26, 1947
> Newsweek, 24:82-3, Nov. 13, 1944
> Newsweek, 30:78, July 28, 1947
> Saturday Review of Literature, 27:10-11, Dec. 30, 1944
> Spectator, 182:45, Jan. 14, 1949
> Theatre Arts, 29:2-6, Jan., 1945
> Theatre Arts, 29:85, Feb., 1945
> Time, 44:60, Nov. 13, 1944

"Midgie Purvis", 1961
> Nation, 192:155-6, Feb. 18, 1961
> New Yorker, 36:75, Feb. 11, 1961
> Saturday Review, 44:41, Feb. 25, 1961
> Time, 77:68, Feb. 10, 1961

"Mrs. McThing", 1952

>Catholic World, 175:68, April, 1952
>Commonweal, 55:567, March 14, 1952
>Life, 32:149-50, March 10, 1952
>Nation, 174:258, March 15, 1952
>New Yorker, 28:58, March 1, 1952
>Newsweek, 39:61, March 3, 1952
>Saturday Review, 35:28, March 15, 1952
>School and Society, 75:182-3, March 22, 1952
>Theatre Arts, 36:28-9, 38-41, May, 1952
>Time, 59:63, March 3, 1952

"Next Half Hour", 1945

>Nathan, George Jean, Theatre Book of the Year, 1945-1946,
>   Knopf, 1946, p. 153-55

>New Republic, 113:639, Nov. 12, 1945
>New Yorker, 21:44, Nov. 10, 1945
>Theatre Arts, 30:12, Jan., 1946

BELLA COHEN

SEE

BELLA SPEWACK

JOHN B. COLTON

"Nine Pine Street", 1933

>Catholic World, 137:336-7, June, 1933
>Newsweek, 1:28, May 6, 1933

JOHN B. COLTON AND CLEMENCE RANDOLPH

"Rain", 1922

>Catholic World, 141:86-7, April, 1935
>Commonweal, 21:513, March 1, 1935
>Golden Book, 22-106-7, July, 1935
>Literary Digest, 119:20, Feb. 23, 1935

Nation, 115:585-6, Nov. 29, 1922
New Republic, 33:349, Feb. 21, 1923
Theatre Arts Monthly, 19:257, April, 1935

ELLSWORTH PROUTY CONKLE

"Prologue to Glory", 1938
McCarthy, Mary Therese, Sights and Spectacles, 1937-1956,
Farrar, Straus, 1956, p. 30-38

Catholic World, 147:213-14, May, 1938
Commonweal, 27:636, April 1, 1938
Theatre Arts Monthly, 22:329-30, May, 1938
Time, 31:24, March 28, 1938

"Two Hundred Were Chosen", 1936
Catholic World, 144:472, Jan., 1937
Commonweal, 25:162, Dec. 4, 1936
Literary Digest, 122:19, Dec. 5, 1936
Newsweek, 8:19, Nov. 28, 1936
Survey Graphic, 26:41, Jan., 1937
Theatre Arts Monthly, 21:17-18, Jan., 1937
Time, 28:54, Nov. 30, 1936

MARCUS COOK CONNELLY

"Flowers of Virtue", 1942
Catholic World, 154:732, March, 1942
Commonweal, 35:437, Feb. 20, 1942
New Yorker, 17:28, Feb. 14, 1942
Theatre Arts, 26:225, April, 1942

"Green Pastures", 1930
Brown, John Mason, As They Appear, McGraw, 1952,
p. 193-98
Brown, John Mason, Dramatis Personae; a Retrospective
Show, Viking, 1963, p. 85-89
Ford, N.A., "How Genuine is 'The Green Pastures'",
Phylon Quarterly, 20:67-70, 1959, and 20:193-4, 1959
McNeir, Waldo F., Studies in Comparative Literature,
Louisiana State Univ. Press, 1962, p. 199-218

Moses, Montrose Jonas and Brown, John Mason, eds.,
American Theatre as Seen by its Critics, 1752-1934,
Norton, 1934, p. 278-81 and 292-94
Nathan, George Jean, Theatre Book of the Year, 1950-1951,
Knopf, p. 255-57
Oppenheimer, George, ed., Passionate Playgoer, a
Personal Scrapbook, Viking, 1958, p. 547-49
Steiner, E.A., "Fashion Play of 1930; 'Green Pastures' and
the Oberammergau Passion play", Christian Century,
47:985-6, Aug. 13, 1930
Theatre Arts Anthology; a Record and a Prophecy, ed. by
Rosamond Gilder and others, Theatre Arts Books, 1950,
p. 613-15
Young, Stark, Immortal Shadows; a Book of Dramatic
Criticism, Scribner, 1948, p. 119-22
Arts & Decoration, 33:105, May, 1930
Bookman, 71:340, June, 1930
Bookman, 73:294-5, May, 1931
Catholic World, 131:210-11, May, 1930
Catholic World, 133:596-8, Aug., 1931
Catholic World, 173:145, May, 1951
Christian Century, 47:1278-81, Oct. 22, 1930
Christian Century, 49:1316, Oct. 26, 1932
Commonweal, 11:561, March 19, 1930
Commonweal, 17:481, March 1, 1933
Commonweal, 53:646, April 6, 1951
Colliers, 85:23, May 10, 1930
Golden Book, 11:102-3, May, 1930
Homiletic Review, 100:19-21, July, 1930
Ladies Home Journal, 52:8-9, Sept., 1935
Life, 30:67-9, April 16, 1951
Literary Digest, 104:20-1, March 22, 1930
Literary Digest, 105:22-3, June 21, 1930
Literary Digest, 107:19-20, Dec. 20, 1930
Literary Digest, 119:255, March 9, 1935
Living Age, 338:501, June 15, 1930
Nation (Lond), 47:564, Aug. 2, 1930
Nation, 130:376, March 26, 1930
Nation, 130:415, April 9, 1930
Nation, 172:305, March 31, 1951
New Republic, 62:128-9, March 19, 1930
New Republic, 124:30, April 16, 1951
New Yorker, 27:56, March 24, 1951

Newsweek, 5:28-9, March 9, 1935
Newsweek, 37:90, March 26, 1951
Outlook, 154:429, March 12, 1930
Review of Reviews, 81:145, April, 1930
Saturday Review of Literature, 34:28-30, April 7, 1951
School and Society, 73:246-7, April 21, 1951
Survey, 64:156, May 1, 1930
Theatre Arts, 14:369-70, May, 1930
Theatre Arts, 35:22, May, 1951
Theatre Arts, 42:64-6, Nov., 1958
Theatre Magazine, 53:14, March, 1931
Time, 57:67, March 26, 1951

"Story for Strangers", 1948

Nathan, George Jean, Theatre Book of the Year, 1948-1949,
Knopf, p. 88-91
Commonweal, 46:618, Oct. 8, 1948
Nation, 167:381, Oct. 2, 1948
New Yorker, 24:51, Oct. 2, 1948
Time, 52:59, Oct. 4, 1948

"Wisdom Tooth", 1926
New Republic, 46:45, March 3, 1926

SEE ALSO

GEORGE S. KAUFMAN AND MARC CONNELLY

AND

ARNOLD SUNGAARD AND MARC CONNELLY

LOUIS OSBORNE COXE

"Billy Budd" (dramatization of novel by H. Melville), 1951
Brown, John Mason, As They Appear, McGraw, 1952,
p. 186-92
Gassner, John, Theatre at the Crossroads, Plays and
Playwrights of the Mid-century American Stage, Holt,
1960, p. 139-41
Nathan, George Jean, Theatre Book of the Year, 1950-1951,
Knopf, p. 219-21

Catholic World, 173:227-8, June, 1951
Commonweal, 53:518, March 2, 1951
Life, 30:87, March 26, 1951
Nation, 172:189, Feb. 24, 1951
New Republic, 124:23, March 19, 1951
New Yorker, 27:70, Feb. 17, 1951
Newsweek, 37:82-3, Feb. 19, 1951
Partisan Review, 18:331-3, May, 1951
Saturday Review of Literature, 34:31-3, March 17, 1951
School and Society, 73:248-9, April 21, 1951
Theatre Arts, 35:18, April, 1951
Theatre Arts, 35:73, Sept., 1951
Time, 57:68, Feb. 19, 1951

RUSSEL CROUSE

SEE

HOWARD LINDSAY AND RUSSEL CROUSE

AUGUSTIN DALY

"Last Word" (drama adapted from German of F. Schonthan), 1890

Atheneum, 98:425, Sept. 26, 1891
Critic, 17 (ns 14):238, Nov. 8, 1890

"Little Miss Million", 1892

Critic 21, (ns 18):213, Oct. 15, 1892

"Love in Tandem" (adapted from H. Bocage and C. deCourcy's
La vie a deux), 1892

Atheneum, 102:139, July 22, 1893
Critic, 20 (ns 17):118, Feb. 20, 1892

"Love on Crutches" (adapted from H. Stobitzer's Ihre ideale), 1894

Critic, 25 (ns 22):437, Dec. 22, 1894

"Peg Woffington", 1892

Critic, 20 (ns 17):223, April 16, 1892

DONALD DAVIS

SEE

OWEN DAVIS AND DONALD DAVIS

OWEN DAVIS

"Donovan Affair", n. d.

Harsnell, H. , Outlook (Lond), 59:211, Feb. 26, 1927

"Insect Comedy" (dramatization of Insect Comedy by Josef and Karel Capek), 1948

Commonweal, 48:235, June 18, 1948
Forum, 110:20-2, July, 1948
New Republic, 118:28-9, June 21, 1948
School and Society, 67:478, June 26, 1948

"Jezebel", 1934

Catholic World, 138:604-5, Feb. 1934
Commonweal, 19:273, Jan. 5, 1934
Nation, 138:28, Jan. 3, 1934
New Republic, 77:226, Jan. 3, 1934
Newsweek, 2:30, Dec. 30, 1933
Theatre Arts, 18:95-7, Feb. , 1934

"Just to Remind You", 1931

Arts & Decoration, 36:73, Nov. , 1931
Literary Digest, 110:15, Sept. 26, 1931
Nation, 133:316, Sept. 23, 1931
Outlook, 159:119, Sept. 23, 1931
Theatre Arts, 15:891-2, Nov. , 1931

"Mr. and Mrs. North" (dramatization of stories by F. Lockridge and R. Lockridge), 1941

Catholic World, 152:727-8, March 1941
Commonweal, 33:375, Jan. 31, 1941
Nation, 152:109, Jan. 25, 1941
New Republic, 104:116, Jan. 27, 1941
Theatre Arts, 25:189, March, 1941

"Nervous Wreck", 1923

>Outlook (Lond), 54:226, Sept. 27, 1924
>Saturday Review, 138:307-8, Sept. 27, 1924

"No Way Out", 1944

>Nathan, George Jean, Theatre Book of the Year, 1944-1945, Knopf, p. 122-124

"Sandalwood", 1926

>Krutch, J. W., Nation, 123:384-5, Oct. 13, 1926

"Saturday Night", 1933

>Arts & Decoration, 38:49, April, 1933
>Catholic World, 137:78-9, April, 1933
>Commonweal, 17:553, March 15, 1933
>Theatre Arts, 17:343, May, 1933

"Sinners", 1915

>Nation, 100:61, Jan. 14, 1915

"Snark Was A Boojum" (dramatization of novel by R. Shattuck), 1943

>Nathan, George Jean, Theatre Book of the Year, 1943-1944, Knopf, p. 44-47

>New Yorker, 19:44, Sept. 11, 1943

OWEN DAVIS AND DONALD DAVIS

"Ethan Frome" (dramatization of novel by E. Wharton), 1936

>O'Hara, Frank Hurburt, Today in American Drama, Univ. Chicago Pr., 1943, p. 1-52
>Young, Stark, Immortal shadows; a book of dramatic criticism, Scribner, 1948, p. 178-80

>Catholic World, 142:723-4, March, 1936
>Commonweal, 23:414, Feb. 7, 1936
>Literary Digest, 121:19, 1936
>Nation, 142:167-8, Feb. 5, 1936
>New Republic, 86:78, Feb. 26, 1936

Newsweek, 7:33, Feb. 1, 1936
Theatre Arts, 20:181-2, March, 1936
Time, 27:25, Feb. 3, 1936

"The Good Earth" (dramatization of novel by P. Buck), 1932

Young, Stark, Immortal Shadows, a Book of Dramatic
Criticism, Scribner, 1948, p. 140-44

Arts & Decoration, 38:57, Dec., 1932
Catholic World, 136:338-9, Dec., 1932
Commonweal, 17:23-4, Nov. 2, 1932
Literary Digest, 114:17, Nov. 5, 1932
Nation, 135:438, Nov. 2, 1932
New Republic, 72:330-1, Nov. 2, 1932
Theatre Arts, 17:16-17, Jan., 1933

KATHARINE DAYTON

SEE

GEORGE S. KAUFMAN AND KATHARINE DAYTON

PAUL HENRY DEKRUIF

SEE

SIDNEY COE HOWARD AND PAUL HENRY DEKRUIF

HENRY CHURCHILL DE MILLE

SEE

DAVID BELASCO AND HENRY CHURCHILL DEMILLE

WILLIAM DUNLAP

"Darby's Return", 1789

Moses, Montrose Jonas and Brown, John Mason, eds.,
American Theatre as seen by its Critics, 1752-1934,
Norton, 1934, p. 26-27

"Father", 1789

> Moses, Montrose Jonas and Brown, John Mason, eds.,
> American Theatre as seen by its Critics, 1752-1934,
> Norton, 1934, p. 26

PHILIP DUNNING

"Night Hostess", 1928

> Nation, 127:327-8, Oct. 3, 1928

PHILIP DUNNING AND GEORGE ABBOTT

"Broadway", 1926

> Nation (Lond), 40:508-9, Jan. 8, 1927
> New Statesman, 28:505, Feb. 5, 1927
> Saturday Review, 143:81-2, Jan. 15, 1927
> Spectator, 138:107-8, Jan. 22, 1927

PHILIP DUNNING AND PHILIP HIGLEY

"Remember the Day", 1935

> Catholic World, 142:213-14, Nov., 1935
> Commonweal, 22:585, Oct. 11, 1935
> Theatre Arts Monthly, 19:825, Nov., 1935
> Time, 26:38, Oct. 7, 1935

PHILIP DUNNING AND JOSEPH SCHRANK

"Page Miss Glory", 1934

> Catholic World, 140:469, Jan., 1935
> Golden Book, 21:28a, Feb., 1935
> Newsweek, 4:26, Dec. 8, 1934

SEE ALSO

GEORGE ABBOTT AND PHILIP DUNNING

ARNAUD D'USSEAU

SEE

JAMES GOW AND ARNAUD D'USSEAU

HENRY AND PHOEBE EPHRON

"Howie", 1958

New Yorker, 34:74, Sept. 27, 1958
Theatre Arts, 42:9, Nov. , 1958

"Take Her, She's Mine", 1961

America, 106:540, Jan. 20, 1962
New Yorker, 37:57, Jan. 6, 1962
Newsweek, 59:48, Jan. 1, 1962
Seventeen, 21:142-3, April, 1962
Theatre Arts, 46:58-60, March, 1962
Time, 79:52, Jan. 5, 1962

"Three's A Family", 1943

Nathan, George Jean, Theatre Book of the Year, 1942-1943,
Knopf, p. 292-93

EDNA FERBER

SEE

GEORGE S. KAUFMAN AND EDNA FERBER

CLYDE FITCH

"The City", 1909

Bookman, 31:63-6, 1910

"Girl and the Judge", 1902

Bookman, 14:526, Jan. , 1902
Critic, 40:41, Jan. , 1902

"Last of the Dandies", n. d.

    Atheneum, 2:603, 1901

"Masked Ball", n. d.

    Atheneum, 1:58, 1900

"Nathan Hale", 1898

    Dial, 28:250, 1900

"Sapho", 1902

    Beerbohm, Max, Around Theatres, British Book Center, 1953, p. 205-08

"The Truth", 1907

    Beerbohm, Max, Around Theatres, British Book Center, 1953, p. 471-74

GENE FOWLER

SEE

BEN HECHT AND GENE FOWLER

ZONA GALE

"Miss Lulu Bett", 1920

    Colliers, 67:13, Jan. 29, 1921
    Nation, 112:189, Feb. 2, 1921
    New Republic, 25:204-5, Jan. 12, 1921
    Outlook, 127:579-80, April 13, 1921

HERB GARDNER

"A Thousand Clowns", 1962

    Commonweal, 76:116-17, April 27, 1962
    Life, 52:57-8, June 15, 1962
    Nation, 194:408, May 5, 1962

New Yorker, 38:106, April 14, 1962
Newsweek, 59:100, April 16, 1962
Saturday Review, 45:46, April 21, 1962
Theatre Arts, 46:57-8, June, 1962
Time, 79:82, April 13, 1962

MICHAEL VINCENTE GAZZO

"Hatful of Rain", 1955

America, 94:286, Dec. 3, 1955
Commonweal, 63:331, Dec. 30, 1955
English, 11:186, Summer, 1957
Illustrated London News, 230:470, March 23, 1957
Life, 39:85-6, Dec. 19, 1955
N. Y. Times Mag., p. 76, Oct. 30, 1955
Nation, 181:465, Nov. 26, 1955
New Republic, 134:20, Jan. 2, 1956
New Statesman, 53:336, March 16, 1957
New Yorker, 31:121-3, Nov. 19, 1955
Newsweek, 46:44, Nov. 21, 1955
Saturday Review, 38:26, Nov. 26, 1955
Spectator, 201:249, Aug. 22, 1958
Theatre Arts, 40:22, Jan., 1956
Time, 66:110, Nov. 21, 1955

"Night Circus", 1958

New Yorker, 34:106-7, Dec. 13, 1958
Saturday Review, 41:32, Dec. 20, 1958
Theatre Arts, 43:71-2, Feb., 1959
Time, 72:44, Dec. 15, 1958

JACK GELBER

"The Apple", 1961

Abel, Lionel, Metatheatre; a New View of Dramatic Form,
Hill and Wang, 1963, p. 128-34

Kerr, Walter, The Theatre in Spite of Itself, Simon and
Schuster, 1963, p. 178-82

Kostelanetz, Richard, ed., The New American Arts, N. Y.,
Horizon Press, 1965, p. 66-67

Christian Century, 79:233-4, Feb. 21, 1962
Commentary, 33:331-4, April, 1962
Commonweal, 75:364-5, Dec. 29, 1961
Hudson Review, 15:119-20, Spring, 1962
National Review, 12:68, Jan. 30, 1962
New Republic, 145:20, Dec. 25, 1961
New Yorker, 37:97-8, Dec. 16, 1961
Newsweek, 58:72, Dec. 18, 1961
Theatre Arts, 46:13-14, Feb., 1962

"The Connection", 1959

Dukore, Bernard F., "The new dramatists: Jack Gelber",
Drama Survey, 2:146-57, Spring, 1962

Eskin, Stanley, G., "Theatrically in the avant-garde drama:
A reconsideration of a theme in the light of 'The Balcony'
and 'The Connection' ", Modern Drama, 7:213-22, 1964

Kerr, Walter, The Theatre in spite of Itself, Simon and
Schuster 1963, p. 182-85

Kostelanetz, Richard C., " 'The Connection': Heroin as
Existential Choice" Texas Quarterly (Univ. of Texas),
5:159-62, 1962

Kostelanetz, Richard, ed., The New American Arts, N. Y.,
Horizon Press, 1965, p. 62-66

Weales, Gerald Clifford, American Drama since World
War II, Harcourt, 1962, p. 203-23

Esquire, 55:45-7, April, 1961
Harper, 220:26-8, April, 1960
Illustrated London News, 238:408, March 11, 1961
Nation, 189:80, Aug. 15, 1959
New Republic, 141:29-30, Sept. 28, 1959
New Yorker, 35:126-9, Oct. 10, 1959
Partisan Review, 27:131-6, Winter, 1960
Saturday Review, 42:27, Sept. 26, 1959
Time, 75:61, Jan. 25, 1960

"Square in the Eye", 1965

Commonweal, 82:474, July 2, 1965
New Republic, 152:30, June 26, 1965
New Yorker, 41:56, May 29, 1965

Newsweek, 65:76, May 31, 1965
Reporter, 33:42, July 1, 1965
Time, 85:83, May 28, 1965
Vogue, 146:38, July, 1965

GEORGE GERSHWIN

SEE

DUBOSE HEYWARD AND GEORGE GERSHWIN

WOLCOTT GIBBS

"Season in the Sun", 1950

Nathan, George Jean, Theatre Book of the Year, 1950-1951, Knopf, p. 45-48

Catholic World, 172:149-50, Nov., 1950
Christian Science Monitor Mag., p. 11, Oct. 7, 1950
Commonweal, 53:42, Oct. 20, 1950
Life, 29:111-14, Oct. 9, 1950
Nation, 171:320-1, Oct. 7, 1950
New Republic, 123:22, Oct. 16, 1950
New Yorker, 26:54, Oct. 7, 1950
Newsweek, 36:84, Oct. 9, 1950
Saturday Review, 33:26-7, Oct. 21, 1950
School and Society, 73:184, March 24, 1951
Theatre Arts, 34:15, Nov., 1950
Theatre Arts, 35:82, Sept., 1951
Time, 56:85, Oct. 9, 1950

WILLIAM GIBSON

"Dinny and the Witches", 1959

America, 102:482, Jan. 16, 1960
New Yorker, 35:82, Dec. 19, 1959
Saturday Review, 42:24-5, Dec. 26, 1959

"The Miracle Worker", 1959

Kerr, Walter, The Theatre in Spite of Itself, Simon and Schuster, 1963, p. 255-57

Tynan, Kenneth, <u>Curtains; Selections from the Drama</u>
<u>Criticism and Related Writings,</u> Atheneum, 1961,
p. 327-30

<u>America,</u> 102:217, Nov. 14, 1959
<u>Christian Century,</u> 76:1470, Dec. 16, 1959
<u>Commonweal,</u> 71:289, Dec. 4, 1959
<u>Illustrated London News,</u> 238:514, March 25, 1961
<u>Life,</u> 47:127-8, Sept. 28, 1959
<u>Nation,</u> 189:366, Nov. 14, 1959
<u>New Republic,</u> 141:28-9, Nov. 9, 1959
<u>New Statesman,</u> 61:448, March 17, 1961
<u>New Yorker,</u> 35:132-4, Oct. 31, 1959
<u>Newsweek,</u> 54:97, Nov. 2, 1959
<u>Saturday Review,</u> 42:28, Nov. 7, 1959
<u>Spectator,</u> 206:364, March 17, 1961
<u>Theatre Arts,</u> 43:14, Dec., 1959
<u>Theatre Arts,</u> 44:26-9, Jan., 1960
<u>Time,</u> 74:51, Oct. 5, 1959
<u>Time,</u> 74:30, Nov. 2, 1959
<u>Time,</u> 74:46-8, Dec. 21, 1959
<u>Vogue,</u> 135:112-13, Jan. 1, 1959

"Two for the Seesaw", 1958

Gassner, John, <u>Theatre at the Crossroads; Plays and Play-</u>
<u>wrights of the Mid-century American Stage,</u> Holt, 1960,
p. 211-17
Tynan, Kenneth, <u>Curtains; Selections from the Drama</u>
<u>Criticism and Related Writings,</u> Atheneum, 1961,
p. 316-19

<u>America,</u> 98:552, Feb. 8, 1958
<u>Catholic World,</u> 187:67-8, April, 1958
<u>Christian Century,</u> 75:168, Feb. 5, 1958
<u>Commonweal,</u> 67:540-1, Feb. 21, 1958
<u>Illustrated London News,</u> 234:34, Jan. 3, 1959
<u>Life,</u> 44:95-6, Feb. 17, 1958
<u>Nation,</u> 186:107, Feb. 1, 1958
<u>New Statesman,</u> 56:906, Dec. 27, 1958
<u>New Yorker,</u> 33:56, Jan. 25, 1958
<u>Newsweek,</u> 51:63, Jan. 27, 1958
<u>Reporter,</u> 18:36, March 6, 1958

Saturday Review, 41:25, Feb. 1, 1958
Spectator, 201:912, Dec. 26, 1958
Theatre Arts, 42:9, March, 1958
Time, 71:86, Jan. 27, 1958

BRENDAN GILL

SEE

MAXWELL ANDERSON AND BRENDAN GILL

WILLIAM HOOKER GILLETTE

"Clarice", 1905

Beerbohm, Max, Around Theatres, British Book Center, 1953, p. 388-92

"Sherlock Holmes", 1899

Brown, John Mason, Two on the Aisle; Ten Years of the American Theatre in Performance, Norton, 1938, p. 231-33
Skinner, R. D., "Concerning Sherlock Holmes", Commonweal, 11:198, Dec. 18, 1930

FRANK GILROY

"The Subject Was Roses", 1964

America, 110:853, June 20, 1964
Hudson Review, 17:427-8, Autumn, 1964
Life, 56:17, June 19, 1964
Life, 57:71-3, Sept. 4, 1964
Nation, 198:611, June 15, 1964
New Yorker, 40:86, June 6, 1964
Newsweek, 63:69, June 8, 1964
Saturday Review, 47:44, June 13, 1964
Time, 83:75, June 5, 1964
Vogue, 144:30, Aug. 1, 1964

"Who'll Save the Plowboy?", 1962

>America, 106:605, Feb. 3, 1962
>Educational Theatre Journal, 14:72, March, 1962
>Hudson Review, 15:266-7, Summer, 1962
>Nation, 194:127, Feb. 10, 1962
>National Review, 146:29-30, Feb. 5, 1962
>New Yorker, 37:69, Jan. 20, 1962
>Reporter, 26:48, March 1, 1962
>Theatre Arts, 46:61, March, 1962
>Time, 79:56, Jan. 26, 1962

SUSAN GLASPELL

"Alison's House", 1930

>Bookman, 72:514, Jan., 1931
>Catholic World, 132:591-2, Feb., 1931
>Commonweal, 13:187, Dec. 17, 1930
>Drama, 21:13, Jan., 1931
>Nation, 132:590-1, May 27, 1931
>Outlook, 156:711, Dec. 31, 1930
>Theatre Arts Monthly, 15:99, 101-2, Feb., 1931
>Theatre Magazine, 53:25, Feb., 1931

"Comic Artist", 1927

>Commonweal, 18:49-50, May 12, 1933
>Nation, 136:539-40, May 10, 1933
>New Republic, 74:365-6, May 10, 1933
>Newsweek, 1:26, April 29, 1933
>Theatre Arts Monthly, 17:418, June, 1933

"Inheritors", 1921

>English Review, 42:268-9, Feb., 1926
>Nation, 112:515, April 6, 1921
>Outlook (Lond), 57:25, Jan. 9, 1926
>Review, 4:344-6, April 13, 1921
>Spectator, 136:80-1, Jan. 16, 1926

"Verge", 1921

>Moses, Montrose Jonas and Brown, John Mason, eds.,
>American Theatre as Seen by its Critics, 1752-1934, Norton,
>1934, p. 252-55

Nation, 113:708-9, Dec. 14, 1921
New Republic, 29:47, Dec. 7, 1921
New Statesman, 24:746, April 4, 1925

THOMAS GODFREY

"Prince of Parthia", 1767
Quinn, A.D., "First American Play", Nation, 100:415,
April 15, 1915

AUGUSTUS AND RUTH GOODMAN GOETZ

"Heiress" (dramatization of novel Washington Square by Henry
James), 1947
Illustrated London News, 221:71, July 12, 1952
Theatre Arts, 34:18, April, 1950
Theatre Arts, 47:14-17, Jan., 1963

FRANCES GOODRICH AND ALBERT HACKETT

"Bridal Wise", 1932

Catholic World, 135:464-5, July, 1932
Commonweal, 16:188, June 15, 1932

"Diary of Anne Frank", 1955

America, 94:110, Oct. 22, 1955
Catholic World, 182:223, Dec., 1955
Commentary, 20:464-7, Nov., 1955
Commentary, 21:183-4, Feb., 1956
Commonweal, 63:91-2, Oct. 28, 1955
Commonweal, 65:87, Oct. 26, 1956
Illustrated London News, 229:1050, Dec. 15, 1956
Life, 39:162-3, Oct. 17, 1955
N.Y. Times Mag., p. 15, Feb. 17, 1957
N.Y. Times Mag., p. 47, Sept. 25, 1955
Nation, 181:370, Oct. 29, 1955
New Republic, 134:20, Jan. 2, 1956
New Statesman, 52:742, Dec. 8, 1956
New Yorker, 31:75-6, Oct. 15, 1955

Newsweek, 46:103, Oct. 17, 1955
Newsweek, 48:112, Oct. 15, 1956
Reporter, 13:31, Dec. 29, 1955
Saturday Review, 38:27, Oct. 22, 1955
Theatre Arts, 39:24, Dec., 1955
Theatre Arts, 41:29-30, May, 1957
Time, 66:51, Oct. 17, 1955
Time, 68:50, Oct. 15, 1956

"Great Big Doorstep" (dramatization of novel by E. P. O'Donnell), 1942

Nathan, George Jean, Theatre Book of the Year, 1942-1943, Knopf, p. 151-2

Catholic World, 156:474, Jan., 1943
Commonweal, 37:206, Dec. 11, 1943
Current History, n. s. 3:457, Jan., 1943
Newsweek, 20:76, Dec. 7, 1942
Theatre Arts, 27:17, Jan., 1943

"Up Pops the Devil", 1930

Arts and Decoration, 34:96, Nov., 1930
Catholic World, 132:205, Nov., 1930

JAY GORNEY

SEE

WALTER FRANCIS KERR, JEAN KERR AND JAY GORNEY

JAMES GOW AND ARNAUD D'USSEAU

"Deep Are the Roots", 1945

Catholic World, 162:164, Nov., 1945
Commonweal, 42:624, Oct. 12, 1945
Life, 19:51-2, Oct. 15, 1945
Nation, 161:384, Oct. 13, 1945
New Republic, 113:499, Oct. 15, 1945
New Republic, 114:446, April 1, 1946
New Yorker, 21:46, Oct. 6, 1945

Newsweek, 26:94-5, Oct. 8, 1945
Saturday Review of Literature, 28:38, Oct. 13, 1945
Theatre Arts, 29:622-4, Nov., 1945
Theatre Arts, 29:678, Dec., 1945
Time, 46:77, Oct. 8, 1945

"Legend of Sarah", 1950

Christian Science Monitor Mag., p. 6, Oct. 21, 1950
Commonweal, 53:95, Nov. 3, 1950
Nation, 171:370, Oct. 21, 1950
New Yorker, 26:55-7, Oct. 21, 1950
Newsweek, 36:85, Oct. 23, 1950
Theatre Arts, 34:14, Dec., 1950
Time, 56:58, Oct. 23, 1950

"Tomorrow the World", 1943

Catholic World, 157:298-9, June, 1943
Commonweal, 38:40, April 30, 1943
Life, 14:63-4, May 31, 1943
Nation, 156:642, May 1, 1943
New Republic, 108:637, May 10, 1943
New Yorker, 19:28, April 24, 1943
Newsweek, 21:86, April 26, 1943
Theatre Arts, 27:331-3, June, 1943
Time, 41:66, April 26, 1943

PAUL ELIOT GREEN

"Common Glory", 1947

Green, Paul, Dramatic Heritage, French, 1953, p. 67-72

"Field God", 1927

Krutch, J. W., Nation, 124:5, 10-11, May 4, 1927

"House of Connelly", 1931

Theatre Arts Anthology, a Record and a Prophecy, ed. by
Rosamond Gilder and others, Theatre Arts Books, 1950,
p. 616-19
Young, Stark, Immortal Shadows, a Book of Dramatic
Criticism, Scribner, 1948, p. 127-31

Arts & Decoration, 36:68, Dec., 1931
Bookman, 74:298-9, Nov., 1931
Catholic World, 134:207-8, Nov., 1931
Commonweal, 14:583-4, Oct. 14, 1931
Literary Digest,111:17, Oct. 24, 1931
Nation, 133:408, Oct. 14, 1931
New Republic, 68:234-6, Oct. 14, 1931
Saturday Review of Literature, 8:199, Oct. 17, 1931
Theatre Arts Monthly, 15:975-7, Dec., 1931

"In Abraham's Bosom, " 1927

Block, Anita Cahn, Changing World in Plays and Theatre,
Little, 1939, p. 194-250
Young, Stark, Immortal Shadows, a Book of Dramatic
Criticism, Scribner, 1948, p. 88-90
Drama, 17:136, Feb., 1927
Literary Digest, 93:27-8, May 28, 1927
London Mercury, 17:91-3, Nov., 1927
New Republic, 50:46-7, March 2, 1927
Survey, 57:591-2, Feb. 1, 1927

"Johnny Johnson", 1937

Catholic World, 144:468-9, Jan., 1937
Commonweal, 25:162, Dec. 4, 1936
Forum, 97:354, June, 1937
Literary Digest, 123:23, Jan. 2, 1937
Nation, 143:674, Dec. 5, 1936
Nation, 183:439, Nov. 17, 1936
New Republic, 89:179, Dec. 9, 1936
Newsweek, 8:19, Nov. 28, 1936
Scribner's Magazine, 101:65-7, June, 1937
Theatre Arts Monthly, 21:15-17, Jan., 1937
Theatre Arts Monthly, 21:426-7, June, 1937
Time, 28:54, Nov. 30, 1936

"Lost Colony", 1937

Green, Paul, Dramatic Heritage, French, 1953, p. 42-48
Magazine of Art, 31:690-3, Dec., 1938
Readers Digest, 37:30, July, 1940
Saturday Review, 39:31, Aug. 4, 1956
Theatre Arts Monthly, 23:518-22, July, 1939
Time, 34:48, July 10, 1939

"Peer Gynt", 1951

>   Nathan, George Jean, Theatre Book of the Year, 1950-1951, Knopf,
>   p. 197-201

"Roll, Sweet Chariot", 1934

>   Theatre Arts Anthology, a Record and a Prophecy, ed. by
>   Rosamond Gilder and others, Theatre Arts Books, 1950,
>   p. 627-29
>   Isaacs, E. J. R., Theatre Arts Monthly, 18:813-14, November,
>   1934

"Wilderness Road", 1955

>   Saturday Review, 39:30, Aug. 4, 1956

SEE ALSO

RICHARD WRIGHT AND PAUL GREEN

BERTRAM GREENE

"Summer of Daisy Miller" (dramatization of Daisy Miller by Henry
James), 1963

>   New Yorker, 39:126, June 8, 1963
>   Theatre Arts, 47:11, Aug., 1963

ALBERT HACKETT

SEE

FRANCES GOODRICH AND ALBERT HACKETT

WILLIAM WISTER HAINES

"Command Decision", 1947

>   Brown, John Mason, Seeing More Things, McGraw, 1948,
>   p. 273-81

Dusenbury, Winifred Loesch, The Theme of Loneliness in
   Modern American Drama, Univ. Florida Press, 1960,
   p. 179-96
Nathan, George Jean, Theatre Book of the Year, 1947-1948,
   Knopf, p. 62-66
McCarthy, Mary Therese, Sights and Spectacles, 1937-1956,
   Farrar, Straus, 1956, p. 121-30

Catholic World, 166:170, Nov. 1947
Commonweal, 47:16, Oct. 17, 1947
Forum, 108:368-70, Dec., 1947
Life, 23:107-8, Oct. 20, 1947
Nation, 165:480-1, Nov. 1, 1947
New Republic, 117:36, Oct. 13, 1947
N. Y. Times Mag., p. 30-1, Sept. 28, 1947
New Yorker, 23:50, Oct. 11, 1947
Newsweek, 30:80, Oct. 13, 1947
Saturday Review of Literature, 30:30-3, Oct. 25, 1947
School and Society, 66:326-7, Oct. 25, 1947
Theatre Arts, 31:13-14, Dec., 1947
Theatre Arts, 32:30, April, 1948
Time, 50:70, Oct. 13, 1947

OSCAR HAMMERSTEIN

"Carmen Jones", 1943

   Thomson, Virgil, Art of Judging Music, Knopf, 1948,
      p. 125-27
   Nathan, George Jean, Theatre Book of the Year, 1943-44,
      Knopf, p. 150-54

"New Moon", 1942

   Nathan, George Jean, Theatre Book of the Year, 1942-43,
      Knopf, p. 44-45

OSCAR HAMMERSTEIN AND JEROME DAVID KERN

"Music in the Air", 1932

   Arts and Decoration, 38:50, Jan., 1933

Catholic World, 136:462-3, Jan., 1933
Commonweal, 17:131, Nov. 30, 1932
Saturday Review, 155:514, May 27, 1933
Theatre Arts Monthly, 17:4-5, Jan., 1933

"Show Boat", 1927

Nathan, George Jean, Theatre Book of the Year, 1945-1946, Knopf, p. 260-64

OSCAR HAMMERSTEIN AND RICHARD RODGERS

"Allegro", 1947

Brown, John Mason, Seeing More Things, McGraw, 1948, p. 134-41
Nathan, George Jean, Theatre Book of the Year, 1947-1948, Knopf, p. 100-03

"Carousel", 1945

Brown, John Mason, Seeing Things, McGraw, 1946, p. 231-36
Nathan, George Jean, Theatre Book of the Year, 1944-1945, Knopf, p. 332-35
Theatre Arts Anthology, a Record and a Prophecy, ed. by Rosamond Gilder and others, Theatre Arts Books, 1950, p. 657-61

"The King and I", 1951

Brown, John Mason, As They Appear, McGraw, 1952, p. 221-27
Nathan, George Jean, Theatre Book of the Year, 1950-1951, Knopf, p. 258-61

"Oklahoma", 1943

Nathan, George Jean, Theatre Book of the Year, 1942-1943, Knopf, p. 269-70
Oppenheimer, George, ed., Passionate Playgoer, a Personal Scrapbook, Viking, 1958, p. 470-75
Theatre Arts Anthology, a Record and a Prophecy, ed. by Rosamond Gilder and others, Theatre Arts Books, 1950, p. 655-57

OSCAR HAMMERSTEIN AND SIGMUND ROMBERG

"Sunny River", 1942
    Catholic World, 154:474, Jan., 1942

                    WILLIAM HANLEY

"Mrs. Dally", 1965
    America, 113:508, Oct. 30, 1965
    Commonweal, 83:61-2, Oct. 15, 1965
    New Yorker, 41:176, Oct. 2, 1965
    Newsweek, 66:94, Oct. 4, 1965
    Saturday Review, 48:34, Oct. 9, 1965
    Time, 86:67, Oct. 1, 1965

"Mrs. Dally Has a Lover", 1962
    Commonweal, 77:123, Oct. 26, 1962
    New Yorker, 38:183, Oct. 13, 1962

"Slow Dance on the Killing Ground", 1964
    America, 112:231-2, Feb. 13, 1965
    Commonweal, 81:485-6, Jan. 8, 1965
    Life, 58:10, Jan. 15, 1965
    Nation, 199:523-4, Dec. 28, 1964
    New Republic, 152:32, Jan. 23, 1965
    Newsweek, 64:84, Dec. 14, 1965
    Reporter, 32:50-1, Feb. 11, 1965
    Saturday Review, 47:24-5, Dec. 19, 1964
    Time, 84:73, Dec. 11, 1964
    Vogue, 145:27, Jan. 15, 1965

"Whisper Into My Good Ear", 1962
    Commonweal, 77:123, Oct. 26, 1962
    New Yorker, 38:182, Oct. 13, 1962

                    LORRAINE HANSBERRY

"Raisin in the Sun", 1959
    Tynan, Kenneth, Curtains; Selections from the Drama
        Criticism and Related Writings, Atheneum, 1961,
        p. 306-09

America, 101:286-7, May 2, 1959
Catholic World, 189:159, May, 1959
Catholic World, 190:31-5, Oct., 1959
Commentary, 27:527-30, June, 1959
Commonweal, 70:81, April 17, 1959
Illustrated London News, 235:246, Sept. 12, 1959
Life, 46:137-8, April 27, 1959
Nation, 188:301-2, April 4, 1959
New Republic, 140:21, April 13, 1959
New Statesman, 58:190, Aug. 15, 1959
New Yorker, 35:100-2, March 21, 1959
Newsweek, 53:76, March 23, 1959
Reporter, 20:34-5, April 16, 1959
Saturday Review, 42:28, April 4, 1959
Spectator, 203:189, Aug. 14, 1959
Theatre Arts, 43:22-3, May, 1959
Theatre Arts, 43:58-61, July, 1959
Time, 73:58, March 23, 1959

"Sign in Sidney Brustein's Window", 1964

America, 111:758, Dec. 5, 1964
Commonweal, 81:197, Nov. 6, 1964
Nation, 199:340, Nov. 9, 1964
National Review, 17:250, March 23, 1965
New Yorker, 40:93, Oct. 24, 1964
Newsweek, 64:101, Oct. 26, 1964
Saturday Review, 47:31, Oct. 31, 1964
Time, 84:67, Oct. 23, 1964

EDWARD HARRIGAN

"Notoriety", 1894

"Mr. Harrigan's new play", Critic (ns 22):418, Dec. 15, 1894

MOSS HART

"Christopher Blake", 1946

Nathan, George Jean, Theatre Book of the Year, 1946-1947, Knopf, p. 217-20

Catholic World, 164:357-8, Jan., 1947
Commonweal, 45:255, Dec. 20, 1946
Life, 22:95-6, Jan. 13, 1947
Nation, 163:738, Dec. 21, 1946
New Republic, 115:824, Dec. 16, 1946
New Yorker, 22:67-9, Dec. 7, 1946
Newsweek, 28:92, Dec. 9, 1946
Theatre Arts, 31:12-13, Feb., 1947
Time, 48:83, Dec. 9, 1946

"Climate of Eden" (dramatization of Shadows Move Among Them by
E. Mittelholzer), 1952

Nathan, George Jean, Theatre in the Fifties, Knopf, 1953,
p. 65-67

Commonweal, 57:223, Dec. 5, 1952
Nation, 175:473, Nov. 22, 1952
New Yorker, 28:69, Nov. 15, 1952
Newsweek, 40:74, Nov. 17, 1952
Saturday Review, 35:37-8, Nov. 22, 1952
Theatre Arts, 37:23-4, Jan., 1953
Time, 60:102, Nov. 17, 1952

"Lady in the Dark", 1941

Catholic World, 152:726-7, March, 1941
Commonweal, 33:401, Feb. 7, 1941
Commonweal, 37:542, March 19, 1943
Nation, 152:164, Feb. 8, 1942
New Republic, 104:179, Feb. 10, 1942
New Yorker, 16:27, Feb. 1, 1941
Theatre Arts, 25:177-8, March, 1941
Theatre Arts, 25:265-75, April, 1941

"Light Up the Sky", 1948

Nathan, George Jean, Theatre Book of the Year, 1948-1949,
Knopf, P. 181-84

Catholic World, 168:324, Jan.,1949
Commonweal, 49:196, Dec. 3, 1948
Forum, 111:92, Feb., 1949
Life, 25:115-16, Dec. 6, 1948
Nation, 167:674, Dec. 11, 1948
New Republic, 119:37-8, Dec. 6, 1948

New Yorker, 24:55, Nov. 27, 1948
Newsweek, 32:82, Nov. 29, 1948
Saturday Review of Literature, 31:24-5, Dec. 11, 1948
School and Society, 69:154, Feb. 26, 1949
Time, 52:78, Nov. 29, 1948

"Winged Victory", 1943

Nathan, George Jean, Theatre Book of the Year, 1943-1944, Knopf, p. 138-142

American Magazine, 137:28-9, June, 1944
Catholic World, 158:392, Jan., 1944
Commonweal, 39:204-5, Dec. 10, 1943
Life, 15:58-64, Nov. 29, 1943
Nation, 157:675, Dec. 4, 1943
New Republic, 109:808, Dec. 6, 1943
N. Y. Times Mag., p. 8-9, Nov. 7, 1943
New Yorker, 19:51-2, Dec. 4, 1943
Newsweek, 22:86, Nov. 29, 1943
Theatre Arts, 27:723-6, Dec., 1943
Theatre Arts, 28:6-8, Jan., 1944
Time, 42:43-4, Nov. 29, 1943

MOSS HART AND IRVING BERLIN

"As Thousands Cheer", 1933

Canadian Forum, 15:274, April, 1935
Catholic World, 138:337, Dec., 1933
Commonweal, 18:591-2, Oct. 20, 1933
New Republic, 76:279, Oct. 18, 1933
Review of Reviews, 89:40, Feb., 1934
Theatre Arts, 17:919, Dec., 1933

"Face the Music", 1932

Arts & Decoration, 36:45, April, 1932
Bookman, 74:666, March, 1932
Catholic World, 135:75-6, April, 1932
Commonweal, 15:495, March 2, 1932
New Republic, 70:97, March 9, 1932
Outlook, 160:189, March, 1932

MOSS HART AND GEORGE SIMON KAUFMAN

"The American Way" , 1939

> Catholic World, 148:728-9, March, 1939
> Commonweal, 29:441, Feb. 10, 1939
> Nation, 148:157-8, Feb. 4, 1939
> New Republic, 98:14, Feb. 8, 1939
> Newsweek, 13:24, Feb. 6, 1939
> North American Review, 247:153-5, March, 1939
> Theatre Arts, 23:162-4, March, 1939

"Fabulous Invalid", 1938

> Brown, John Mason, Broadway in Review, Norton, 1940,
> p. 169-76

> Catholic World, 148:211-12, Nov. , 1938
> Commonweal, 28:677, Oct. 21, 1938
> Independent Woman, 17:347, Nov. , 1938
> Nation, 147:432, Oct. 22, 1938
> New Republic, 96:334, Oct. 26, 1938
> Publishers Weekly, 134:1581, Oct. 29, 1938
> Theatre Arts, 22:862-4, Dec. , 1938
> Time, 32:50, Oct. 17, 1938

"George Washington Slept Here", 1940

> American Mercury, 51:483-5, Dec. , 1940
> Catholic World, 152:335, Dec. , 1940
> Commonweal, 33:80, Nov. 8, 1940
> Nation, 151:430, Nov. 2, 1940
> New Republic, 103:629, Nov. 4, 1940
> New Yorker, 16:36, Oct. 26, 1940
> Newsweek, 16:62, Nov. 4, 1940
> Theatre Arts, 24:849, Dec. , 1940

"I'd Rather Be Right", 1937

> Brown, John Mason, Two on the Aisle; Ten Years of the
> American Theatre in Performance, Norton, 1938,
> p. 286-89

> Catholic World, 146:339-40, Dec. , 1937
> Commonweal, 27:106, Nov. 19, 1937
> Independent Woman, 16:351, Nov. , 1937

New Republic, 93:44, Nov. 17, 1937
Newsweek, 10:24-6 Oct. 25, 1937
Newsweek, 10:29, Nov. 15, 1937
Scholastic, 31:2, Oct. 30, 1937
Scribner's Magazine, 103:70, Jan., 1938
Theatre Arts, 21:924, Dec., 1937
Time, 30:45, Oct. 25, 1937
Time, 30:25, Nov. 15, 1937

"Man Who Came to Dinner", 1939

Brown, John Mason, Broadway in Review, Norton, 1940,
p. 85-95
Catholic World, 150:339-40, Dec., 1939
Commonweal, 31:47, Nov. 3, 1939
Nation, 149:474-5, Oct. 28, 1939
New Republic, 100:368, Nov. 1, 1939
Theatre Arts, 23:779, 788-98, Nov., 1939
Theatre Arts, 23:851-2, Dec., 1939
Theatre Arts, 24:407, June, 1940
Time, 34:42, Oct. 30, 1939

"Merrily We Roll Along", 1934

Catholic World, 140:209, Nov., 1934
Commonweal, 20:589, Oct. 19, 1934
Golden Book, 20:636, Dec., 1934
Literary Digest,118:18, Oct. 13, 1934
Nation, 139:460, Oct. 17, 1934
Scholastic, 25:3, Oct. 20, 1934
Theatre Arts, 18:815-16, Nov., 1934

"Once in a Life Time", 1930

Catholic World, 132:204-5, Nov., 1930
Commonweal, 12:584, Oct. 8, 1930
Nation, 131:386, Oct. 8, 1930
Sociology and Social Research, 15:498, May, 1931
Spectator, 150:284-5, March 3, 1933

"You Can't Take It With You", 1936

Brown, John Mason, Two on the Aisle; Ten Years of the
American Theatre in Performance, Norton, 1938,
p. 177-80

Kaplan, Charles, "Two depression plays and Broadway's
   popular idealism", American Quarterly, 15:579-85, 1963
Nathan, George Jean, Theatre Book of the Year, 1944-1945,
   Knopf, p. 320-21
O'Hara, Frank H., Today in American drama, Univ. of
   Chicago Press, 1939, p. 190-234

America, 113:762-3, Dec. 11, 1965
Catholic World, 144:597-8, Feb., 1937
Commonweal, 25:249, Dec. 25, 1936
Life, 59:16, Dec. 17, 1965
Literary Digest, 122:22, Dec. 26, 1936
Nation, 201:484, Dec. 13, 1965
New Republic, 153:29, Dec. 18, 1965
New Republic, 89:273, Dec. 30, 1936
Newsweek, 66:92, Dec. 6, 1965
Newsweek, 8:38, Dec. 26, 1936
New Yorker, 41:106, Dec. 4, 1965
Saturday Review, 48:51, Dec. 11, 1965
Theatre Arts, 21:96-7, Feb., 1937
Time, 28:33, Dec. 28, 1936
Time, 86:54, Dec. 3, 1965

MOSS HART AND COLE PORTER

"Jubilee", 1935

Catholic World, 142:340, Dec., 1935
Commonweal, 22:642, Oct. 25, 1935
Newsweek, 6:26-7, Oct. 19, 1935
Theatre Arts, 19:901-2, Dec., 1935
Time, 26:51, Oct. 21, 1935

JAN DE HARTOG

"The Fourposter", 1951

Nathan, George Jean, Theatre in the Fifties, Knopf, 1953,
   p. 170-72

America, 92:463, Jan. 29, 1955
Catholic World, 174:227, Dec., 1951
Catholic World, 180:468, March, 1955
Commonweal, 55:118, Nov. 9, 1951

Life, 31:125-6, Nov. 26, 1951
New Republic, 132:22, Feb. 7, 1955
New Yorker, 27:91, Nov. 3, 1951
Newsweek, 38:64, Nov. 5, 1951
Saturday Review, 35:27, July 5, 1952
Theatre Arts, 35:3, Dec., 1951
Theatre Arts, 36:21, Jan., 1952
Theatre Arts, 39:91, March, 1955
Time, 58:66, Nov. 5, 1951

"Skipper Next to God", 1945

Nathan, George Jean, Theatre Book of the Year, 1947-1948,
Knopf, p. 211-16

"This Time Tomorrow", 1947

Nathan, George Jean, Theatre Book of the Year, 1947-1948,
Knopf, p. 131-34

GEORGE COCHRANE HAZELTON, JR.

"Mistress Nell", 1912

Personal Book Buyer, 22:93-4, March, 1901

GEORGE COCHRANE HAZELTON, JR.

AND

J. HARRY BENRIMO

"Yellow Jacket", 1912

Craftsman, 31:154-64, Nov., 1916
English Review, 14:319-22, May, 1913
New Republic, 9:189, Dec. 16, 1916

BEN HECHT

"A Flag is Born", 1946

Nathan, George Jean, Theatre Book of the Year, 1946-1947,
Knopf, p. 52-56

Catholic World, 164:71, Oct., 1946
Life, 21:87-8, Sept. 30, 1946
New Republic, 115:351, Sept. 23, 1946
New Yorker, 22:48, Sept. 14, 1946
Newsweek, 28:92, Sept. 16, 1946
Time, 48:85, Sept. 16, 1946

"Lily of the Valley", 1942

Catholic World, 154:732, March, 1942
Commonweal, 35:418, Feb. 13, 1942
New Republic, 106:204, Feb. 9, 1942
Theatre Arts, 26:225, April, 1942

"To Quito and Back", 1937

McCarthy, Mary Therese, Sights and Spectacles, 1937-1956,
Farrar, Straus, 1956, p. 3-8

Catholic World, 146:218-19, Nov. 1937
Commonweal, 26:606, Oct. 22, 1937
Independent Woman, 16:368, Nov., 1937
Nation, 145:412, Oct. 16, 1937
New Republic, 92:342, Oct. 27, 1937
Theatre Arts, 21:919-20, Dec., 1937
Time, 30:324, Oct. 18, 1937

"Winkelberg", 1958

New Republic, 138:21, Feb. 3, 1958
Saturday Review, 41:25, Feb. 1, 1958

BEN HECHT AND GENE FOWLER

"Great Magoo", 1932

Nathan, George Jean, Passing Judgments, Knopf, 1935,
p. 140-176

Nation, 135:625-6, Dec. 21, 1932
Theatre Arts, 17:112, Feb., 1933

BEN HECHT AND CHARLES MACARTHUR

"Front Page", 1928

> Nathan, George Jean, <u>Theatre Book of the Year, 1946-1947</u>, Knopf, p. 43-46
>
> <u>Catholic World</u>, 128:211-2, Nov., 1928
> <u>Catholic World</u>, 164:72, Oct., 1946
> <u>Life</u>, 21:78-80, Sept. 23, 1946
> <u>New Republic</u>, 56:73-4, Sept. 5, 1928
> <u>New Republic</u>, 115:351, Sept. 23, 1946
> <u>New Yorker</u>, 22:46, Sept. 14, 1946
> <u>Newsweek</u>, 28:92, Sept. 16, 1946
> <u>Outlook</u>, 149:705, Aug. 29, 1928
> <u>Saturday Review of Literature</u>, 5:706, Feb. 23, 1939
> <u>Saturday Review of Literature</u>, 29:24-6, Oct. 26, 1946
> <u>Time</u>, 48:85, Sept. 16, 1946

"Swan Song", 1946

> Nathan, George Jean, <u>Theatre Book of the Year, 1946-1947</u>, Knopf, p. 17-20
>
> <u>Catholic World</u>, 163:360, July, 1946
> <u>New Yorker</u>, 22:46-7, May 25, 1946
> <u>Time</u>, 47:66, May 27, 1946

"Twentieth Century", 1933

> <u>Arts & Decoration</u>, 38:63, March, 1933
> <u>Catholic World</u>, 136:580, Feb., 1933
> <u>Catholic World</u>, 172:387-8, Feb., 1951
> <u>Christian Science Monitor Mag.</u>, p. 9, Dec. 30, 1950
> <u>Commonweal</u>, 17:329, Jan. 18, 1933
> <u>Commonweal</u>, 53:349, Jan. 12, 1951
> <u>Life</u>, 30:117-18, Feb. 19, 1951
> <u>Nation</u>, 172:18, Jan. 6, 1951
> <u>New Republic</u>, 124:22, Jan. 8, 1951
> <u>New Yorker</u>, 26:54, Jan. 6, 1951
> <u>Newsweek</u>, 37:80, Jan. 22, 1951
> <u>Saturday Review of Literature</u>, 34:25-7, March 24, 1951

Theatre Arts, 17:178, March, 1933
Theatre Arts, 35:12, 22-3, March, 1951
Time, 57:30, Jan. 8, 1951

THOMAS HEGGEN AND JOSHUA LOGAN

"Mister Roberts", 1948

Brown, John Mason, Seeing More Things, McGraw, 1948,
  p. 282-88
Nathan, George Jean, Theatre Book of the Year, 1947-1948,
  Knopf, p. 283-86
Oppenheimer, George, ed., Passionate Playgoer, a
  Personal Scrapbook, Viking, 1958, p. 574-80

Catholic World, 167:70, April, 1948
Commonweal, 47:521, March 5, 1948
Christian Science Monitor Mag., p. 7, Aug. 5, 1950
Illustrated London News, 217:254, Aug. 12, 1950
Life, 24:93-6, March 1, 1948
Nation, 166:402-3, April 10, 1948
New Republic, 118:29, March 8, 1948
N.Y. Times Mag., p. 12-13, Feb. 8, 1948
New Yorker, 24:46, Feb. 28, 1948
Newsweek, 31:65-6, March 1, 1948
Saturday Review of Literature, 31:24-6, March 6, 1948
Spectator, 185:113, July 28, 1950
Theatre Arts, 32:28-9, April, 1948
Theatre Arts, 33:12, 15, Nov., 1949
Theatre Arts, 41:25, Feb., 1957
Time, 51:63, March 1, 1948

SEE ALSO

JOSHUA LOGAN AND THOMAS HEGGEN

LILLIAN HELLMAN

"Another Part of the Forest", 1946

Nathan, George Jean, Theatre Book of the Year, 1946-1947,
  Knopf, p. 201-04

Catholic World, 164:600, Jan., 1947
Commonweal, 45:201, Dec. 6, 1946
Life, 21:71-2, Dec. 9, 1946
Nation, 163:671, Dec. 7, 1946
New Republic, 115:822, Dec. 16, 1946
N. Y. Times Mag., p. 68-9, Nov. 17, 1946
New Yorker, 22:58, Nov. 30, 1946
Newsweek, 28:94, Dec. 2, 1946
Saturday Review of Literature, 29:20-3, Dec. 14, 1946
School and Society, 65:251, April 5, 1947
Theatre Arts, 31:14, 17, Jan., 1947
Time, 48:56, Dec. 2, 1946

"Autumn Gardens", 1951

Nathan, George Jean, Theatre Book of the Year, 1950-1951, Knopf, p. 241-44
Catholic World, 173:67, April, 1951
Commonweal, 53:645, April 6, 1951
Nation, 172:257, March 17, 1951
New Republic, 124:21-2, March 26, 1951
New Yorker, 27:52, March 17, 1951
Newsweek, 37:84, March 19, 1951
Theatre Arts, 35:18, May, 1951
Theatre Arts, 35:17, Sept., 1951
Time, 57:51, March 19, 1951

"Children's Hour", 1934

Bentley, Eric Russel, Dramatic Event, Horizon Press, 1954, p. 74-77
Block, Anita Cahn, Changing World in Plays and Theatre, Little, 1939, p. 76-132
Nathan, George Jean, Theatre in the Fifties, Knopf, 1953, p. 49-52
Catholic World, 140:466-7, Jan., 1935
Catholic World, 176:388, Feb., 1953
Commonweal, 57:377, Jan. 16, 1953
Golden Book, 21:28a, Feb., 1935
Life, 34:51, Jan. 19, 1953
Literary Digest, 118:20, Dec. 1, 1934
Nation, 139:656-7, Dec. 5, 1934
Nation, 176:18, Jan. 3, 1953

New Republic, 81:169, Dec. 19, 1934
New Republic, 128:30-1, Jan. 5, 1953
New Statesman and Nation, 12:810, Nov. 21, 1936
New Yorker, 28:30, Jan. 3, 1953
Newsweek, 40:40, Dec. 29, 1952
Saturday Review, 162:671, Nov. 21, 1936
Saturday Review of Literature, 11:523, 548, March 2, 16,
   1935
Saturday Review of Literature, 36:30, Jan. 10, 1953
School and Society, 77:117-18, Feb. 21, 1953
Spectator, 157:905, Nov. 20, 1936
Theatre Arts, 19:113-15, 270, Jan., and April, 1935
Time, 60:55, Dec. 29, 1952

"Days to Come", 1936

Commonweal, 25:276, Jan. 1, 1937
Literary Digest, 122:22, Dec. 26, 1936
Nation, 143:769-70, Dec. 26, 1936
New Republic, 89:274, Dec. 30, 1936

"Little Foxes", 1939

Brown, John Mason, Broadway in Review, Norton, 1940,
   p. 116-20
Krutch, Joseph Wood, American drama since 1918,
   Braziller, 1957, p. 73-133
O'Hara, Frank Hurburt, Today in American drama, Univ.
   Chicago Press, 1939, p. 53-141

Catholic World, 149:87-8, April, 1939
Commweal, 29:525, March 3, 1939
Nation, 148:244, Feb. 25, 1939
New Republic, 98:279, April 12, 1939
Newsweek, 13:26, Feb. 27, 1939
New Statesman and Nation, 24:304, Nov. 7, 1942
Theatre Arts Monthly, 23:244, April, 1939
Time, 33:38, Feb. 27, 1939

"Montserrat" (adapted from Montserrat by Emmanuel Robles), 1949

Nathan, George Jean, Theatre Book of the Year, 1949-1950,
   Knopf, p. 63-71

America, 104:577, Jan. 28, 1961
New Yorker, 36:68-70, Jan. 21, 1961

"My Mother, My Father, and Me" (dramatization of How much? by
B. Blechman), 1963

Nation, 196:334, April 20, 1963
New Yorker, 39:108, March 30, 1963
Newsweek, 61:85, April 8, 1963
Reporter, 28:48, April 25, 1963
Saturday Review, 46:27, April 27, 1963
Theatre Arts, 47:69-70, May, 1963
Time, 81:56, April 5, 1963

"Searching the Wind", 1944

Nathan, George Jean, Theatre Book of the Year, 1943-1944,
Knopf, p. 295-99
Catholic World, 159:170-1, May, 1944
Commonweal, 40:40, April 28, 1944
Life, 16:43-44, May 1, 1944
Nation, 158:494, April 22, 1944
New Republic, 110:604, May 1, 1944
N. Y. Times Mag., p. 19, April 23, 1944
New Yorker, 20:42, April 22, 1944
Newsweek, 23:86, April 24, 1944
Theatre Arts, 28:331-3, June, 1944
Time, 43:72, April 24, 1944

"Toys in the Attic", 1960

Kerr, Walter, The Theatre in Spite of Itself, Simon and
Schuster, 1963, p. 235-38
America, 103:323, May 28, 1960
Christian Century, 77:511, April 27, 1960
Life, 48:53-4, April 4, 1960
Nation, 190:261, March 19, 1960
New Republic, 142:22, March 14, 1960
Illustrated London News, 237:964, Nov. 26, 1960
New Yorker, 36:124-5, March 5, 1960
Newsweek, 55:89, March 7, 1960
Reporter, 22:43, March 31, 1960

"Watch on the Rhine", 1941

Theatre Arts Anthology, Theatre Arts Books, 1950, p. 649-51

Catholic World, 153:215-16, May, 1941
Commonweal, 34:15-16, April 25, 1941

Life, 10:81-2, April 14, 1941
Nation, 152:453, April 12, 1941
New Republic, 104:498-9, April 14, 1941
New Statesman and Nation, 23:288, May 2, 1942
New Yorker, 17:32, April 12, 1941
Newsweek, 17:70, April 14, 1941
Spectator, 168:419, May 1, 1942
Theatre Arts, 25:409-11, June, 1941
Theatre Arts, 25:791, Nov., 1941
Time, 37:64, April 14, 1941

FREDERICK HUGH HERBERT

"Best House in Naples" (adapted from the play by E. deFilippo),
1956

New Yorker, 32:73, Nov. 3, 1956
Theatre Arts, 41:20, Jan., 1957

"For Keeps", 1944

Nathan, George Jean, Theatre Book of the Year, 1944-1945,
Knopf, p. 20-21

Catholic World, 159:459, Aug., 1944
Commonweal, 40:255, June 30, 1944
New Yorker, 20:47, June 24, 1944

"For Love or Money", 1947

Nathan, George Jean, Theatre Book of the Year, 1947-1948,
Knopf, p. 135-40

Catholic World, 166:267, Dec., 1947
New Republic, 117:32, Nov. 17, 1947
New Yorker, 23:54, Nov. 15, 1947
Newsweek, 30:84, Nov. 17, 1947
School and Society, 66:421-2, Nov. 29, 1947
Time, 50:87, Nov. 17, 1947

"A Girl Can Tell", 1953

America, 90:215, Nov. 21, 1953
Catholic World, 178:231, Dec., 1953
Commonweal, 59:164, Nov. 20, 1953

Nation, 177:434, Nov. 21, 1953
New Yorker, 29:76, Nov. 7, 1953
Newsweek, 42:60, Nov. 9, 1953
Saturday Review, 36:38, Nov. 14, 1953
Theatre Arts, 38:17, Jan., 1954
Time, 62:72, Nov. 9, 1953

"Kiss and Tell", 1943

Nathan, George Jean, Theatre Book of the Year, 1942-1943, Knopf, p. 255-57

Catholic World, 157:185-6, May 1943
Commonweal, 37:590, April 2, 1943
Independent Woman, 22:155, May, 1943
Life, 14:41-2, April 12, 1943
Newsweek, 21:58, March 29, 1943
Theatre Arts, 27:276, May, 1943

"The Moon is Blue", 1951

Nathan, George Jean, Theatre Book, of the Year, 1950-1951, Knopf, p. 245-48

Catholic World, 173:147, May, 1951
Commonweal, 53:618, March 30, 1951
Life, 30:87-8, April 2, 1951
New Republic, 124:21, April 9, 1951
New Yorker, 27:56, March 17, 1951
Newsweek, 37:84, March 19, 1951
Theatre Arts, 35:19, May, 1951
Time, 57:52, March 19, 1951

FREDERICK HUGH HERBERT AND HANS KRALY

"Quiet, Please", 1940

Commonweal, 33:127, Nov. 22, 1940

JAMES A. HERNE

"Drifting Apart", 1888

Harper's Monthly, 81:154, June, 1890

"Margaret Fleming", 1890

> Moses, Montrose Jonas and Brown, John Mason, American
> Theatre as Seen by its Critics, 1752-1934, Norton 1934,
> p. 142-47

> Arena, 4:247-8, July, 1891
> Critic, 19 (ns16) :352-3, Dec. 19, 1891

"Reverend Griffith Davenport", 1899

> Arena, 22:375-82, Sept., 1899

DOROTHY HARTZELL HEYWARD

"Set My People Free", 1948

> Nathan, George Jean, Theatre Book of the Year, 1948-1949,
> Knopf, p. 153-57

> Catholic World, 168:241-2, Dec., 1948
> Commonweal, 49:142, Nov. 19, 1948
> Forum, 110:353-4, Dec., 1948
> Nation, 167:586, Nov. 20, 1948
> New Republic, 119:28-9, Nov. 22, 1943
> New Yorker, 24:60, Nov. 13, 1948
> Newsweek, 32:82, Nov. 15, 1948
> School and Society, 68:389, Dec. 4, 1948
> Time, 52:84, Nov. 14, 1948

DOROTHY HARZELL HEYWARD AND DUBOSE HEYWARD

"Mamba's Daughters", 1939

> Davidson, Donald, The Spyglass; Views and Reviews, 1924-
> 1930, Vanderbilt Univ. Press, 1963, p. 29-34

> O'Hara, Frank Hurburt, Today in American Drama, Univ.
> Chicago Press, 1939, p. 142-89

> Catholic World, 148:597-8, Feb., 1939
> Commonweal, 29:358, Jan. 20, 1939
> Nation, 148:74, Jan. 14, 1939
> New Republic, 97:315, Jan. 18, 1939
> Newsweek, 13:26, Jan. 16, 1939

Theatre Arts, 23:169, March, 1939
Time, 33:41, Jan. 16, 1939

"Porgy", 1927

Ludwig, Richard Milton, Essays Today, Harcourt, 1955,
p. 56-64

Moses, Montrose Jonas and John Mason Brown, eds.,
American Theatre as Seen by its Critics, 1752-1934,
Norton, 1934, p. 323-26

Literary Digest, 95:27-8, Nov. 5, 1927
Nation (Lond), 45:75, April 20, 1929
New Republic, 52:261-2, Oct. 26, 1927
New Statesman, 33:81, April 27, 1929
Outlook, 147:402-3, Nov. 30, 1927
Saturday Review of Literature, 4:251, Oct. 29, 1927
Spectator, 142:615-16, April 20, 1929
Survey, 59:465-6, Jan. 1, 1928

DOROTHY HARTZELL HEYWARD AND HOWARD RIGSLEY

"South Pacific", 1944

Commonweal, 39:328-9, Jan. 14, 1944
New Yorker, 19:38, Jan. 8, 1944
Newsweek, 23:89, Jan. 10, 1944
Theatre Arts, 28:136-7, March, 1944
Time, 43:72, Jan. 10, 1944

DUBOSE HEYWARD

"Brass Ankle", 1931

Arts & Decoration, 35:82, July, 1931
Catholic World, 133:335-7, June, 1931
Commonweal, 14:16, May 6, 1931
Drama, 21:10-11, May, 1931
Nation, 132:538-9, May 13, 1931
New Republic, 66:359, May 13, 1931
Outlook, 158:26, May 6, 1931
Sociology and Social Research, 16:97, Sept., 1931

DUBOSE HEYWARD AND GEORGE GERSHWIN

"Porgy and Bess", 1935
  South Atlantic Quarterly, 53:497-507, Oct., 1954

SEE ALSO

DOROTHY HARTZELL HEYWARD AND DUBOSE HEYWARD

HAROLD HICKERSON

SEE

MAXWELL ANDERSON AND HAROLD HICKERSON

PHILIP HIGLEY

SEE

PHILIP DUNNING AND PHILIP HIGLEY

J. E. HOARE

SEE

JOHN LLOYD BALDERSTON AND J. E. HOARE

JOHN CECIL HOLM

SEE

GEORGE ABBOTT AND JOHN CECIL HOLM

BRONSON CROCKER HOWARD

"Banker's Daughter", 1873
  Matthews, Brander, Papers on Playmaking, Hill and Wang,
  1957, p. 25-42

"Shenandoah", 1888

Moses, Montrose Jonas, and Brown, John Mason, eds.,
American Theatre as Seen by its Critics, 1752-1934,
Norton, 1934, p. 141-42

SIDNEY COE HOWARD

"Alien Corn", 1933

Arts & Decoration, 38:48-9, April, 1933
Catholic World, 137:77, April, 1933
Commonweal, 17:553, March 15, 1933
Literary Digest, 115:20, March 11, 1933
Nation, 136:299-300, March 15, 1933
New Republic, 74:101-2, March 8, 1933
New Statesman and Nation, 18:85, July 15, 1939
Newsweek, 1:26, Feb. 25, 1933
Theatre Arts Monthly, 17:342, May, 1933

"Dodsworth" (dramatization of the novel by Sinclair Lewis), 1934

Lewis, Sinclair, Sinclair Lewis Reader, Random House, 1953,
p. 219-27
Catholic World, 139:86-7, April, 1934
Colliers, 95:16, Jan. 12, 1935
Commonweal, 19:554, March 16, 1934
Golden Book, 20:376, Oct., 1934
Literary Digest, 117:22, March 17, 1934
Nation, 139:311-12, March 14, 1934
New Outlook, 163:44, April, 1934
New Republic, 78:134, March 14, 1934
New Statesman and Nation, 15:368, March 5, 1938
Newsweek, 3:34, March 3, 1934
Review of Reviews, 89:48, April, 1934
Theatre Arts Monthly, 18:325-6, May, 1934

"Ghost of Yankee Doodle", 1937

Catholic World, 146:467, Jan., 1938
Commonweal, 27:191, Dec. 10, 1937
Nation, 145:664, Dec. 11, 1937
Newsweek, 10:32, Dec. 6, 1937
Theatre Arts, 22:20-1, Jan., 1938
Time, 30:41, Dec. 6, 1937

"Half-Gods", 1930

>   Drama, 20:138, Feb., 1930
>   Nation, 130:52, Jan. 8, 1930

"Late Christopher Bean" (adaptation of Prenez garde a la peinture
by R. Fauchois), 1933

>   Arts & Decoration, 38:50, Jan., 1933
>   Catholic World, 136:335-6, Dec., 1932
>   Commonweal, 17:75, Nov. 16, 1932
>   Nation, 135:484, Nov. 16, 1932
>   Theatre Arts Monthly, 17:17-18, Jan., 1933

"Lute Song", 1946

>   Nathan, George Jean, Theatre Book of the Year, 1945-1946,
>   Knopf, p. 304-10

>   American Mercury, 62:587-90, May, 1946
>   Catholic World, 162:553, March, 1946
>   Commonweal, 43:479, Feb. 22, 1946
>   Life, 20:53-6, March 4, 1946
>   Modern Music, 23:no. 2:145, April, 1946
>   Nation, 162:240, Feb. 23, 1946
>   New Republic, 114:254, Feb. 18, 1946
>   New Yorker, 22:48, Feb. 16, 1946
>   Saturday Review of Literature, 29:28-9, March 2, 1946
>   Theatre Arts, 30:199-200, April, 1946
>   Time, 47:49, Feb. 18, 1946

"Madam, Will You Walk", 1939

>   America, 90:346, Dec. 26, 1953
>   Catholic World, 178:307, Jan., 1954
>   Commonweal, 59:330, Jan. 1, 1954
>   Nation, 177:554, Dec. 19, 1953
>   New Yorker, 29:87-8, Dec. 12, 1953
>   Newsweek, 42:61, Dec. 14, 1953
>   Saturday Review, 36:28, Dec. 19, 1953
>   Time, 62:94, Dec. 14, 1953

"Ned McCobb's Daughter", 1926

>   Nation, 123:697, Dec. 29, 1926
>   New Republic, 49:108-9, Dec. 16, 1926

"Ode to Liberty" (Adapted from Liberte provisoire by M. Duran),
1935

    Wyatt, E. V., Catholic World, 140:598-9, Feb., 1935

"Paths of Glory" (dramatization of novel by H. Cobb), 1935

    Catholic World, 142:212-13, Nov., 1935
    Commonweal, 22:585, Oct. 11, 1935
    Literary Digest, 121:19, Jan. 4, 1936
    New Republic, 84:302, Oct. 23, 1935
    Theatre Arts, 19:813-15, Nov., 1935
    Theatre Arts, 20:74-6, Jan., 1936
    Time, 26:38, Oct. 7, 1935

"Quest" (masque), 1920

    Morris, M., Drama, 11:41-4, Nov., 1920

"The Silver Cord", 1926

    Dusenbury, Winifred Loesch, The Theme of Loneliness in
    Modern American Drama, Univ. Florida Press, 1960,
    p. 57-85

    Moses, Montrose Jonas and Brown, John Mason, eds.,
    American Theatre as Seen by its Critics, 1752-1934, Nor-
    ton, 1934, p. 313-15

    O'Hara, Frank Hurburt, Today in American Drama, Univ.
    Chicago Press, 1939, p. 53-141

    Oppenheimer, George, ed., Passionate Playgoer; a personal
    Scrapbook, Viking, 1958, p. 562-64

    Young, Stark, Immortal Shadows, Scribner, 1948, p. 76-79

    Drama, 17:171, March, 1927
    Nation, 124:20-1, Jan. 5, 1927
    Nation (Lond), 41:804, Sept. 24, 1927
    New Republic, 49:328, Feb. 9, 1927
    New Statesman, 30:171-3, Nov. 19, 1927
    Outlook (Lond), 60:408, Sept. 24, 1927
    Saturday Review, 144:394-5, Sept. 24, 1927
    Spectator, 139:1083, Dec. 17, 1927

"Swords", 1921

    Hackett, F., New Republic, 28:77, Sept. 14, 1921

"They Knew What They Wanted", 1924

    Krutch, Joseph Wood, American drama since 1918, Braziller,
    1957, p. 26-72

    Nathan, George Jean, Theatre Book of the year, 1948-1949,
    Knopf, p. 286-95

    American Review, 3:220-1, March, 1925
    Catholic World, 150:217, Nov., 1939
    Catholic World, 169:64, April, 1949
    Commonweal, 30:587, Oct. 20, 1939
    Commonweal, 49:591, March 25, 1949
    Forum, 111-287-8, May, 1949
    Independent, 114:51, Jan. 10, 1925
    London Mercury, 14:301-2, July, 1926
    Nation (Lond), 39:207, May 29, 1926
    Nation, 119:662-3, Dec. 10, 1924
    Nation, 168:312, March 12, 1949
    New Statesman, 27:231, June 12, 1926
    New Yorker, 25:50-1, Feb. 26, 1949
    Newsweek, 14:44, Oct. 16, 1939
    Newsweek, 33:73, Feb. 28, 1949
    Saturday Review, 141:647, May 29, 1926
    School and Society, 69:233, March 26, 1949
    Spectator, 136:946, June 5, 1926
    Theatre Arts, 23:862, December, 1939
    Theatre Arts, 33:24, 26, May, 1949
    Time, 34:35, Oct. 16, 1939
    Time, 53:57, Feb. 28, 1949

"Yellow Jack", 1934

    Nathan, George Jean, Theatre Book of the Year, 1946-1947,
    Knopf, p. 321-25

    Catholic World, 139:89-90, April, 1934
    Catholic World, 165:71, April, 1947
    Commonweal, 19:580, March 23, 1934
    Commonweal, 45:566, March 21, 1947
    Literary Digest, 117:32, March 31, 1934

Nation, 138:340-1, March 21, 1934
Nation, 164:312-13, March 15, 1947
New Outlook, 163:44, April, 1934
New Republic, 116:41, March 17, 1947
New Yorker, 23:56, March 8, 1947
Newsweek, 3:38, March 17, 1934
Newsweek, 29:82, March 10, 1947
Review of Reviews, 89:49, May, 1934
School and Society, 65:252, April 5, 1947
Survey Graphic, 23:241, May, 1934
Theatre Arts, 18:326-8, May, 1934
Time, 49:46, March 10, 1947

SIDNEY COE HOWARD AND CHARLES GORDON MACARTHUR

"Salvation", 1927

Young, S., New Republic, 54:18-19, Feb. 22, 1928

SEE ALSO

EDWARD SHELDON AND SIDNEY HOWARD

WILLIAM DEAN HOWELLS

"The Rise of Silas Lapham"

Edwards, Herbert, "The dramatization of 'The Rise of
Silas Lapham'", New England Quarterly, 30:235-243,
1957

HATCHER HUGHES

"Hell-bent For Heaven", 1924

Arts & Decoration, 20:24, April, 1924
Nation, 118:68-9, Jan. 16, 1924
Journal of Applied Sociology, 9:127, Nov., 1924

HATCHER HUGHES AND ALAN WILLIAMS

"It's a Grand Life", 1930

>Commonweal, 11:480, Feb. 26, 1930
>New Republic, 62:47, Feb. 26, 1930

HATCHER HUGHES AND ELMER L. RICE

"Wake Up, Jonathan", 1920

>Firkins, O. W., Review, 4:112-14, Feb. 2, 1921
>
>Hogan, Robert, The Independence of Elmer Rice, Sou. Ill. Univ. Press, 1965, p. 27-29

WILLIAM MOTTER INGE

"Bus Stop", 1955

>America, 93:54, April 9, 1955
>Catholic World, 181:147, May, 1955
>Commonweal, 62:14, April 8, 1955
>Life, 38:77-80, March 28, 1955
>N. Y. Times Mag., p. 59, March 20, 1955
>Nation, 180:245, March 19, 1955
>New Republic, 132:22, May 2, 1955
>New Yorker, 31:62, March 12, 1955
>Newsweek, 45:99, March 14, 1955
>Saturday Review, 38:24, March 19, 1955
>Theatre Arts, 39:16, 22, May, 1955
>Time, 65:58, March 14, 1955

"Come Back, Little Sheba", 1950

>Dusenbury, Winifred Loesch, The Theme of Loneliness in Modern American Drama, Univ. Florida Press, 1960, p. 8-37
>
>Nathan, George Jean, Theatre Book of the Year, 1949-1950, Knopf, p. 232-36
>
>Catholic World, 171:67, April, 1950
>Chris. Science Monitor Mag., p. 4, Feb. 25, 1950

Commonweal, 51:558, March 3, 1950
Life, 28:93, April 17, 1950
New Republic, 122:22-3, March 13, 1950
New Yorker, 26:68, Feb. 25, 1950
Newsweek, 35:74, Feb. 27, 1950
School and Society, 71:345, June 3, 1950
Theatre Arts, 34:20, April, 1950
Time, 55:81, Feb. 27, 1950

"Dark at the Top of the Stairs", 1957

America, 98:436, Jan. 11, 1958
Catholic World, 186:386, Feb., 1958
Christian Century, 75:17-18, Jan. 1, 1958
Commonweal, 67:616, March 14, 1958
N.Y. Times Mag., p. 80-1, Nov. 24, 1957
Nation, 185:483, Dec. 21, 1957
New Republic, 137:21, Dec. 30, 1957
Newsweek, 50:81, Dec. 16, 1957
Reporter, 17:34, Dec. 26, 1957
Saturday Review, 40:27, Dec. 21, 1957
Theatre Arts, 42:20-1, Feb., 1958
Theatre Arts, 42:62-4, July, 1958
Time, 70:42, Dec. 16, 1957

"A Loss of Roses", 1959

Kerr, Walter, The Theater in Spite of Itself, Simon and
Schuster, 1963, p. 238-42

Tynan, Kenneth, Curtains, Selections from the Drama
Criticism and Related Writings, Atheneum, 1961,
p. 333-35

America, 102:402, Jan. 2, 1960
Christian Century, 77:15, Jan. 6, 1960
Commonweal, 71:392, Jan. 1, 1960
Nation, 189:475, Dec. 19, 1959
New Republic, 141:23-4, Dec. 21, 1959
New Yorker, 35:99-100, Dec. 12, 1959
Newsweek, 54:96, Dec. 7, 1959
Saturday Review, 42:24, Dec. 19, 1959
Theatre Arts, 44:10-13, Feb., 1960
Time, 74:56, Dec. 7, 1959

"Natural Affection", 1963

>Commonweal, 77:598, March 1, 1963
>Educational Theatre Journal, 15:185-6, May, 1963
>Nation, 196:148, Feb. 16, 1963
>New Republic, 148:29, Feb. 23, 1963
>New Yorker, 38:66, Feb. 9, 1963
>Newsweek, 61:84, Feb. 11, 1963
>Reporter, 28:48-9, April 25, 1963
>Saturday Review, 46:25, Feb. 16, 1963
>Theatre Arts, 47:58-9, March, 1963
>Time, 81:56, Feb. 8, 1963

"Picnic", 1953

>Bentley, Eric Russell, Dramatic Event, Horizon Press,
>1954, p. 102-106

>America, 88:632, March 7, 1953
>America, 89:147, May 2, 1953
>Catholic World, 171:69, April, 1953
>Commonweal, 57:603, March 20, 1953
>Life, 34:136-7, March 16, 1953
>Nation, 176:213, March 7, 1953
>New Republic, 128:22-3, March 16, 1953
>New Yorker, 29:65, Feb. 28, 1953
>Newsweek, 41:84, March 2, 1953
>Saturday Review, 36:33, March 7, 1953
>Theatre Arts, 37:14-15, May, 1953
>Theatre Arts, 37:28-9, Oct., 1953
>Theatre Arts, 37:66-7, July, 1953
>Time, 61:72, March 2, 1953

W. H. IRWIN

SEE

SIDNEY COE HOWARD AND W. H. IRWIN

HENRY JAMES

"American", 1891

>Atheneum, 98:461, Oct. 3, 1891

"Daisy Miller"

>   Mendelsohn, Michael J., " 'Drop a Tear....': Henry James
>   dramatizes 'Daisy Miller' ", Modern Drama, 7:60-64
>   May, 1964

"Guy Domville", 1895

>   Shaw, George B., Plays and Players; Essays on the
>   Theatre, Harcourt, 1958, p. 1-9

>   Atheneum, 105:57, Jan. 12, 1895
>   Harper's Weekly, 39:199, March 2, 1895

"High Bid", 1909

>   Beerbohm, Sir Max, Around Theatres, British Book Center,
>   1953, p. 540-45

"Tenants", 1894

>   Atheneum, 104:685, Nov. 17, 1894
>   Critic, 26 (ns23):38, Jan. 12, 1895
>   Harper Monthly, 90:654 sup. 1, March, 1895
>   Nation, 58:491, June 28, 1894

ROBINSON JEFFERS

"Cretan Woman" (adaptation of Medea by Euripides), 1954

>   Catholic World, 179:469-71, Sept., 1954
>   Commonweal, 60:558, Sept. 10, 1954
>   Life, 37:142, Sept. 13, 1954
>   Saturday Review, 37:25, June 5, 1954

"Dear Judas", 1947

>   Commonweal, 47:71, Oct. 31, 1947
>   Forum, 108:371, Dec., 1947
>   New Yorker, 23:59-61, Oct. 18, 1947
>   Newsweek, 30:91, Oct. 20, 1947
>   Time, 50:73, Oct. 20, 1947

"Medea" (adaptation of play by Euripides), 1946

>   Brown, John Mason, Seeing More Things, McGraw, 1948,
>   p. 231-37

Ransome, John Crowe, ed. , Kenyon Review, Kenyon
Critics, World Pub. Co. , 1951, p. 307-12

Theatre Arts Anthology, a Record and a Prophecy, ed. by
Rosamond Gilder and others, Theatre Arts Books, 1950,
p. 669-72

Weales, Gerald Clifford, American Drama Since World
War II, Harcourt, 1962, p. 182-202

Catholic World, 166:263-4, Dec. , 1947
Catholic World, 169:228-9, June, 1949
Commonweal, 47:94, Nov. 7, 1947
Life, 23:112-14, Nov. 17, 1947
Nation, 165:509-10, Nov. 8, 1947
New Republic, 117:36, Nov. 3, 1947
New Statesman and Nation, 36:303, Oct. 9, 1948
New Yorker, 23:44, Nov. 1, 1947
Newsweek, 30:76, Nov. 3, 1947
Saturday Review of Literature, 30:24-7, Nov. 22, 1947
School and Society, 67:163-4, Feb. 28, 1948
Theatre Arts, 31:10-12, 36, Dec. , 1947
Time, 50:68, Nov. 3, 1947

"Tower Beyond Tragedy", 1950

Nathan, George Jean, Theatre Book of the Year, 1950-1951,
Knopf, p. 136-38

Catholic World, 172:308, Jan. , 1951
Christian Science Monitor Mag. , p. 5, Dec. 9, 1950
Commonweal, 53:279, Dec. 22, 1950
New Republic, 124:22, Jan. 8, 1951
New Yorker, 26:62, Dec. 9, 1950
School and Society, 72:416-19, Dec. 23, 1950
Theatre Arts, 35:15, Feb. , 1951
Time, 56:65, Dec. 4, 1950

THOMAS JOB

"Land's End", 1946

Nathan, George Jean, Theatre Book of the Year, 1946-1947,
Knopf, p. 227-30

"Therese", 1945

>Brown, John Mason, Seeing Things, McGraw, 1946,
>p. 174-80
>
>Nathan, George Jean, Theatre Book of the Year, 1945-1946,
>Knopf, p. 124-26

LEROI JONES

"The Dutchman", 1964

>Hudson Review, 17:424, Autumn, 1964
>New Yorker, 40:78-9, April 4, 1964
>Newsweek, 63:60, April 13, 1964
>Partisan Review, 31:389-94, Summer, 1964
>Vogue, 144:32, July, 1964

"The Slave", 1964

>Nation, 200:16-17, Jan. 4, 1965
>National Review, 17:249, March 23, 1965
>New Republic, 152:32-3, Jan. 23, 1965
>New Yorker, 40:50, Dec. 26, 1964
>Newsweek, 64:56, Dec. 28, 1964
>Saturday Review, 48:46, Jan. 9, 1965
>Time, 84:62-3, Dec. 25, 1964
>Vogue, 145:98, Feb. 1, 1965

"The Toilet", 1964

>Nation, 200:16, Jan. 4, 1965
>National Review, 17:249, March 23, 1965
>New Republic, 152:32-3, Jan. 23, 1965
>New Yorker, 40:50, Dec. 26, 1964
>Newsweek, 64:56, Dec. 28, 1964
>Saturday Review, 48:46, Jan. 9, 1965
>Time, 84:62, Dec. 25, 1964
>Vogue, 145:98, Feb. 1, 1965

GEORGE SIMON KAUFMAN

"Butter and Egg Man", 1925

>Young, Stark, New Republic, 44:202, Oct. 14, 1925
>
>Nation (Lond), 41:747, Sept. 10, 1927

"Hollywood Pinafore", n. d.

> Nathan, George Jean, Theatre Book of the Year, 1945-1946, Knopf, p. 14-17

GEORGE S. KAUFMAN AND MARC CONNELLY

"Beggar on Horseback", 1923

> Freeman, 8:617-18, March 5, 1924
> Nation, 118:238-9, Feb. 27, 1924
> New Republic, 38:45-6, March 5, 1924
> Outlook (Lond), 55:329, May 16, 1925
> Saturday Review, 139:552, May 23, 1925
> Saturday Review, 140:63-4, July 18, 1925

"Dulcy", 1921

> Hackett, F., New Republic, 28:23, Aug. 31, 1921

"Merton of the Movies", 1922

> Nation (Lond), 33:130-2, April 28, 1923

GEORGE S. KAUFMAN AND KATHARINE DAYTON

"First Lady", 1952

> Catholic World, 175:309, July, 1952
> Commonweal, 56:269, June 20, 1952
> Theatre Arts, 36:72, Aug., 1952

GEORGE S. KAUFMAN AND EDNA FERBER

"Bravo!", 1948

> Commonweal, 49:195, Dec. 3, 1948
> New Republic, 119:28-9, Nov. 29, 1948
> New Yorker, 24:58, Nov. 20, 1948
> Newsweek, 32:80, Nov. 22, 1948
> School and Society, 68:454-5, Dec. 25, 1948
> Time, 52:85, Nov. 22, 1948

"Dinner at Eight", 1932

>
> MacCarthy, Sir Desmond, <u>Humanities</u>, Oxford, 1954,
>   p. 113-17
>
> New Statesman and Nation, 5:41-2, Jan. 4, 1933
> Saturday Review, 155:38, Jan. 14, 1933
> Sociology and Social Research, 17:297, Jan., 1933
> Spectator, 150:40, Jan. 13, 1933

"Land is Bright", 1941

>
> Catholic World, 154:337-8, Dec., 1941
> Commonweal, 35:93, Nov. 14, 1941
> Current History, ns. 1:378-80, Dec., 1941
> Life, 11:53-6, Dec. 1, 1941
> Nation, 153:491, Nov. 15, 1941
> New Yorker, 17:36, Nov. 8, 1941
> Newsweek, 18:70, Nov. 10, 1941
> Theatre Arts, 26:10, Jan., 1942
> Time, 38:55, Nov. 10, 1941

"Royal Family", 1927

>
> Nathan, George Jean, <u>Theatre Book of the Year, 1950-1951</u>,
>   Knopf, p. 181-84
>
> Commonweal, 32:390, Aug. 30, 1940
> Literary Digest, 96:26-7, Jan. 21, 1928
> Outlook, 148:67, Jan. 11, 1928
> Saturday Review of Literature, 4:531-2, Jan. 21, 1928
> School and Society, 73:102-3, Feb. 17, 1951
> Spectator, 153:670, Nov. 2, 1934
> Theatre Arts, 35:18, March, 1951

"Stage Door", 1936

>
> Catholic World, 144:471, Jan., 1937
> Commonweal, 25:51, Nov. 6, 1936
> Nation, 143:557, Nov. 7, 1936
> New Republic, 89:50, Nov. 11, 1936
> Newsweek, 8:24, Oct. 31, 1936
> Theatre Arts, 20:923-4, Dec., 1936
> Time, 28:46, Nov. 2, 1936

GEORGE S. KAUFMAN AND LEUEEN MACGRATH

"Fancy Meeting You Again", 1952

Nathan, George Jean, Theatre in the Fifties, Knopf, 1953,
p. 67-69

Commonweal, 55:423, Feb. 1, 1952
New Yorker, 27:54, Jan. 26, 1952
Saturday Review, 35:30, Feb. 2, 1952
Theatre Arts, 36:71, March, 1952

"Small Hours", 1951

Nathan, George Jean, Theatre Book of the Year, 1950-1951,
Knopf, p. 225-26

Commonweal, 53:542, March 9, 1951
New Yorker, 27:66, Feb. 24, 1951
Newsweek, 37:49, Feb. 26, 1951
Theatre Arts, 35:20, April, 1951
Time, 57:50, Feb. 26, 1951

GEORGE S. KAUFMAN AND MORRIS RYSKIND

"Let 'Em Eat Cake", 1933

Catholic World, 138:338, Dec., 1933
Commonweal, 19:47, Nov. 10, 1933

"Of Thee I Sing", 1931

Arts and Decoration, 36:39, Feb., 1932
Bookman, 74:561-2, Jan., 1932
Catholic World, 134:587-8, Feb., 1932
Commonweal, 15:302, Jan. 13, 1932
New Republic, 69:243, Jan. 13, 1932
New Republic, 70:97, March, 1932
Outlook, 160:54, Jan. 13, 1932
Sociology and Social Research, 16:593, July, 1932

GEORGE S. KAUFMAN AND ALEXANDER WOOLLCOTT

"Dark Tower", 1933

Catholic World, 138:475-6, Jan., 1934
Commonweal, 19:160, Dec. 8, 1933
Spectator, 152:774, May 18, 1934

SEE ALSO

MOSS HART AND GEORGE S. KAUFMAN
AND
JOHN PHILIPS MARQUAND AND GEORGE S. KAUFMAN

GEORGE EDWARD KELLY

"Craig's Wife", 1925

> Dusenbury, Winifred Loesch, The Theme of Loneliness in Modern American Drama, Univ. Florida Press, 1960, p. 155-78
>
> Nathan, George Jean, Theatre Book of the Year, 1946-1947, Knopf, p. 307-10
>
> O'Hara, Frank Hurburt, Today in American Drama, Univ. Chicago Press, 1939, p. 53-141
>
> Catholic World, 165:72, April, 1947
> Commonweal, 45:492, Feb. 28, 1947
> Nation, 164:256, March 1, 1947
> New Yorker, 23:53, Feb. 22, 1947
> Newsweek, 29:92, Feb. 24, 1947
> Saturday Review of Literature, 30:32-4, March 8, 1947
> Theatre Arts, 31:19, April, 1947
> Time, 49:58, Feb. 24, 1947

"Deep Mrs. Sykes", 1945

> Nathan, George Jean, Theatre Book of the Year, 1944-1945, Knopf, p. 305-309
>
> Commonweal, 41:625, April 6, 1945
> Nation, 160:395, April 7, 1945
> New Republic, 112:447, April 2, 1945
> New Yorker, 21:40, March 31, 1945
> Newsweek, 25:84, April 2, 1945
> Theatre Arts, 29:271, May, 1945
> Time, 45:58, April 2, 1945

"Fatal Weakness", 1946

> Nathan, George Jean, Theatre Book of the Year, 1946-1947, Knopf, p. 197-200

Catholic World, 164:359, Jan., 1947
Commonweal, 45:201, Dec. 6, 1946
Nation, 164:81, Jan. 18, 1947
New Republic, 115:764, Dec. 9, 1946
New Yorker, 22:60, Nov. 30, 1946
Newsweek, 28:94, Dec. 2, 1946
Saturday Review of Literature, 29:23, Dec. 21, 1946
Theatre Arts, 31:21, 30, Jan., 1947
Time, 48:54, Dec. 2, 1946

"Maggie the Magnificent", 1929
Commonweal, 11:21, Nov. 6, 1929
New Republic, 60:323-5, Nov. 6, 1929
Review of Reviews, 80:158-9, Dec., 1929
Theatre Arts, 14:17-18, Jan., 1930

"Reflected Glory", 1936
Catholic World, 144:217-18, Nov., 1936
Commonweal, 24:532, Oct. 2, 1936
Literary Digest, 122:18-19, Aug. 8, 1936
Literary Digest, 122:19, Oct. 3, 1936
Nation, 143:401-2, Oct. 3, 1936
New Republic, 88:257, Oct. 7, 1936
Newsweek, 8:22, Aug. 1, 1936
Theatre Arts, 20:849-50, Nov., 1936
Time, 28:42, Oct. 5, 1936

"Show-off", 1924
Moses, Montrose Jonas and Brown, John Mason, eds.,
American Theatre as Seen by its Critics, 1752-1934,
Norton, 1934, p. 211-13

Catholic World, 171:309, July, 1950
Christian Science Monitor Mag., p. 9, June 17, 1950
Commonweal, 17:187, 245, Dec. 14, 28, 1932
Freeman, 8:592-3, Feb. 27, 1924
Nation, 170:603, June 17, 1950
New Republic, 122:21, June 19, 1950
Newsweek, 35:83, June 12, 1950
Time, 55:57, June 12, 1950

"Torch Bearers", 1922
Young, Stark, Immortal Shadows, a Book of Dramatic
Criticism, Scribner, 1948, p. 5-7

Independent, 109:397-8, Dec. 23, 1922
New Republic, 32:100-1, Sept. 20, 1922
Playground, 16:357-60, Nov., 1922

JEROME DAVID KERN

SEE

OSCAR HAMMERSTEIN, II, AND JEROME DAVID KERN

JEAN KERR

"Jenny Kissed Me", 1948

Nathan, George Jean, Theatre Book of the Year, 1948-1949,
Knopf, p. 216-219

"King of Hearts", 1954

Bentley, Eric Russell, Dramatic Event; an American
Chronicle, Horizon Press, 1959, p. 226-29

America, 91:114, April 24, 1954
Catholic World, 179:149, May, 1954
Commonweal, 60:143, May 14, 1954
Life, 36:97-8, April 26, 1954
Nation, 178:342, April 17, 1954
New Republic, 130:21, May 31, 1954
New Yorker, 30:60, April 10, 1954
Newsweek, 43:92, April 12, 1954
Saturday Review, 37:22, April 17, 1954
Theatre Arts, 38:17, June, 1954
Theatre Arts, 38:17, July, 1954
Time, 63:74, April 12, 1954

"Mary, Mary", 1961

America, 105:27, April 1, 1961
Commonweal, 74:79-80, April 14, 1961
Coronet, 50:16, June, 1961
Drama, no. 69:21, Summer, 1963
Illustrated London News, 242:398, March 16, 1963
Nation, 192:311, April 8, 1961
New Yorker, 37:124, March 18, 1961

Newsweek, 57:88, March 20, 1961
Reporter, 24:46, April 13, 1961
Saturday Review, 44:35, March 25, 1961
Saturday Review, 44:27, March 18, 1961
Spectator, 210:296, March 8, 1963
Theatre Arts, 45:58, May, 1961
Time, 77:42, March 17, 1961

"Poor Richard", 1964

Look, 29:67-70, March 9, 1965
New Yorker, 40:152, Dec. 12, 1964
Newsweek, 64:84, Dec. 14, 1964
Saturday Review, 47:25, Dec. 19, 1964
Time, 84:73, Dec. 11, 1964
Vogue, 145:27, Jan. 15, 1965

SEE ALSO

WALTER FRANCIS KERR AND JEAN KERR AND JAY GORNEY

W. T. KERR

SEE

WALTER F. KERR AND W. T. KERR

WALTER FRANCIS KERR

"Sing Out, Sweet Land!", 1944

Nathan, George Jean, Theatre Book of the Year, 1944-1945, Knopf, p. 206-09

WALTER FRANCIS KERR AND LEO BRADY

"Count Me In", 1942

Nathan, George Jean, Theatre Book of the Year, 1945-1946, Knopf, p. 344-46

WALTER FRANCIS KERR, JEAN KERR AND JAY GORNEY

"Heaven on Earth", 1948

> Nathan, George Jean, Theatre Book of the Year, 1948-1949, Knopf, p. 77-83

"Touch and Go", 1949

> Nathan, George Jean, Theatre Book of the Year, 1949-1950, Knopf, p. 56-62

WALTER FRANCIS KERR AND W. T. KERR

"Song of Bernadette" (dramatization of novel by F. Werfel), 1958

> America, 99:179, May 3, 1958

JOSEPH KESSELRING

"Arsenic and Old Lace", 1941

> Nathan, George Jean, Theatre Book of the Year, 1943-1944, Knopf, p. 169-170

> Catholic World, 152:599, Feb. , 1941
> Commonweal, 33:351, Jan. 24, 1941
> Life, 16:57-8, April 3, 1944
> Nation, 152:108-9, Jan. 25, 1941
> New Republic, 104:116, Jan. 27, 1941
> New Statesman and Nation, 25:8, Jan. 2, 1943
> New Yorker, 16:34, Jan. 18, 1941
> Newsweek, 17:63, Jan. 20, 1941
> Newsweek, 19:56, May 18, 1942
> Theatre Arts, 25:185-6, March, 1941
> Time, 37:40, Jan. 20, 1941

"Four Twelves Are 48", 1951

> Nathan, George Jean, Theatre Book of the Year, 1950-1951, Knopf, p. 189-93

> Commonweal, 53:447, Feb. 9, 1951
> New Yorker, 26:54, Jan. 27, 1951

Newsweek, 37:83, Jan. 29, 1951
Theatre Arts, 35:20, March, 1951
Time, 57:49, Jan. 29, 1951

"There's Wisdom in Women", 1935

Commonweal, 23:76, Nov. 15, 1935
Catholic World, 142:343, Dec., 1935

SIDNEY KINGSLEY

"Darkness at Noon" (dramatization of the novel by A. Koestler), 1951

Brown, John Mason, As They Appear, McGraw, 1952,
    p. 172-77
Brown, John Mason, Dramatis Personae, a Retrospective
    Show, Viking, 1963, p. 328-31
Gassner, John, Theatre at the Crossroads, Plays and Play-
    wrights of the Mid-century American Stage, Holt, 1960,
    p. 141-43
Nathan, George Jean, Theatre Book of the Year, 1950-1951,
    Knopf, p. 185-88

Catholic World, 172:465, March, 1951
Commonweal, 53:425, Feb. 2, 1951
Life, 30:77-8, Feb. 5, 1951
Nation, 172:92-3, Jan. 27, 1951
New Republic, 124:22-3, Feb. 5, 1951
New Yorker, 26:54, Jan. 20, 1951
Newsweek, 37:80, Jan. 22, 1951
Partisan Review, 18:331, May, 1951
Saturday Review of Literature, 34:22-4, Feb. 3, 1951
School and Society, 73:105-6, Feb. 17, 1951
Theatre Arts, 35:19, 42, March, 1951
Theatre Arts, 35:41, 373, Sept., 1951
Time, 57:38, Jan. 22, 1951

"Dead End, 1935

Catholic World, 142:339-40, Dec., 1935
Commonweal, 23:48, 76, Nov. 8, 15, 1935
Literary Digest, 120:17, Nov. 9, 1935
Nation, 141:575-7, Nov. 13, 1935
New Republic, 85:21, 49, Nov. 13, 20, 1935

Newsweek, 6:26, Nov. 9, 1935
Survey Gazette, 25:52, Jan., 1936
Theatre Arts, 19:888-93, Dec., 1935
Theatre Arts, 20:462-3, June, 1936
Time, 26:40, Nov. 11, 1935

"Detective Story", 1949

Nathan, George Jean, Theatre Book of the Year, 1948-1949,
   Knopf, p. 325-32

Catholic World, 169:144, May, 1949
Christian Science Monitor Mag., p. 7, April 15, 1950
Commonweal, 49:638, April 8, 1949
Life, 26:131-2, May 2, 1949
Nation, 168:424-5, April 9, 1949
New Republic, 120:25, April 11, 1949
Saturday Review of Literature, 32:50-2, April 16, 1949
School and Society, 70:362-3, Dec. 3, 1949
Theatre Arts, 33:11, June, 1949
New Yorker, 25:50, April 2, 1949
Newsweek, 33:78, April 4, 1949
Time, 53:75-6, April 4, 1949

"Lunatics and Lovers", 1954

America, 92:366, Jan. 1, 1955
Catholic World, 180:388, Feb., 1955
Commonweal, 61:406, Jan. 14, 1955
Life, 38:57-8, Jan. 17, 1955
Nation, 180:18, Jan. 1, 1955
New Republic, 132:20, March 7, 1955
New Yorker, 30:44-6, Dec. 25, 1954
Newsweek, 45:43, Jan. 3, 1955
Saturday Review of Literature, 38:62, Jan. 1, 1955
Theatre Arts, 39:17, 90, Feb., 1955
Time, 64:32, Dec. 27, 1954

"Men in White", 1934

Brown, John Mason, Two on the Aisle, Ten Years of the
   American Theatre in Performance, Norton, 1938, p. 171-73
Dusenbury, Winifred Loesch, The Theme of Loneliness in
   Modern American Drama, Univ. of Florida Press, 1960,
   p. 179-96

Catholic World, 138:215-17, Nov., 1933
Commonweal, 18:563-4, Oct. 13, 1933
Hygeia, 12:358-60, April, 1934
Literary Digest, 116:19, Nov. 4, 1933
Nation, 137:419-20, Oct. 11, 1933
New Republic, 76:241-2, Oct. 11, 1933
Newsweek, 2:29, Oct. 7, 1933
Spectator, 153:14, July 6, 1934
Review of Reviews, 89:39, Feb., 1934
Theatre Arts, 17:915-16, Dec., 1933

"Night Life", 1962

Catholic World, 196:199, Dec., 1962
Commonweal, 77:232, Nov. 23, 1962
New Yorker, 38:111, Nov. 3, 1962
Newsweek, 60:75, Nov. 5, 1962
Saturday Review, 45:28, Nov. 10, 1962
Theatre Arts, 46:12-13, Dec., 1962
Time, 80:82, Nov. 2, 1962

"Patriots", 1943

Nathan, George Jean, Theatre Book of the Year, 1942, -1943, Knopf, p. 174-75

American Mercury, 56:486-7, April, 1943
Catholic World, 156:726-7, March, 1943
Commonweal, 37:422, Feb. 12, 1943
Current History, ns. 4:88-91, March, 1943
Independent Woman, 22:143, May, 1943
Life, 14:57-8, March 8, 1943
Nation, 156:248, Feb. 13, 1943
New Republic, 108:211, Feb. 15, 1943
N.Y. Times Mag., p. 16-17, Jan. 31, 1943
New Yorker, 18:31, Feb. 6, 1943
Newsweek, 21:82, Feb. 8, 1943
Saturday Review of Literature, 26:26, April 17, 1943
Scholastic, 42:20, March 15, 1943
Theatre Arts, 27:201-4, April, 1943
Time, 41:36, Feb. 8, 1943

"World We Make" (dramatization of Outward Room by M. Brand), 1939
Catholic World, 150:470, Jan., 1940
Forum, 103:32-3, Jan., 1940

Life, 8:27-9, Jan. 1, 1940
Nation, 149:627-9, Dec. 2, 1939
Newsweek, 14:39, Dec. 4, 1939
North American Review, 248 no. 2:402-3, Dec., 1939
Theatre Arts, 24:15, Jan., 1940
Time, 34:38, Dec. 4, 1939

JACK KIRKLAND

"Mr. Adam", 1949

Nathan, George Jean, Theatre Book of the Year, 1949-1950, Knopf, p. 14-15

"Suds in Your Eye", 1944

Nathan, George Jean, Theatre Book of the Year, 1943-1944, Knopf, p. 213-15

"Tobacco Road" (dramatization of the novel by Erskine Caldwell), 1933

Krutch, Joseph, American Drama Since 1918; an Informal History, Random House, 1939, p. 73-133

Nathan, George Jean, Theatre Book of the Year, 1942-1943, Knopf, p. 48-49
Nathan, George Jean, Theatre Book of the Year, 1943-1944, Knopf, p. 43
Nathan, George Jean, Theatre Book of the Year, 1949-1950, Knopf, p. 247-8
Theatre Arts Anthology, a Record and a Prophecy, ed. by Rosamond Gilder and others, Theatre Arts Books, 1950, p. 623-25

Catholic World, 138:603-4, Feb., 1934
Commonweal, 39:140-1, Nov. 26, 1943
Golden Book, 20:246, Sept., 1934
Life, 9:30, Dec. 16, 1940
Literary Digest, 118:18, Dec. 15, 1934
Nation, 137:718, Dec. 20, 1933
New Republic, 77:168-9, Dec. 20, 1933
Newsweek, 8:22, Dec. 5, 1936
Newsweek, 14:32-3, Nov. 27, 1939
Review of Reviews, 89:47, March, 1934
Theatre Arts, 18:93-5, Feb., 1934

Theatre Arts, 31:67-9, April, 1947
Theatre Arts, 34:16, May, 1950
Time, 55:61, March 20, 1950

ARTHUR L. KOPIT

"The Day the Whores Came Out to Play Tennis", 1965

Nation, 200:374, April 5, 1965
New Republic, 152:24, April 10, 1965
New Yorker, 41:146-7, March 27, 1965
Newsweek, 65:82, March 29, 1965
Time, 85:58, March 26, 1965
Vogue, 145:142, May, 1965

"Oh, Dad, Poor Dad, Mamma's Hung You in the Closet and I'm
Feelin' so Sad", 1960

Kostelanetz, Richard, ed., The New American Arts, N.Y.,
Horizon Press, 1965, p. 71-2

Commonweal, 76:41, April 6, 1962
Educational Theatre Journal, 14:169-71, May, 1962
Hudson Review, 15:267-8, Summer, 1962
Nation, 194:289, March 31, 1962
National Review, 12:416-17, June 5, 1962
New Republic, 146:31, March 19, 1962
New Statesman, 62:64, July 14, 1961
New Statesman, 70:576, Oct. 15, 1965
New Yorker, 38:84-5, March 10, 1962
Saturday Review, 45:35, March 17, 1962
Spectator, 207:60, July 14, 1961
Theatre Arts, 46:60-1, May, 1962
Time, 78:72, July 14, 1961

"Sing to Me Through the Open Window", 1965

Nation, 200:373-4, April 5, 1965
New Republic, 152:24, April 10, 1965
Newsweek, 65:82, March 29, 1965

HARRY KURNITZ

"Once More, With Feeling", 1958

America, 100:298, Nov. 29, 1958
Catholic World, 188:334, Jan., 1959
New Yorker, 34:98-9, Nov. 1, 1958
Newsweek, 52:62, Nov. 3, 1958
Theatre Arts, 43:10-11, Jan., 1959
Time, 72:50, Nov. 3, 1958

"Reclining Figure", 1954

America, 92:138, Oct. 30, 1954
Catholic World, 180:226, Dec., 1954
Commonweal, 61:166, Nov. 12, 1954
Nation, 179:371, Oct. 23, 1954
New Republic, 131:23, Nov. 1, 1954
New Yorker, 30:67, Oct. 16, 1954
Newsweek, 4:96, Oct. 18, 1954
Saturday Review, 37:32, Oct. 23, 1954
Theatre Arts, 38: 21, Dec., 1954
Time, 64:76, Oct. 18, 1954

"Shot in the Dark" (adaptation of L'Idiote by M. Achard), 1961

Christian Century, 78:1533, Dec. 20, 1961
Commonweal, 75:176-7, Nov. 10, 1961
Nation, 193:362, Nov. 4, 1961
New Republic, 145:23, Nov. 6, 1961
New Yorker, 37:135, Oct. 28, 1961
Newsweek, 58:73, Oct. 30, 1961
Saturday Review, 44:32, Nov. 4, 1961
Theatre Arts, 45:10, Dec., 1961
Time, 78:79, Oct. 27, 1961

JEROME LAURENCE AND ROBERT E. LEE

"Auntie Mame" (dramatization of novel by E. E. Tanner), 1956

America, 96:310, Dec. 8, 1956
Catholic World, 184:305-6, Jan., 1957
Commonweal, 65:382, Jan. 11, 1957

Life, 41:129-30, Nov. 12, 1956
Nation, 183:485, Dec. 1, 1956
New Yorker, 32:110, Nov. 10, 1956
Newsweek, 48:54, Nov. 12, 1956
Saturday Review, 39:28, Nov. 17, 1956
Theatre Arts, 41:22-3, Jan. , 1957
Time, 68:71, Nov. 12, 1956

"Call on Kuprin" (dramatization of novel by M. Edelman), 1961

Nation, 192:504, June 10, 1961
New Yorker, 37:94, June 10, 1961
Newsweek, 57:85, June 5, 1961
Theatre Arts, 45:9-11, July, 1961
Time, 77:85, June 2, 1961

"Gang's All Here", 1959

America, 102:213-14, Nov. 14, 1959
Commonweal, 71:186, Nov. 6, 1959
Nation, 189:239, Oct. 17, 1959
New Yorker, 35:125-6, Oct. 10, 1959
Newsweek, 54:70, Oct. 12, 1959
Reporter, 21:37, Nov. 12, 1959
Saturday Review, 42:65, Oct. 17, 1959
Theatre Arts, 43:15, Dec. , 1959
Time, 74:70, Oct. 12, 1959

"Inherit the Wind", 1955

America, 93:250, May 28, 1955
Catholic World, 181:225-6, June, 1955
Commonweal, 62:278, June 17, 1955
English, 13:61, Summer, 1960
Illustrated London News, 236:566, April 2, 1960
Life, 38:119-20, May 9, 1955
Nation, 180:410, May 7, 1955
New Statesman, 59:286, Feb. 27, 1960
New Yorker, 31:67, April 30, 1955
Newsweek, 45:82, May 2, 1955
Saturday Review, 38:25, May 14, 1955
Spectator, 204:429, March 25, 1960
Theatre Arts, 39:18-19, 23, July, 1955
Time, 65:78, May 2, 1955

"Only In America" (dramatization of book by H. Golden), 1959

>Commonweal, 71:321, Dec. 11, 1959
>Nation, 189:427, Dec. 5, 1959
>New Yorker, 35:97, Dec. 5, 1959
>Newsweek, 54:100, Nov. 30, 1959
>Saturday Review, 42:29, Dec. 5, 1959
>Time, 74:64, Nov. 30, 1959

ARTHUR LAURENTS

"Bird Cage", 1950

>Nathan, George Jean, Theatre Book of the Year, 1949-1950,
>Knopf, p. 237-41

>Commonweal, 51:607, March 17, 1950
>Nation, 170:236, March 11, 1950
>New Republic, 122:23, March 13, 1950
>New Yorker, 26:58, March 4, 1950
>Newsweek, 35:82, March 6, 1950
>Theatre Arts, 34:14, May, 1950
>Time, 55:71, March 6, 1950

"A Clearing in the Woods", 1957

>Gassner, John, Theatre at the Crossroads, Plays and
>Playwrights of the Mid-century American Stage, Holt,
>1960, p. 164-65

>America, 96:510, Feb. 2, 1957
>Catholic World, 184:470, March, 1957
>Christian Century, 74:235, Feb. 20, 1957
>Commonweal, 65:489, Feb. 8, 1957
>New Yorker, 32:57, Jan. 26, 1957
>Saturday Review, 42:25, Feb. 28, 1959
>Saturday Review, 40:23, Jan. 26, 1957
>Theatre Arts, 41:20, March, 1957
>Time, 69:72, Jan. 21, 1957

"Home of the Brave", 1945

>Nathan, George Jean, Theatre Book of the Year, 1945-1946,
>Knopf, p. 253-59

Catholic World, 162:457, Feb., 1946
Forum, 105:657-9, March, 1946
New Yorker, 21:42-4, Jan. 12, 1946
Newsweek, 27:82, Jan. 7, 1946
Theatre Arts, 30:141, 145-6, March, 1946
Time, 47:88, Jan. 7, 1946

"Invitation to a March", 1960

America, 104:352, Dec. 3, 1960
Christian Century, 71:1382, Nov. 23, 1960
Educational Theatre Journal, 13:51, March, 1961
Nation, 191:420-1, Nov. 26, 1960
New Republic, 143:20-1, Nov. 14, 1960
New Yorker, 36:116, Nov. 5, 1960
Newsweek, 56:61, Nov. 14, 1960
Saturday Review, 43:73, Nov. 12, 1960
Theatre Arts, 45:73, Jan., 1961
Time, 76:84, Nov. 14, 1960

"Time of the Cuckoo", 1952

Nathan, George Jean, Theatre in the Fifties, Knopf, 1953,
    p. 100-03

Catholic World, 176:229-30, Dec., 1952
Commonweal, 57:118, Nov. 7, 1952
Nation, 175:413, Nov. 1, 1952
New Yorker, 28:77-8, Oct. 25, 1952
Newsweek, 40:77, Oct. 27, 1952
Saturday Review, 35:28, Oct. 18, 1952
Saturday Review, 35:26, Nov. 1, 1952
School and Society, 77:117, Feb. 21, 1953
Theatre Arts, 36:26-7, Dec., 1952
Time, 60:75, Oct. 27, 1952

JOHN HOWARD LAWSON

"Gentlewoman", 1934

Krutch, J. W., Nation, 138:424, April 11, 1934

"Ghosts", n.d.

Downer, Alan S., ed., American Drama and its Critics,
Univ. Chicago Pr., 1965, p. 128-32

"Hidden Heritage", n. d.

>Science and Sociology,16 no. 1:60-5, 1951

"Loud Speaker", 1927

>Krutch, J. W. , Nation, 124:324, March 23, 1927

"Marching Song", 1937

>Catholic World, 145:85-6, April, 1937
>Commonweal, 25:528, March 5, 1937
>Nation, 144:248-9, Feb. 27, 1937
>New Republic, 90:166-7, March 17, 1937
>Theatre Arts, 21:265, April, 1937
>Time, 29:47, March 1, 1937

"Nirvana", 1926

>Krutch, J. W. , Nation, 122:295, March 17, 1926

"Processional", 1925

>Block, Anita Cahn, Changing World in Plays and Theatre,
>Little, 1939, p. 194-250
>Mendelsohn, Michael, "The social critics on stage",
>Modern Drama 6:279, 1963-64
>Moses, Montrose Jonas and Brown, John Mason, eds. ,
>American theatre as seen by its critics, 1752-1934,
>Norton, 1934, p. 311-313

>American Review, 3:387-8, July, 1925
>Drama, 15:129-30, March, 1925
>Independent, 114:275, March 7, 1925
>Independent Woman, 16:368, Nov. , 1937
>Catholic World, 146:341-2, Dec. , 1937
>Nation, 120:99-100, Jan. 28, 1925
>New Republic, 41:261, Jan. 28, 1925

"Success Story", 1932

>Catholic World, 136:207-8, Nov. , 1932
>Commonweal, 16:566, Oct. 12, 1932
>Nation, 135:336-7, Oct. 12, 1932
>New Republic, 72-233-5, Oct. 12, 1932
>Sociology and Social Research, 17:398, March, 1933
>Theatre Arts, 16:955-7, Dec. , 1932

LORELEI LEE, PSEUD

SEE

ANITA LOOS

R. E. LEE

SEE

JEROME LAWRENCE AND R. E. LEE

IRA LEVIN

"Critic's Choice", 1960

America, 104:548, Jan. 21, 1961
Nation, 191:531, Dec. 31, 1960
New Yorker, 36:38, Dec. 24, 1960
Newsweek, 56:53, Dec. 26, 1960
Saturday Review, 43:28, Dec. 31, 1960
Theatre Arts, 45:11, Feb., 1961

"General Seeger", 1962

New Yorker, 38:83, March 10, 1962

"Interlock", 1958

New Republic, 138:22, March 3, 1958
New Yorker, 33:58, Feb. 15, 1958
Theatre Arts, 42:25, April, 1958

"No Time For Sergeants" (dramatization of novel by M. Hyman), 1955

America, 94:167, Nov. 5, 1955
Catholic World, 182:226, Dec., 1955
Colliers, 137:6, March 2, 1956
Commonweal, 63:141-2, Nov. 11, 1955
Life, 39:113, Nov. 7, 1955

N.Y. Times Mag., p. 38, Oct. 9, 1955
Nation, 181:406, Nov. 5, 1955
New Yorker, 31:88, Oct. 29, 1955
Newsweek, 46-55, Oct. 31, 1955
Saturday Review, 38:26, Nov. 5, 1955
Theatre Arts, 39:28-9, Dec., 1955
Time, 66:73, Oct. 31, 1955

SAUL LEVITT

"Andersonville Trial", 1959

Tynan, Kenneth, Curtains; selections from the drama
criticism and related writings, Atheneum, 1961, p. 337-40

America, 102:482-3, Jan. 16, 1960
Christian Century, 77:136-7, Feb. 3, 1960
Commonweal, 71:469, Jan. 22, 1960
Drama, no. 62:20, Fall, 1961
Illustrated London News, 238:1044, June 17, 1961
Life, 48:125-6, Feb. 8, 1960
Nation, 190:87-8, Jan. 23, 1960
New Republic, 142:21-2, Jan. 18, 1960
New Statesman, 61:1018, June 23, 1961
New Yorker, 35:69-70, Jan. 9, 1960
Newsweek, 55:60, Jan. 11, 1960
Saturday Review, 43:54, Jan. 16, 1960
Theatre Arts, 44:12, March, 1960
Spectator, 206:882-3, June 16, 1961
Time, 75:46, Jan. 11, 1960

HOWARD LINDSAY

"She Loves Me Not" (dramatization of novel by E..Hope), 1933

Catholic World, 138:477, January, 1934
Nation, 137:662, Dec. 6, 1933
Newsweek, 2:32, Nov. 25, 1933
Review of Reviews, 89:49, June, 1934
Spectator, 152:737, May 11, 1934
Theatre Arts, 18:9-11, January, 1934

HOWARD LINDSAY AND RUSSEL CROUSE

"Great Sebastians", 1956

> America, 94:515, Feb. 4, 1956
> Commonweal, 63:428, Jan. 27, 1956
> Life, 40:107-8, Jan. 30, 1956
> Nation, 182:58, Jan. 21, 1956
> New Yorker, 31:60, Jan. 14, 1956
> Newsweek, 47:50, Jan. 16, 1956
> Saturday Review, 39:40, Jan 21, 1956
> Theatre Arts, 40:18, February, 1956
> Theatre Arts, 40:16, March, 1956
> Time, 67:79, Jan. 16, 1956

"Life With Father", 1939

> Brown, John Mason, Broadway in Review, Norton, 1940,
>   p. 96-101.
> Woollcott, Alexander, Portable Woollcott, Viking, 1946,
>   p. 684-92
> Woollcott, Alexander, Long, Long Ago, Viking, 1943,
>   p. 235-43

> Catholic World, 150:336, Dec., 1939
> Catholic World, 156:90, Oct., 1942
> Catholic World, 161:508-9, Sept., 1945
> Catholic World, 163:554, Sept., 1946
> Colliers, 115:18, April 21, 1945
> Commonweal, 31:118, Nov. 24, 1939
> Commonweal, 40:399-400, Aug. 11, 1944
> Forum, 103:33, January, 1940
> Ladies Home Journal, 58:20-1, May, 1941
> Nation, 149:560, Nov. 18, 1939
> N.Y. Times Mag., p. 34-5, Nov. 3, 1946
> New Republic, 101:169, Nov. 29, 1939
> New Yorker, 21:16-17, June 16, 1945
> Newsweek, 14:36, Nov. 20, 1939
> Newsweek, 29:86, June 16, 1947
> North American Review, 248 no. 2:401, Dec., 1939
> Saturday Review of Literature, 21:8-9, Nov. 18, 1939
> Theatre Arts, 24:13-15, Jan., 1940
> Theatre Arts, 31:69, April, 1947
> Time, 34:69, Nov. 20, 1939
> Time, 49:74, June 16, 1947

"Life with Mother", 1948
> Nathan, George Jean, Theatre Book of the Year, 1948-1949,
> Knopf, p. 144-46

> Catholic World, 168:241, Dec. , 1948
> Commonweal, 49:118, Nov. 12, 1948
> Life, 25:53-4, July 5, 1948
> Life, 25:149-50, Nov. 15, 1948
> Life, 26:41, Feb. 7, 1949
> Nation, 167:528, Nov. 6, 1948
> New Republic, 119:26, Nov. 8, 1948
> N. Y. Times Mag. , p. 16-17, June 27, 1948
> New Yorker, 24:40, Oct. 30, 1948
> Newsweek, 32:74, Nov. 1, 1948
> Saturday Review of Literature, 31:25-8, Nov. 20, 1948
> School and Society, 68:455-6, Dec. 25, 1948
> Theatre Arts, 32:10-44, Aug. , 1948
> Theatre Arts, 32:28-9, Oct. , 1948
> Time, 52:51, Nov. 1, 1948

"Prescott Proposals", 1953
> America, 90:385, Jan. 9, 1954
> Catholic World, 178:386-7, Feb. , 1954
> Commonweal, 59:404, Jan. 22, 1954
> Life, 36:75-7, Jan. 18, 1954
> Nation, 178:57, Jan. 16, 1954
> New Republic, 130:21, Jan. 4, 1954
> New Yorker, 29:46-7, Dec. 26, 1953
> Newsweek, 42:47, Dec. 28, 1953
> Saturday Review, 37:55-6, Jan. 2, 1954
> Theatre Arts, 38:21, March, 1954
> Time, 62:34, Dec. 28, 1953

"Remains to be Seen", 1951

> Catholic World, 174:148, Nov. , 1951
> Commonweal, 55:37-8, Oct. 19, 1951
> Life, 31:169-70, Oct. 15, 1951
> Nation, 173:334, Oct. 20, 1951
> New Yorker, 27:84, Oct. 13, 1951
> Newsweek, 38:85, Oct. 15, 1951
> Saturday Review of Literature, 34:25-6, Oct. 20, 1951
> School and Society, 75:185, March 22, 1952
> Theatre Arts, 35:378, Dec. , 1951
> Time, 58:74, Oct. 15, 1951

"State of the Union", 1945

> Nathan, George Jean, Theatre Book of the Year, 1945-1946, Knopf, p. 184-86

> Catholic World, 162:357, Jan., 1946
> Commonweal, 43:169, Nov. 30, 1945
> Forum, 105:466-8, Jan., 1946
> Free World, 11:71-2, Jan., 1946
> Life, 19:85-6, Dec. 10, 1945
> Nation, 161:604, Dec. 1, 1945
> New Republic, 113:711, Nov. 26, 1945
> N. Y. Times Mag., p. 24-5, Nov. 4, 1945
> New Yorker, 21:48, Nov. 24, 1945
> Newsweek, 26:96, Nov. 26, 1945
> Saturday Review of Literature, 28:18-20, Nov. 24, 1945
> Sociology and Social Research, 30:522, July, 1946
> Theatre Arts, 29:677, Dec., 1945
> Theatre Arts, 30:5-6, Jan., 1946
> Time, 46:48, Nov. 26, 1945

"Strip for Action", 1942

> Nathan, George Jean, Theatre Book of the Year, 1942-1943, Knopf, p. 83-85

> New Republic, 107:545, Oct. 26, 1942
> Theatre Arts, 26:741, Dec., 1942

"Tall Story" (dramatization of Homecoming Game by H. Nemerov), 1959

> America, 100:614, Feb. 21, 1959
> Catholic World, 189:60-1, April, 1959
> Commonweal, 69:600, March 6, 1959
> New Yorker, 34:87-8, Feb. 7, 1959
> Newsweek, 53:56, Feb, 9, 1959
> Saturday Review, 42:34, Feb. 21, 1959
> Theatre Arts, 43:21-2, April, 1959
> Time, 73:73, Feb. 9, 1959

HOWARD LINDSAY, RUSSEL CROUSE AND IRVING BERLIN

"Call Me Madam", 1950

> Nathan, George Jean, Theatre Book of the Year, 1950-1951, Knopf, 1951, p. 64-66

HOWARD LINDSAY AND DAMON RUNYON

"Slight Case of Murder", 1935

Commonweal, 22:528, Sept. 27, 1935
Literary Digest, 120:22, Sept, 28, 1935
Nation, 141:364, Sept. 25, 1935
Theatre Arts, 19:822, Nov., 1935
Time, 26:54, Sept. 23, 1935

HOWARD LINDSAY AND BERTRAND ROBINSON

"O Promise Me", 1930

Commonweal, 13:218, Dec. 24, 1930
Drama, 21:12-13, Jan, 1931

"Your Uncle Dudley", 1929

Commonweal, 11:145, Dec. 4, 1929

FRANK LOESSER

"Greenwillow", 1960

Tynan, Kenneth, Curtains; Selections from the Drama
Criticism and Related Writings, Atheneum, 1961,
p. 344-46

"Guys and Dolls", 1950

Brown, John Mason, As They Appear, McGraw, 1952,
p. 228-32
Nathan, George Jean, Theatre Book of the Year, 1950-1951,
Knopf, p. 130-33
Tynan, Kenneth, Curtains; Selections from the Drama
Criticism and Related Writings, Atheneum, 1961,
p. 252-53

"Where's Charley?", 1948

Nathan, Georgy Jean, Theatre Book of the Year, 1948-1949,
Knopf, p. 125-27

JOSHUA LOCKWOOD LOGAN

"The Wisteria Trees", 1950

> Brown, John Mason, Dramatis Personae; A Retrospective
> Show, Viking, 1963, p. 246-52
> Brown, John Mason, Still Seeing Things, McGraw, 1950,
> p. 233-40
> Nathan, George Jean, Theatre Book of the Year, 1949-1950,
> Knopf, p. 258-61

> Catholic World, 171:147, May, 1950
> Christian Science Monitor Mag., p. 4, April 1, 1950
> Commonweal, 52:69-70, April, 1950
> Life, 28:68-70, April 24, 1950
> Nation, 170:354-5, April 15, 1950
> New Republic, 122:22, April 10, 1950
> New York Times Mag., p. 32-3, March 5, 1950
> New Yorker, 26:63, April 8, 1950
> Newsweek, 35:77, April 10, 1950
> Theatre Arts, 34:15, June, 1950
> Time, 55:68, April 10, 1950

SEE ALSO

THOMAS HEGGEN AND JOSHUA LOCKWOOD LOGAN

ANITA LOOS

"Cheri" (dramatization of novel by S. G. Colette), 1959

> America, 102:214, Nov. 14, 1959
> Nation, 189:339, Nov. 7, 1959
> New Republic, 141:19-20, Oct. 26, 1959
> New Yorker, 35:91-2, Oct. 24, 1959
> Newsweek, 54:116, Oct. 26, 1959
> Saturday Review, 42:26, Oct. 31, 1959
> Theatre Arts, 43:14-16, Nov., 1959
> Theatre Arts, 43:84, Dec., 1959
> Time, 74:102, Oct. 26, 1959

"Darling, Darling", 1954

> Theatre Arts, 38:75, Oct., 1954

"Gigi" (dramatization of novel by G. C. Colette), 1951

> Catholic World, 174:309-10, Jan. 1952
> Commonweal, 55:254, Dec. 14, 1951
> Illustrated London News, 228:704, June 9, 1956
> Nation, 173:530, Dec. 15, 1951
> New Yorker, 27:87, Dec. 1, 1951
> Newsweek, 38:60, Dec. 3, 1951
> Saturday Review of Literature, 34:32-3, Dec. 15, 1951
> School and Society, 75:107-8, Feb. 16, 1952
> Theatre Arts, 36:31, Feb., 1952
> Theatre Arts, 36:41-7, July, 1952
> Time, 58:49, Dec. 3, 1951

"Happy Birthday", 1946

> Nathan, George Jean, Theatre Book of the Year, 1946-1947,
> Knopf, p. 146-49

JAMES LORD AND MARGUERITE DURAS

"Beast in the Jungle" (dramatization of story by Henry James), 1963

> New Yorker, 38:104, Jan 12, 1963

CLARE BOOTHE LUCE

"Abide with Me", 1935

> Commonweal, 23:162, Dec. 6, 1935
> Theatre Arts, 20:20, Jan., 1936
> Time, 26:68, Dec. 2, 1935

"Chill of the Morning", 1951

> America, 99:151, April 26, 1958
> Catholic World, 187:311, July, 1958
> Commonweal, 68:153-4, May 9, 1958

"Kiss the Boys Good-bye", 1938

> O'Hara, Frank Hurburt, Today in American drama, Univ. of
> Chicago Press, 1939, p. 190-234

> Catholic World, 148:212-13, Nov., 1938
> Commonweal, 28:644, Oct. 14, 1938

Independent Woman, 17:348, Nov., 1938
Nation, 147:362, Oct. 8, 1938
New Republic, 96:331, Oct. 26, 1938
Theatre Arts, 22:778, Nov., 1938
Time, 32:48, Oct. 10, 1938

"Margin for Error", 1939

Catholic World, 150:339, Dec., 1939
Commonweal, 31:118, Nov. 24, 1939
Forum, 103:33, Jan., 1940
Newsweek, 14:36, Nov. 20, 1939
Theatre Arts, 24:18-19, Jan., 1940
Time, 34:58, Nov. 13, 1939

"The Women", 1936

Brown, John Mason, Two on the Aisle; Ten Years of
American Theatre in Performance, Norton, 1938,
p. 180-83

Catholic World, 144:599-600, Feb., 1937
Commonweal, 25:332, Jan. 15, 1937
L'Illustration, 201:357, Nov. 12, 1938
Life and Letters Today, 22:94-8, July, 1939
Literary Digest, 123:24-5, Jan. 9, 1937
New Republic, 90:263, April 7, 1937
New States and Nation, 19:646, April 29, 1939
Newsweek, 9:22, Jan. 2, 1937
Theatre Arts, 21:101-2, Feb., 1937
Time, 29:30, Jan. 4, 1937
Time, 86:94, Nov. 12, 1965

CHARLES G. MACARTHUR

SEE

BEN HECHT AND CHARLES G. MACARTHUR

AND

HOWARD SIDNEY COE AND CHARLES G. MACARTHUR

CARSON SMITH MCCULLERS

"Member of the Wedding", 1950

Cole, Toby and Chinoy, Helen Kirch, eds., <u>Actors on Acting; the Theories, Techniques, and Practices of the Great Actors of all Times as Told in Their Own Words</u>, Crown, 1950, p. 311-20

Cole, Toby and Chinoy, Helen Kirch, eds., <u>Directors on Directing</u>, Rev. ed., Bobbs, 1963, p. 380-89

Dusenbury, Winifred Loesch, <u>The Theme of Loneliness in Modern American Drama</u>, Univ. of Florida Press, 1960, p. 57-85

Nathan, George Jean, <u>Theatre Book of the Year, 1949-1950</u>, Knopf, p. 164-66

Weales, Gerald Clifford, <u>American Drama since World War II</u>, Harcourt, 1962, p. 154-81

<u>Catholic World</u>, 170:467, March 1950
<u>Commonweal</u>, 51:437-8, Jan. 27, 1950
<u>English</u>, 11:185, Summer, 1957
<u>Illustrated London News</u>, 230:276, Feb, 1957
<u>Nation</u>, 170:44, Jan. 14, 1950
<u>New Republic</u>, 122:28, Jan. 30, 1950
<u>New Statesman</u>, 53:201, Feb., 16, 1957
<u>New Yorker</u>, 25:46, Jan. 14, 1950
<u>Newsweek</u>, 35:74, Jan. 16, 1950
<u>Saturday Review of Literature</u>, 33:27-9, Jan. 28, 1950
<u>School and Society</u>, 71:213-14, April 8, 1950
<u>Theatre Arts</u>, 34:13, March, 1950
<u>Time</u>, 55:45, Jan. 16, 1950

"Square Root of Wonderful", 1958

<u>America</u>, 98:299, Nov. 30, 1957
<u>Catholic World</u>, 186:306, Jan., 1958
<u>Christian Century</u>, 74:1425, Nov. 27, 1957
<u>Commonweal</u>, 67:288-9, Dec. 13, 1957
<u>Nation</u>, 185:394, Nov. 23, 1957
<u>New Yorker</u>, 33:103-5, Nov. 9, 1957
<u>Theatre Arts</u>, 42:24, Jan., 1958
<u>Time</u>, 70:93-4, Nov. 11, 1957

SOPHIE MCGEEHAN

SEE

SOPHIE TREADWELL

LEUEEN MACGRATH

SEE

GEORGE S. KAUFMAN AND LEUEEN MACGRATH

PERCY MACKAYE

"George Washington", n. d.

> Firkins, O. W. , Review of Reviews, 2:288-9, March 20,
> 1920

"The Scarecrow", 1910

> Austin, S. , "'Scarecrow' ; a discussion of its performance",
> Drama, no. 4:216-22, November, 1911
> Bentley,Eric Russell, Dramatic Event; an American
> Chronicle, Horizon, 1954, p. 136-39
> Hamilton, C. , "Supernatural plays", Bookman, 33:28-9,
> March, 1911

> New Republic, 128:23, June 29, 1953

ARCHIBALD MACLEISH

"Fall of the City", 1937

> "'Fall of the city': verse drama for radio; with study
> analysis" Scholastic, 31:17E-23E, Nov. 13, 1937

"J. B.", 1958

> Abel, Lionel, Metatheatre; a new veiw of dramatic form,
> Hill and Wang, 1963, p. 116-22
> Bond, Charles M. , "J. B. is not Job", Bucknell Review,
> 9:272-80, 1961

Campbell, Colin C., "The transformation of the Biblical myth; MacLeish's use of the Adam and Job stories", Myth and Symbol, 15:79-88, 1963

Casper, Leonard, "The Godmask of MacLeish", Critique: Review of Theatre Arts and Literature, 1:iii, 11-12, 1958

Christensen, Parley A., " 'J. B. ', the critics, and me", Western Humanities Review, 15:111-26, 1961

Donoghue, Denis, Third verse; modern British and American verse drama, Princeton, 1959, p. 193-212

Gassner, John, Theatre at the crossroads; plays and playwrights of the mid-century American stage, Holt, 1960, p. 298-403

Grebstein, S. N. " 'J. B. ' and the problem of evil", University of Kansas City Review, 29:253-61, 1963

Hamilton, Kenneth, "The patience of J. B.", Dalhousie Review, 41:32-39, 1961

Slote, Bernice, ed., Myth and symbol; critical approaches and applications, Univ. of Nebraska Press, 1963, p. 79-88.

Tynan, Kenneth, Curtains; selections from the drama criticism and related writings, Atheneum, 1961, p. 290-94

Vann, J. Don, "Macleish's 'J. B. ' ", American Notes and Queries, 11:150, 1964

America, 100:13, Oct. 4, 1958
America, 100:502, Jan. 24, 1959
Catholic World, 188:505, March, 1959
Catholic World, 190:81-5, Nov., 1959
Christian Century, 75:692-3, June 11, 1958
Christian Century, 75:926, Aug. 13, 1958
Christian Century, 76:21-2, Jan. 7, 1959
Commentary, 26:183-4, Aug., 1958
Commentary, 27:153-8, Feb., 1959
Commonweal, 70:153-4, May 8, 1959
Educational Theatre Journal, 11:29-32, 1959
Harper, 218:77-8, April, 1959
Illustrated London News, 238:600, April 8, 1961
Library Journal, 84:36-7, Jan. 1, 1959
Life, 45:171, Dec. 22, 1958
Life, 46:124-5, May 18, 1959
Nation, 186:425-6, May 10, 1958
Nation, 188:19, Jan 1959
New Yorker, 34:70-2, Dec. 20, 1958
Reporter, 20:37, Jan 8, 1959

Saturday Review, 41:11-12, March 8, 1958
Saturday Review, 41:22, May 10, 1958
Saturday Review, 42:22-3, Jan. 3, 1959
Saturday Review, 43:39, Jan. 30, 1960
Theatre Arts, 42:9-11, August, 1958
Theatre Arts, 43:9, Feb. , 1959
Theatre Arts, 43:60-3, April 1959
Theatre Arts, 44:29-30, Feb. , 1960
Theology Today, 16:65-9, 1959
Time, 71:87-8, March 24, 1958
Time 72:53-4, Dec. 22, 1958
Time 73:95, April 13, 1959

"Panic", 1935

Saturday Review of Literature, 11:545, March 16, 1935
Nation, 140:369-70, March 27, 1935
New Republic, 82:190, 217, March 27, 1935
Theatre Arts, 19:325-7, May, 1935
Theatre Arts, 21:104-6, Feb. , 1937

LORING MANDEL

"Advise and Consent" (dramatization of novel by A. Drury), 1960

Christian Century, 77:1512-14, Dec. 21, 1960
Commonweal, 73:280-1, Dec. 9, 1960
Educational Theatre Journal, 13:49-50, March, 1961
Hudson Review, 41:260-1, Summer, 1961
Life, 49:48, Dec. 12, 1960
Nation, 191:444, Dec. 3, 1960
National Review, 10:25, Jan. 14, 1961
New Republic, 143:20, Dec. 26, 1960
New Yorker, 36:104, Nov. 26, 1960
Newsweek, 56:81, Nov. 28, 1960
Reporter, 23:35-6, Dec. 22, 1960
Saturday Review, 43:37, Dec. 3, 1960
Theatre Arts, 45:59, Jan. , 1961
Time, 76:40, Nov. 28, 1960

JOHN HARTLEY MANNERS

"Peg-o-My-Heart", 1912

English Review, 18:523-4, Nov. , 1914

V. MAPES

SEE

WINCHELL SMITH AND V. MAPES

GEORGE MARION, JR.

SEE

GEORGE ABBOTT AND GEORGE MARION, JR.

JOHN PHILIPS MARQUAND AND GEORGE SIMON KAUFMAN
"Late George Apley", 1944

> Atlantic Monthly, 198:71-4, Sept. 1956
> Catholic World, 160:355, Jan., 1945
> Commonweal, 41:230, Dec. 15, 1944
> Life, 17:41-4, Dec. 4, 1944
> Nation, 159:725, Dec. 9, 1944
> New Republic, 111:798, Dec. 11, 1944
> N. Y. Times Mag., p. 28-9, Nov. 19, 1944
> New Yorker, 20:44, Dec. 2, 1944
> Newsweek, 23:110, Dec. 4, 1944
> Saturday Review of Literature, 27:24, Dec. 9, 1944
> Scholastic, 46:18, March 5, 1945
> Theatre Arts, 29:7, January, 1945
> Theatre Arts, 29:221-5, April, 1945
> Time, 44:48, Dec. 4, 1944

WILLIAM MASS, PSEUD.

SEE

WILLIAM GIBSON

EDWIN JUSTUS MAYER

"Children of Darkness", 1930

> Catholic World, 130:722, March, 1930
> Catholic World, 187:145, May, 1958

Commonweal, 68:105, April 25, 1958
Nation, 130:134, Jan. 29, 1930
New Republic, 62:20, Feb. 19, 1930

"Firebrand of Florence", 1924

Nathan, George Jean, Theatre Book of the Year, 1944-1945,
Knopf, p. 314-17

"Last Love of Don Juan", 1955

Saturday Review, 38:25, Dec. 10, 1955

GIAN-CARLO MENOTTI

"Amahl and the Night Visitors", 1952

Lillich, Meredith, "Menotti's music dramas", Educational
Theatre Journal, 11:271-9, 1959

Catholic World, 175:227-8, June, 1952
Colliers, 130:52-3, Dec. 27, 1952
House and Garden, 102:116-17, Dec., 1952
Life, 33:102-3, Dec. 15, 1952
Musical America, 72:5, April 15, 1952
Musical Quarterly, 38:296-8, April, 1952
New Yorker, 27:56, Jan. 5, 1952
New Yorker, 28:91, April 19, 1952
Newsweek, 39:36-7, Jan. 7, 1952
Saturday Review, 35:30, Jan. 12, 1952
Saturday Review, 35:30, April 26, 1952
Time, 58:30, Dec. 31, 1951

"Amelia Goes to the Ball", 1937

Commonweal, 27:581, March 18, 1938
Musical America, 71:9, Aug., 1951
Musical America, 74:7, April, 1954
Musical America, 77:47, March, 1957
Musician, 43:45, March, 1938
New Yorker, 89:96, May 18, 1963
Newsweek, 9:19, April 10, 1937
Time, 29:28, April 12, 1937

"The Consul", 1950

> Lillich, Meredith, "Menotti's music dramas", <u>Educational
> Theatre Journal</u>, 11:271-9, 1959
> Nathan, George Jean, <u>Theatre Book of the Year, 1949-1950</u>,
> Knopf, p. 249-54
> Thompson, Virgil, <u>Music Right and Left</u>, Knopf, 1948,
> p. 79-81
> Tynan, Kenneth, Curtains; <u>Selections from the Drama
> Criticism and Related Writings</u>, Atheneum, 1961,
> p. 246-47

> <u>Catholic World</u>, 171:148, May, 1950
> <u>Christian Science Monitor Mag.</u>, p. 5, March 18, 1950
> <u>Commentary</u>, 9:472-4, May, 1950
> <u>Commonweal</u>, 51:677, April 7, 1950
> <u>Illustrated London News</u>, 218:346, March 3, 1951
> <u>Life</u>, 28:61-3, April 10, 1950
> <u>Music and Letters</u>, 32:247-51, and 400, 1951
> <u>Musical America</u>, 70:7, March, 1950
> <u>Musical America</u>, 71:6, Oct., 1951
> <u>Musical Quarterly</u>, 36:447-50, July, 1950
> <u>Nation</u>, 170:305, April 1, 1950
> <u>Nation</u>, 170:557-8, June 3, 1950
> <u>New Republic</u>, 122:21-2, April 10, 1950
> <u>New Statesman and Nation</u> 41:183, Feb. 17, 1951
> <u>New Yorker</u>, 26:54, March, 1950
> <u>New Yorker</u>, 28:149, Oct. 18, 1952
> <u>Saturday Review of Literature</u>, 33:28-30, April 22, 1950
> <u>School and Society</u>, 72:183, Sept. 16, 1950
> <u>Theatre Arts</u>, 34:28-9, March, 1950
> <u>Theatre Arts</u>, 34:17, May, 1950

"Labyrinth", 1963

> <u>Hudson Review</u>, 16:437, 1963
> <u>Opera News</u>, 27:33, April 13, 1963
> <u>Saturday Review</u>, 46:94, March 16, 1963

"Last Savage", 1963

> <u>Life</u>, 56:66A-66B, Feb. 14, 1964
> <u>New Yorker</u>, 39:198-200, Nov. 2, 1963
> <u>New Yorker</u>, 39:60, Feb. 1, 1964

Newsweek, 63:77, Feb. 3, 1964
Opera News, 28:24-5, Feb. 8, 1964
Opera News, 28:30, Dec. 7, 1963
Opera News, 28:13-15, Feb. 8, 1964
Opera News, 28:17-20, Feb. 8, 1964
Saturday Review, 47:27-8, Feb. 8, 1964
Saturday Review, 48:22, Jan. 16, 1965
Time, 83:33, Jan. 31, 1964

"Maria Golovin", 1958

Musical America, 78:17, October, 1958
Musical America, 78:18, Nov. 15, 1958
Nation, 187:395-6, Nov. 22, 1958
New Republic, 139:22-3, Nov. 17, 1958
New Yorker, 34:200-1, Nov. 15, 1958
Newsweek, 52:75, Nov. 17, 1958
Newsweek, 52:54, Sept. 1, 1958
Saturday Review, 41:43, Nov. 22, 1958
Theatre Arts, 43:68, January, 1959
Time, 72:54, Nov. 17, 1958
Time, 72:40, Sept. 1, 1958

"Martin's Lie", 1963

Newsweek, 63:93, June 15, 1964
Spectator, 212:794, June 12, 1964

"The Medium", 1946

Lillich, Meredith, "Menotti's music dramas", Educational
    Theatre Journal, 11:271-9, 1959
Nathan, George Jean, Theatre Book of the Year, 1947-1948,
    Knopf, p. 3-5
Thompson, Virgil, Art of Judging Music, Knopf, 1948,
    p. 127-29
Weales, Gerald Clifford, American Drama since World War
    II, Harcourt, 1962, p. 120-53

Catholic World, 165:265-6, June, 1947
Catholic World, 171:469, Sept. , 1950
Commonweal, 45:518, March 7, 1947
Life, 22:95-6, June 9, 1947
Modern Music, 23 no. 3:223, July, 1946
Musical America, 73:6, April 15, 1953
Musical America, 79:8, May, 1959

Nation, 164:637, May 24, 1947
New Republic, 116:40, March 10, 1947
New Yorker, 23:50, May 10, 1947
New Yorker, 39:96, May 18, 1963
Saturday Review of Literature, 30:22-4, May 31, 1947
Saturday Review of Literature, 31:43-4, Feb. 28, 1948
School and Society, 66:66, July 26, 1947
School and Society, 69:86, Jan. 29, 1949
Spectator, 180:554, May 7, 1948
Theatre Arts, 31:60, May, 1947
Time, 49:69, June 30, 1947

"The Old Maid and the Thief", 1941

Musician, 49:69, April, 1944

"The Saint of Bleecker Street", 1954

Lillich, Meredith, "Menotti's music dramas", Educational
Theatre Journal, 11:271-9, 1959

America, 92:434, Jan. 22, 1955
Catholic World, 180:385, Feb., 1955
Commonweal, 61:476-7, Feb., 4, 1955
Kenyon Review, 17:624-32, 1955
Life, 38:62-3, Feb. 14, 1955
Musical America, 75:3, Jan. 15, 1955
Nation, 180:83, Jan. 22, 1955
New Yorker, 30:74-6, Jan. 8, 1955
New Yorker, 30:77, Jan. 22, 1955
New Yorker, 41:172, March 27, 1965
Newsweek, 45:62, Jan. 10, 1955
Reporter, 12:40, April 7, 1955
Saturday Review, 38:28, Jan. 8, 1955
Theatre Arts, 39:17, 22-3, March, 1955
Time, 65:42, Jan. 10, 1955

"The Telephone", 1947

Nathan, George Jean, Theatre Book of the Year, 1947-1948,
Knopf, p. 3-5
Thompson, Virgil, The Art of Judging Music, Knopf, 1948,
p. 127-29

Catholic World, 165:264-5, June, 1947
Catholic World, 171:469, Sept., 1950

Commonweal, 45:518, March 7, 1947
Nation, 164:637, May 24, 1947
New Republic, 116:40, March 10, 1947
New Yorker, 23:50, May 10, 1947
Saturday Review of Literature, 30:22-4, May 31, 1947
School and Society, 66:66, July 26, 1947
School and Society, 69:86, Jan. 29, 1949
Spectator (Lond), 180:554, May 7, 1948
Theatre Arts, 31:60, May, 1947

"The Unicorn, The Gorgon and the Manticore", 1957
Lillich, Meredith, "Menotti's music dramas", Educational
Theatre Journal 11:271-9, 1959

ARTHUR MILLER

"After the Fall", 1964
Ganz, Arthur, "Arthur Miller: After the silence", Drama
Survey, 3:520-530, Fall, 1964
George, Manfred, and Henry B. Kranz, "Neues Meisterwerk
der modernen Dichtung: Arthur Miller's drama 'After the
Fall' als spiegel unseres Daseins", Universitas
(Stuttgart), 19:349-55, 1964
Huftel, Sheila, Arthur Miller: The Burning Glass, Citadel,
1965, p. 191-216
America, 110:322, March 7, 1964
Commonweal, 79:600-1, Feb. 14, 1964
Educational Theatre Journal, 16:177-9, May, 1964
Hudson Review, 17:234-6, Summer, 1964
Life, 56:64, Feb. 7, 1964
National Review, 16:289-90, April 7, 1964
Nation, 198:153-4, Feb. 10, 1964
New Republic, 150:26-8, Feb. 8, 1964
New Yorker, 39:59, Feb. 1, 1964
Newsweek, 63:49-52, Feb. 3, 1964
Partisan Review, 31:284-7, Spring, 1964 and 324, Summer,
1964
Reporter, 30:46, Feb. 27, 1964
Saturday Review, 47:35, Feb. 15, 1964
Spectator, 212:213, Feb. 14, 1964
Theatre Arts, 48:12-16, Jan., 1964
Time, 83:54, Jan. 31, 1964
Vogue, 143:66, March 15, 1964

"All My Sons", 1947

Boggs, W. Arthur, " 'Oedipus' and 'All my sons' ", The
Personalist, 42:555-560, 1961
Dotzenrath, Theo "Arthur Miller's 'All my Sons' als
Schullekture" Die Neuren Sprachen, 8:33-40, 1959
Huftel, Sheila, Arthur Miller: the Burning Glass, Citadel,
1965 p. 84-102
Lerner, Max, Actions and Passions; Notes on the
Multiple Revolution of Our Time, Simon and Schuster,
1949, p. 20-28
Moss, Leonard, "Arthur Miller and the common man's
language", Modern Drama, 7:52-59, May, 1964
Nathan, George Jean, Theatre Book of the Year, 1946-1947,
Knopf, p. 290-93
Wells, Arvin R. , "The living and the dead in 'All My Sons' ",
Modern Drama, 7:46-51, 1964

New Statesman and Nation, 35:412, May 22, 1948
School and Society, 65:250, April 5, 1947
Spectator, 180:612, May 21, 1948

"Babbitt", 1955

Coachman, G. W. , "Arthur Miller's tragedy of 'Babbitt' ",
Educational Theatre Journal, 7:206-11, Oct. , 1955

"The Crucible", 1953

Bentley,Eric Russell, Dramatic Event; an American
Chronicle, Horizon Press, 1954, p. 90-94
Brossard, Chandler, ed. , Scene Before You; a New Approach
to American Culture, Rinehardt, 1955, p. 191-203
Calendoli, Giovanni, "Il Crogiulo di Miller", La Fiera
Letteraria, #48, Nov. 27, 1955, p. 6
Galinsky, Hans and Lang, Hans-Joachim, eds. , Kleine
Beitrage zur Americanischen literaturgeschichte:
Arbeitsproben aus deutschen Seminarem und Instituten,
Heidelberg, Winter, 1961, p. 114-128.
Ganz, Arthur, "The silence of Arthur Miller", Drama
Survey, 3:224-37, 1963
Gassner, John, Theatre at the crossroads; plays and
playwrights of the mid-century American stage, Holt,
1960, p. 274-78
Huftel, Sheila, Arthur Miller: the burning glass, Citadel,
1965, p. 124-148

Lemarchand, Jacques, "La sorciere de Salem", Nouvelle
  Revue Francaise, 3:309-313, February, 1955

Maulnier, Thierry, "Les sorcieres de Salem d'Arthur
  Miller", Revue de Paris, 62:137-149, February, 1955

Nathan, George Jean, Theatre in the fifties, Knopf, 1953,
  p. 105-09

Popkin, Henry, "Arthur Miller's 'The Crucible'",
  College English, 26:139-46, 1964

Selz, Jean, "Les sorcieres de Salem d'Arthur Miller",
  Lettres Nouvelles, 5:422-426, March, 1955

Tynan, Kenneth, Curtains; selections from the drama
  criticism and related writings, Atheneum, 1961, p. 253,
  54

Walker, Philip, "Arthur Miller's 'The Crucible': tragedy
  or allegory?" Western Speech, 20:222-224, 1956

Warshow, Robert, "The immediate experience; movies,
  comics, theatre and other aspects of popular culture",
  Doubleday, 1962, p. 189-203

Catholic World, 176:465-6, March, 1953
Catholic World, 193:394-5, Sept., 1961
Commentary, 15:265-71, March, 1953
Commentary, 16:83-4, July, 1953
Commonweal, 57:498, Feb. 20, 1953
Illustrated London News, 225:964, Nov. 27, 1954
Life, 34:87-8, Feb. 9, 1953.
Nation, 176:131, Feb. 7, 1953
New Republic, 128:22-3, Feb. 16, 1953
New Statesman, 48:642, Nov. 20, 1954
New Statesman, 51:370, April 14, 1956
New Yorker, 28:47, Jan. 31, 1953
Newsweek, 41:68, Feb. 2, 1953
Saturday Review, 36:41-2, Feb. 14, 1953
School and Society, 77:185-8, March 21, 1953
Spectator, 193:608, Nov. 19, 1954
Spectator, 196:547, April, 20, 1956
Theatre Arts, 37:24-6, 65-9, April, 1953
Theatre Arts, 37:33-4, Oct., 1953
Theatre Arts, 40:80, Feb., 1956
Theatre Arts, 41:27, May, 1957
Time, 61:48, Feb. 2, 1953

"Death of a Salesman", 1949

Bettina, Sister M., "Willy Loman's brother Ben: tragic insight in 'Death of a Salesman'", Modern Drama, 4:409-412, 1962

Brown, John Mason, Dramatis personae; a retrospective show, Viking, 1963, p. 94-100.

Brown, John Mason, Still seeing things, McGraw, 1950, p. 196-204

Cole, Toby, ed., Playwrights on playwriting; the meaning and making of modern drama from Ibsen to Ionesco, Hill and Wang, 1960, p. 261-76.

"'Death of a Salesman'; a symposium", Tulane Drama Review, 2:63-69, May, 1958

DeSchweinitz, George, "'Death of a Salesman': a note on epic and tragedy", Western Humanities Review, 14:91-96, 1960

Dusenbury, Winifred Loesch, The theme of loneliness in modern American drama, Univ, of Florida Press, 1960, p. 8-37

Ganz, Arthur, "The silence of Arthur Miller", Drama Survey, 3:224-237, 1963

Gassner, John, Theatre in our times; a survey of the men, materials, movements in the modern theatre, Crown, 1954, p. 364-73

Huftel, Sheila, Arthur Miller; the burning glass, Citadel, 1965, p. 103-123

Hurrell, John D., Two modern American tragedies: reviews and criticisms of 'Death of a Salesman' and 'A Streetcar Named Desire', Scribner, 1961, p. 54-88

Hynes, Joseph A., "'Attention must be paid...'", College English, 23:574-578, 1962

Kennedy, Sighle, "Who killed the salesman?", Catholic World, 171:110-6, May, 1950

Lawrence, Stephen A., "The right to dream in Miller's 'Death of a Salesman'", College English, 25:547-49, 1964

Lewis, Allan, The contemporary theatre; the significant playwrights of our time, Crown, 1962, p. 282-303

Moss, Leonard, "Arthur Miller and the common man's language," Modern Drama, 7:52-59, May, 1964

Nathan, George Jean, Theatre book of the year, 1948-1949, Knopf, p. 278-85

Oppenheimer, George, ed., Passionate playgoer; a
personal scrapbook, Viking, 1958, p. 600-01
Shea, A.A., "'Death of a Salesman'", Canadian Forum,
29:86-7, July, 1949
"Tragedy and the common man", Theatre Arts, 35:48-50,
March, 1951

American Mercury, 68:679-80, June, 1949
Catholic World, 169:62-3, April, 1949
Commentary, 11:184-6, February, 1951
Commonweal, 49:520-1, March 4, 1949
Fortune, 39:79-80, May, 1949
Forum, 111:219-21, April, 1949
House and Garden, 95:218, May, 1949
Life, 26:115, Feb. 21, 1949
Nation, 168:283-4, March 5, 1949
New Republic, 120:26-8, Feb., 28, 1949
New Statesman and Nation, 38:146, August 6, 1949
New Yorker, 24:58, Feb. 19, 1949
Newsweek, 33:78, Feb. 21, 1949
N.Y. Times Mag., p. 11, Aug. 28, 1949
Partisan Review, 16:631-5, June, 1949
Saturday Review of Literature, 32:30-2, Feb. 26, 1949
Saturday Review, 46:34, Aug. 24, 1963
School and Society, 70:363-4, Dec. 3, 1949
Spectator, 183:173, Aug. 5, 1949
Theatre Arts, 33:14-16, April, 1949
Theatre Arts, 33:18-21, Oct., 1949
Theatre Arts, 33:12-14, Nov., 1949
Time, 53:74-6, Feb. 21, 1949

"Incident at Vichy", 1964

Huftel, Sheila, Arthur Miller: the burning glass, Citadel,
1965, p. 217-236.

America, 112:147-9, Jan. 23, 1965
Life, 58:39-40, Jan. 22, 1965
Nation, 199:504, Dec. 21, 1964
New Republic, 151:26-7, Dec. 26, 1964
N.Y. Times Mag., p. 10-11, Jan. 3, 1965
New Yorker, 40:152, Dec. 12, 1964
Newsweek, 64:86, Dec. 14, 1964

Saturday Review, 47:24, Dec. 19, 1964
Time, 84:73, Dec. 11, 1964
Vogue, 145:27, Jan. 15, 1965

"The Man Who Had All the Luck", 1943

Huftel, Sheila, Arthur Miller: the burning glass, Citadel,
1965, p. 76-83
Nathan, George Jean, Theatre book of the year, 1944-45,
Knopf, p. 171-73

"The Misfits", 1961

Huftel, Sheila, Arthur Miller: the burning glass, Citadel,
1965, p. 165-190
Moss, Leonard, "Arthur Miller and the common man's
language", Modern Drama, 7:52-59, May, 1964

"A View from the Bridge", 1955

Huftel, Sheila, Arthur Miller: the burning glass, Citadel,
1965, p. 149-164

America, 94:223, Nov. 19, 1955
Catholic World, 182:144-5, Nov. 1955
Commonweal, 63:117, Nov. 4, 1955
Commonweal, 81-670, Feb. 19, 1965
Illustrated London News, 229:720, Oct., 1957
Life, 39:166-7, Oct. 17, 1955
Nation, 181:348-9, Oct. 22, 1955
New Republic, 133:21-2, Dec. 17, 1955
New Statesman, 54:482, Oct. 20, 1956
New Yorker, 31:92, Oct. 8, 1955
New Yorker, 40:94, Feb. 6, 1965
Newsweek, 65:93, March 15, 1965
N.Y. Times Mag., p. 78, Sept. 18, 1955
Saturday Review, 38:25-6, Oct. 15, 1955
Spectator, 197:538, Oct. 19, 1956
Theatre Arts, 39:18-19, Dec., 1955
Theatre Arts, 40:31-2, Sept., 1956
Theatre Arts, 41:28-9, May, 1957
Time, 66:53, Oct. 10, 1955
Twentieth Century, 161:56-62, Jan., 1957
Vogue, 145:56, April 15, 1965

LANGDON ELWYN MITCHELL

"Becky Sharp", 1899

> Commonweal, 10:189, June 19, 1929
> Literary Digest, 101:23-4, June 29, 1929

"Major Pendennis", 1916

> "Impossible Thackeray", Literary Digest, 53:1409,
> Nov. 25, 1916
>
> Literary Digest, 53:1328-9, Nov. 18, 1916
> Nation, 103:426-7, Nov. 2, 1916
> New Republic, 9:21, Nov. 4, 1916

"The New York Idea", 1906

> Moses, Montrose Jonas and Brown, John Mason, eds.,
> American Theatre as Seen by Its Critics, 1752-1934,
> Norton, 1934, p. 167-69
>
> Harper's Weekly, 50:1758, Dec. 8, 1906
> Nation, 101:443, Oct. 7, 1915
> New Republic, 119:31, Aug. 30, 1948

WILLIAM VAUGHN MOODY

"The Faith Healer", 1909

> Nation, 88:175-6, Feb. 18, 1909

"The Fire Bringer", 1904

> Shackford, M. H., "Moody's 'The fire bringer' for today",
> Sewanee Review, 26:407-16, October, 1918
>
> Critic, 45:571, Dec., 1904
> Dial, 36:321-3, May, 1916
> Nation, 78:498-9, June 24, 1904
> Reader, 4:108-9, June, 1904
> Sewanee Review, 12:348-53, July, 1904

"The Great Divide", 1906

> Moses, Montrose Jonas and Brown, John Mason, eds.,
> American Theatre as Seen by Its Critics, 1752-1934,
> Norton, 1934, p. 176-78

"The Masque of Judgment", 1900

> Dial, 30:365-8, June 1, 1901
> Nation, 72:259-60, March 28, 1901
> Sewanee Review, 9:332-6, July, 1901

LLOYD R. MORRIS

SEE

JOHN VAN DRUTEN AND LLOYD R. MORRIS

ANNE NICHOLS

"Abie's Irish Rose", 1922

> Brown, John Mason, Two on the Aisle; Ten Years of the American Theatre in Performance, Norton, 1938, p. 92-94
> Littell, Robert, Read America First, Harcourt, 1926, p. 238-45
> Moses, Montrose Jonas and Brown, John Mason, eds., American Theatre as Seen by Its Critics, 1752-1934, Norton, 1934, p. 259-62
> Oppenheimer, George, ed., Passionate Playgoer; a Personal Scrapbook, Viking, 1958, p. 584-87

> Catholic World, 180:309, Jan., 1955
> Colliers, 74:5, July 26, 1924
> Commonweal, 26:160, June 4, 1937
> Current Opinion, 77:192, Aug., 1921
> Journal des Debats, 40, pt. 2:516-18, Sept. 29, 1933
> Ladies Home Journal, 41:32, Sept., 1924
> Literary Digest, 92:30, Feb. 19, 1927
> Literary Digest, 93:27, May 14, 1927
> Nation (Lond), 41:80, April 23, 1927
> Nation, 125:467-8, Nov. 2, 1927
> New Republic, 42:98-9, March 18, 1927
> New Republic, 51:18-19, May 25, 1927
> Newsweek, 9:26, May 22, 1937
> Theatre Arts, 31:66-7, April, 1937
> Theatre Arts, 39:13, 92, Feb., 1955
> Time, 64:50, Nov. 29, 1954

ANNE NICHOLS AND ALFRED VAN RONKEL

"Pre-honeymoon", 1936

Time, 27:28, May 11, 1936

ELLIOTT NUGENT

"Message for Margaret" (adapted from story by James Parish), 1947

New Yorker, 23:46, April 26, 1947
Theatre Arts, 31:52, Jan., 1947
Theatre Arts, 31:44, June, 1947

"Place of Our Own", 1945

Nathan, George Jean, Theatre Book of the Year, 1944-1945, Knopf, p. 328-29

ELLIOTT NUGENT AND J. C. NUGENT

"The Poor Nut", 1925

Krutch, J. W., Nation, 120:556-7, May 13, 1925

ELLIOTT NUGENT AND JAMES THURBER

"The Male Animal", 1940

Nathan, George Jean, Theatre Book of the Year, 1946-1947, Knopf, p. 377

Catholic World, 150:597, Feb., 1940
Catholic World, 175:228, June, 1952
Commonweal, 31:307, Jan. 26, 1940
Commonweal, 56:173, May 23, 1952
Life, 8:27-8, Jan. 29, 1940
Nation, 150:81, Jan. 20, 1940
Nation, 175:58, July 19, 1952
New Republic, 102:116, Jan. 22, 1940
New Statesman and Nation, 37:556, May 28, 1949

New Yorker, 28:58, May 10, 1952
Newsweek, 14:34, Nov. 6, 1939
Newsweek, 15:32-3, Jan. 22, 1940
Newsweek, 39:84, May 26, 1952
Saturday Review, 35:28, May 17, 1952
Spectator (Lond), 183:13, July 1, 1949
Theatre Arts, 24:158-59, March, 1940
Theatre Arts, 24:407, June, 1940
Theatre Arts, 36:17, 32-5, July, 1952
Time, 35:49, Jan. 22, 1940
Time, 59:58, May 12, 1952

J. C. NUGENT

SEE

ELLIOTT NUGENT AND J. C. NUGENT

CLIFFORD ODETS

"Awake and Sing", 1935

Brown, John Mason, Broadway in Review, Norton, 1940,
p. 176-84
Brown, John Mason, Dramatis Personae; a Retrospective
Show, Viking, 1963, p. 69-72
Downer, Alan S., ed., American Drama and Its Critics,
Univ. Chicago Pr., 1965, p. 139
Kaplan, Charles, "Two depression plays and Broadway's
popular idealism", American Quarterly, 15:579-85, 1963
O'Hara, Frank Hurburt, Today in American Drama, Univ.
of Chicago Pr., 1939, p. 53-141
Warshow, R. S., "Poet of the Jewish middle-class; Clifford
Odets voices its conflicts and frustrations; lower middle
class Jewish culture of New York City as portrayed in
'Awake and sing' ", Commentary, 1:17-22, May, 1946

Catholic World, 141:91, April, 1935
Catholic World, 149:217-18, May, 1939
Commonweal, 21:570, March 15, 1935
Commonweal, 29:639, March 31, 1939
Nation, 140:314, March 13, 1935

New Republic, 82:134, March 13, 1935
New Statesman and Nation, 15:328, Feb. 26, 1938
New Statesman and Nation, 23:352, May 30, 1942
Newsweek, 5:31, March 2, 1935
Spectator (Lond), 160:311, Feb. 25, 1938
Spectator (Lond), 168:507, May 29, 1942
Theatre Arts, 19:255-6, April, 1935
Theatre Arts, 23:323, May, 1939
Time, 33:60, March 20, 1939

"The Big Knife", 1949

Brown, John Mason, Still Seeing Things, McGraw, 1950,
   p. 222-26
Downer, Alan S., ed., American drama and Its Critics,
   Univ. Chicago Pr., 1965, p. 143
Nathan, George Jean, Theatre Book of the Year, 1948-49,
   Knopf, p. 296-304

Catholic World, 169:63, April, 1949
Commonweal, 49:590-1, March 25, 1949
Forum, 111:286-7, May, 1949
Illustrated London News, 224:90, Jan. 16, 1954
Nation, 168:340, March 19, 1949
New Republic, 120:28-9, March 14, 1949
New Statesman, 47:40, Jan. 9, 1954
New Yorker, 25:56, March 5, 1949
Newsweek, 33:84, March 7, 1949
Saturday Review of Literature, 32:34-5, March 19, 1949
School and Society, 69:340-1, May 7, 1949
Spectator (Lond), 192:37, Jan. 8, 1954
Theatre Arts, 33:23-5, May, 1949
Time, 53:58, March 7, 1949

"Clash by Night", 1942

Catholic World, 154:601, February, 1942
Commonweal, 35:319-20, Jan. 16, 1942
Current History, 1:566-8, Feb., 1942
Life, 11:53-4, Nov. 24, 1941
Nation, 154:45-6, Jan. 10, 1941
New Yorker, 17:28, Jan. 3, 1942
Newsweek, 19:46, Jan. 12, 1942
Theatre Arts, 26:150-2, March, 1942

"The Country Girl", 1950

    Gassner, John, Theatre at the Crossroads; Plays and
      Playwrights of the Mid-century American Stage, Holt,
      1960, p. 129-30
    Downer, Alan S., American Drama and Its Critics, Univ.
      Chicago Pr., 1965, p. 143-44
    Nathan, George Jean, Theatre Book of the Year, 1950-1951,
      Knopf, p. 95-100

    American Mercury, 72:350-1, March, 1951
    Catholic World, 172:310, Jan., 1951
    Christian Science Monitor Mag., p. 4, Nov. 18, 1950
    Commonweal, 53:196, Dec. 1, 1950
    Life, 29:77-80, Dec. 4, 1950
    Nation, 171:493, Nov. 25, 1950
    New Republic, 123:29-30, Dec. 11, 1950
    New Yorker, 26:77-9, Nov. 18, 1950
    Newsweek, 36:90, Nov. 20, 1950
    Saturday Review of Literature, 33:26-7, Dec. 9, 1950
    School and Society, 73:249-50, April 21, 1951
    Theatre Arts, 35:14, Jan., 1951
    Time, 56:64, Nov. 20, 1950

"The Flowering Peach", 1954

    Gassner, John, Theatre at the Crossroads; Plays and
      Playwrights of the Mid-century American Stage, Holt,
      1960, p. 153-55
    Downer, Alan S., ed., American Drama and Its Critics,
      Univ. Chicago Pr., 1965, p. 144-45

    America, 92:434, Jan. 22, 1955
    Catholic World, 180:387, Feb., 1955
    Commentary, 20:74-6, July, 1955
    Commonweal, 61:502, Feb. 11, 1955
    Hudson Review, 8:263-8, 1955
    Nation, 180:57-9, Jan. 15, 1955
    New Republic, 132:21, Jan. 10, 1955
    New Yorker, 30:62, Jan. 8, 1955
    Newsweek, 45:62, Jan. 10, 1955
    Saturday Review, 38:30, Jan. 15, 1955
    Theatre Arts, 38:24-5, Oct., 1954
    Theatre Arts, 39:18, 23, March, 1955
    Time, 63:34, Jan. 10, 1955

"Golden Boy", 1937

Gassner, John, Theatre in Our Time; a survey of the Men,
  Materials, and Movements in the Modern Theatre, Crown,
  1954, p. 433-37
Downer, Alan S., American drama and Its Critics, Univ.
  Chicago Pr., 1965, p. 140-141
McCarthy, Mary Therese, Sights and Spectacles, 1937-1956,
  Farrar, Straus, 1956, p. 9-12

Catholic World, 146:342, Dec., 1937
Catholic World, 175:148, May, 1952
Commonweal, 27:106, Nov. 19, 1937
Commonweal, 55:614-15, March 28, 1952
Current History, 48:54, April, 1938
Literary Digest, 124:35, Nov. 27, 1937
Nation, 145:540, Nov. 13, 1937
Nation, 174:285, March 22, 1952
New Republic, 93:45, Nov. 17, 1937
New Statesman and Nation, 16:14-15, July 2, 1938
New Yorker, 28:60, March 22, 1952
Newsweek, 39:100, March 24, 1952
Saturday Review, 35:26, March 29, 1952
School and Society, 75:326-7, May 24, 1952
Scribner's, 103:66, May, 1938
Spectator (Lond), 161:16, July 1, 1938
Theatre Arts, 22:11-13, Jan., 1938
Time, 30:25-6, Nov. 15, 1937
Time, 59:56, March 24, 1952

"Night Music", 1948

Brown, John Mason, Broadway in Review, Norton, 1940,
  p. 176-84
Downer, Alan S., ed., American Drama and Its Critics,
  Univ. Chicago Pr., 1965, p. 142
Dusenbury, Winifred Loesch, The Theme of Loneliness in
  Modern American Drama, Univ. of Florida Pr., 1960,
  p. 38-56
Nathan, George Jean, Theatre Book of the Year, 1950-1951,
  Knopf, p. 262-66

Commonweal, 31:435, March 8, 1940
Nation, 150:316-17, March 2, 1940
New Republic, 102:377, March 18, 1940

Newsweek, 15:42, March 4, 1940
Theatre Arts, 24:230, April, 1940
Time, 35:34, March 4, 1940
Commonweal, 54:58, April 27, 1951
New Republic, 124:22, April 30, 1951
New Yorker, 27:62, April 21, 1951

"Paradise Lost", 1935

Burke, Kenneth, Philosophy of Literary Form; Studies in
Symbolic Action, Louisiana State Univ. Press, 1941, p.
429-32
Theatre Arts Anthology; a Record and a Prophecy, ed. by
Rosamond Gilder and others, Theatre Arts Books, 1950,
p. 635-39

Catholic World, 142:600, Feb., 1936
Commonweal, 23:244, Dec. 27, 1935
Forum, 95:347, June, 1936
Literary Digest, 120:20, Dec. 21, 1935
Nation, 141:752, Dec. 25, 1935
Nation, 142:27-8, Jan. 1, 1936
Nation, 142:72-3, Jan. 15, 1936
New Republic, 85:202, Dec. 25, 1935
New Republic, 86:283, April 15, 1936
Newsweek, 6:39, Dec. 21, 1935
Theatre Arts, 20:94-7, Feb., 1936
Theatre Arts, 20:465-6, June, 1936
Time, 26:31-2, Dec. 23, 1935

"Rocket to the Moon", 1938

Brown, John Mason, Broadway in Review, Norton, 1940,
p. 176-84
Downer, Alan S., ed., American Drama and Its Critics,
Univ. Chicago Pr., 1965, p. 141
Dusenbury, Winifred Loesch, The Theme of Loneliness in
Modern American Drama, Univ. of Florida Press, 1960
p. 86-112
O'Hara, Frank Hurburt, Today in American Drama, Univ.
of Chicago Press, 1939, p. 53-141

Catholic World, 148:476, Jan., 1939
Commonweal, 29:190, Dec. 9, 1938
Forum, 101:72, Feb., 1939

Nation, 147:600-1, Dec. 3, 1938
New Republic, 97:173, Dec. 14, 1938
New Statesman and Nation, 35:253, March 27, 1948
North American Review, 247 no. 1:157-8, March, 1939
Spectator (Lond), 180:373, March 26, 1948
Theatre Arts, 28:11-13, Jan., 1939

"Till the day I Die", 1935

Catholic World, 141:214-15, May, 1935
Commonweal, 21:682, April 12, 1935
New Republic, 82:247, April 10, 1935
New Statesman and Nation, 20:111, Aug. 3, 1940
Theatre Arts, 19:328, May, 1935

"Waiting for Lefty", 1935

Brown, John Mason, Dramatis Personae; a Retrospective
Show, Viking, 1963, p. 69-72
Downer, Alan S., ed., American Drama and Its Critics,
Univ. Chicago Pr., 1965, p. 136-38

Catholic World, 141:215, May, 1935
Commonweal, 21:682, April 12, 1935
Nation, 140:427-8, April 10, 1935
New Republic, 82:247, April 10, 1935
Theatre Arts, 19:327-8, May, 1935

"Winter Journey", 1949

Tynan, Kenneth, Curtains; Selections from the Drama
Criticism and Related Writings, Atheneum, 1961,
p. 19-21

New Statesman, 43:432, April 12, 1952

EUGENE GLADSTONE O'NEILL

"Ah Wilderness", 1933

Adler, Jacob H., "The Worth of 'Ah, Wildenress'",
Modern Drama, 3:280-88, 1960
Cargill, Oscar; Fagin, Nathan; and Fisher, William J., eds.,
O'Neill and His Plays; Four Decades of Criticism, New
York Univ. Press, 1961, p. 194-96

O'Hara, Frank Hurburt, Today in American Drama, Univ. of Chicago Pr., 1939, p. 53-141

Canadian Forum, 14:188, Feb., 1934
Catholic World, 138:214-15, Nov., 1933
Catholic World, 154:212-13, Nov., 1941
Commonweal, 18:620, Oct. 27, 1933
Commonweal, 34:613, Oct. 17, 1941
Life, 11:59-61, Nov. 3, 1941
Literary Digest, 116:24, Oct. 28, 1933
Nation, 137:458-9, Oct. 18, 1933
Nation, 153:381, Oct. 18, 1941
New Republic, 76:280, Oct. 18, 1933
Newsweek, 2:29, Oct. 7, 1933
Newsweek, 3:23, May 12, 1934
Review of Reviews, 89:39, Feb., 1934
Saturday Review of Literature, 10:217, Oct. 28, 1933
Spectator, 156:835, May 8, 1936
Theatre Arts, 17:908-10, Dec., 1933
Theatre Arts, 25:867-8, Dec., 1941

"All God's Chillun Got Wings", 1924

Cargill, Oscar; Fagin, Nathan, and Fisher, William J., eds., O'Neill and His Plays; Four Decades of Criticism, New York Univ. Press, 1961, p. 168-69
Downer, Alan S., ed., American drama and Its Critics, Univ. Chicago Pr., 1965, p. 79-80

Mercure de France, 176:549-50, Dec. 1, 1924
Nation, 118:664, June 4, 1924
Nation (Lond), 44:356, Dec. 8, 1928
New Statesman and Nation, 5:321-2, March 18, 1933
New Statesman, 32:253, Dec. 1, 1928
New Statesman, 33:337-8, June 22, 1929
Saturday Review, 147:829-30, June 22, 1929
Saturday Review, 155:258, March 18, 1933
Spectator, 141:812, Dec. 1, 1928
Spectator, 150:372, March 17, 1933
Theatre Arts, 17:423-4, June, 1933

"Anna Christie", 1921

Cargill, Oscar; Fagin, Nathan, and Fisher, William J., Eds., O'Neill and His Plays; Four Decades of Criticism, New York Univ. Press, 1961, p. 152-54

Dusenbury, Winifred Loesch, The Theme of Loneliness
in Modern American Drama, Univ. of Florida Press,
1960, p. 38-56
Gassner, John, ed., O'Neill; a Collection of Critical Essays,
Prentice-Hall, 1964, p. 62-71
Gay, Robert Malcolm, ed., Fact, Fancy and Opinion;
Examples of Present-day Writing, Little, 1923, p. 344-45
McAleer, John J., "Christ Symbolism in 'Anna Christie'",
Modern Drama, 4:389-96, 1962

Catholic World, 174:462-3, March, 1952
Commonweal, 55:399, Jan. 25, 1952
English Review, 36:469-70, May, 1923
Independent, 107:236, Dec. 3, 1921
Life, 32:82-4, Feb. 4, 1952
Literary Digest, 77:28-9, May 26, 1923
Nation, 174:92, Jan. 26, 1952
Nation (Lond), 33:96-8, April 28, 1923
New Republic, 29:20, Nov. 30, 1921
New Statesman, 21:48, April 21, 1923
New Yorker, 27:48, Feb. 2, 1952
Saturday Review, 35:32-4, Feb. 16, 1952
School and Society, 75:107, Feb. 16, 1952
Spectator, 130:708-9, April 28, 1923
Theatre Arts, 36:70, March, 1952
Time, 59:73, Jan. 21, 1952

"Before Breakfast", 1916
      Cargill, Oscar; Fagin, Nathan, and Fisher, William J.,
         eds., O'Neill and His Plays; Four Decades of Criticism,
         New York Univ., 1961, p. 131

"Beyond the Horizon", 1920
      Cargill, Oscar; Fagin, Nathan, and Fisher, William J.,
         eds., O'Neill and His Plays; Four Decades of Criticism,
         New York Univ. Pr., 1961, p. 135-39
      Cole, Toby, Playwrights on Playwriting; the Meaning and
         Making of Modern Drama from Ibsen to Ionesco, Hill and
         Wang, 1960, p. 234
      Hamilton, Clayton Meeker, Seen on the Stage, Holt, 1920,
         p. 184-91
      Loomis, Roger Sherman and Clark, Donald Lemon, eds.,
         Modern English Readings; Biography, Short Stories, Poems
         and Essays and Plays, Reinhart, 1946, p. 274-77

Moses, Montrose Jonas and Brown, John Mason, <u>American Theatre as Seen By Its Critics, 1752-1934</u>, Norton, 1934, p. 209-11

Times, London, Literary Supplement, <u>American Writing Today; its Independence, and Vigor</u>, ed. by Allan Angoff, New York Univ. Press, 1957, p. 341-48

<u>English Review</u>, 42:702-3, May, 1926
<u>New Statesman</u>, 26:746, March 27, 1926
<u>Outlook</u> (Lond), 57:110, Feb. 13, 1926
<u>Saturday Review</u>, 141:399, March 27, 1926

"Bound East for Cardiff", 1916

Cargill, Oscar; Fagin, Nathan, and Fisher, William J., eds., <u>O'Neill and His Plays; Four Decades of Criticism</u>, New York Univ. Pr., 1961, p. 129-30

Nathan, George Jean, <u>Theatre Book of the Year, 1948-1949</u>, Knopf, p. 32-35

"Chris", n.d.

Cargill, Oscar; Fagin, Nathan, and Fisher, William J., eds., <u>O'Neill and His Plays; Four Decades of Criticism</u>, New York Univ. Pr., 1961, p. 140-41

"Curse of the Misbegotten", 1959

<u>Saturday Review</u>, 43:34-5, May 23, 1959

"Days Without End", 1926

Alexander, Doris M. "Eugene O'Neill, 'The Hound of Heaven' and 'The Hell Hole'", <u>Modern Language Quarterly</u>, 20:307-14, 1959

Cargill, Oscar; Fagin, Nathan, and Fisher, William J., eds., <u>O'Neill and His Plays; Four Decades of Criticism</u>, New York Univ. Pr., 1961, p. 200-02 and 415-23

Moses, Montrose Jonas and John Mason Brown, eds., <u>American Theatre as Seen by its Critics, 1752-1934</u>, Norton, 1934, p. 287-89

<u>American Review</u>, 2:491-5, Feb., 1934
<u>Catholic World</u>, 138:513-17, Feb., 1934
<u>Christian Century</u>, 5:191-2, Feb. 7, 1934
<u>Christian Century</u>, 73:950, Aug. 15, 1956
<u>Commonweal</u>, 19:327-9, Jan. 19, 1926

Literary Digest, 117:17, Feb. 10, 1934
Living Age, 347:554-6, Feb., 1935
London Mercury, 31:508, March, 1935
Nation, 138:10-11, Jan. 24, 1934
New Republic, 77:312, Jan. 24, 1934
New Outlook, 163:48, February, 1934
Newsweek, 3:34, Jan. 20, 1934
Saturday Review of Literature, 10:419, Jan. 20, 1934
Spectator, 170:219, March 5, 1943
Theatre Arts, 18:167-9, March, 1934

"Desire Under the Elms", 1924

Cargill, Oscar; Fagin, Nathan, and Fisher, William J.,
    eds., O'Neill and His Plays; Four Decades of Criticism,
    New York Univ. Pr., 1961, p. 170-71
Conlin, Matthew T., "The Tragic Effect in 'Autumn Fire'
    and 'Desire Under the Elms'", Modern Drama, 1:228-35,
    1959
Downer, Alan S., ed., American Drama and its Critics,
    Univ. Chicago Pr., 1965, p. 84-85
Frenz, Horst, "Eugene O'Neill's 'Desire Under the Elms',
    and Henrik Ibsen's 'Rosmersholm'", Jahrbuch fur
    Amerikastudien, 9:160-165, 1964
Gassner, John, ed., O'Neill; a Collection of Critical
    Essays, Prentice-Hall, 1964, p. 57-61
Hartmann, Murray, "'Desire Under the Elms' in the Light
    of Strindberg's Influence", American Literature, 33:360-69,
    1961
Macgowan, Kenneth, "O'Neill and a Mature Hollywood
    Outlook", Theatre Arts, 42:79-81, 1958
Racey, Edgar F., Jr., "Myth as Tragic Structure in
    'Desire Under the Elms'", Modern Drama, 5:42-46, 1962
Winther, Sophus Keith, "'Desire Under the Elms', a Modern
    Tragedy", Modern Drama, 3:326-32, 1960

America, 108:275, Feb. 23, 1963
American Review, 3:219-20, March, 1925
Canadian Magazine, 64:74, April, 1925
Catholic World, 120:519-21, Jan., 1925
Catholic World, 174:464, March, 1952
Commonweal, 55:423, Feb. 1, 1952
Commonweal, 77:543, Feb. 15, 1963

Independent, 114:51, Jan. 10, 1925
Life, 32:82-4, Feb. 4, 1952
Literary Digest, 86:23-4, Aug. 8, 1925
Mercure de France, 179:836-8, May 1, 1925
Nation, 119:578-80, Nov. 26, 1924
Nation, 122:548-9, May 19, 1926
Nation, 196:106-7, Feb. 2, 1963
New Republic, 41:44, Dec. 3, 1924
New Republic, 148:26, Feb. 2, 1963
New Statesman and Nation, 1:62-3, March 7, 1931
New Statesman and Nation, 19:133-4, Feb. 3, 1940
New Yorker, 38:62, Jan. 19, 1963
New Yorker, 27:53, Jan. 26, 1952
Newsweek, 39:83, Jan. 28, 1952
Newsweek, 61:57, Jan. 21, 1963
Saturday Review, 35:32-4, Feb. 16, 1952
Saturday Review, 46:32, Jan. 26, 1963
School and Society, 75:106-7, Feb. 16, 1952
Spectator, 164:144, Feb. 2, 1940
Survey Graphic, 53:421-2, Jan. 1, 1925
Theatre Arts, 9:3-5, Jan., 1925
Theatre Arts, 36:70, March, 1952
Theatre Arts, 36:31-3, April, 1952
Theatre Arts, 47:10-11, Feb., 1963
Time, 81:42, Jan. 18, 1963
Time, 59:44, Jan. 28, 1952

"Diff'rent", 1920

    Cargill, Oscar; Fagin, Nathan, and Fisher, William J.,
      eds., O'Neill and His Plays; Four Decades of Criticism,
    New York Univ. Pr., 1961, p. 147-49 and 104-06

    Nation (Lond), 30:119-20, Oct. 15, 1921
    Nation, 193:459-60, Dec. 2, 1961
    New Yorker, 37:137, Oct. 28, 1961
    Review of Reviews, 4:207-9, March 2, 1921
    Theatre Arts, 45:70-1, Dec., 1961

"The Dreamy Kid", 1919

    Cargill, Oscar; Fagin, Nathan, and Fisher, William J.,
      eds., O'Neill and His Plays; Four Decades of Criticism,
    New York Univ. Pr., 1961, p. 134

"Dynamo", 1929

Cargill, Oscar; Fagin, Nathan, and Fisher, William J.,
eds., O'Neill and His Plays; Four Decades of Criticism,
New York Univ. Pr., 1961, p. 187-89 and 454-58
Downer, Alan S., ed., American Drama and its Critics,
Univ. Chicago Pr., 1965, p. 98-100
Young, Stark, Immortal Shadows; a Book of Dramatic
Criticism, Scribner, 1948, p. 91-95

Arts and Decoration, 30:72, April, 1929
American Mercury, 16:119-20, Jan., 1929 and
16:373-8, March, 1929
Bookman, 69:179-80, April, 1929
Catholic World, 129:80-2, April, 1929
Commonweal, 9:489-90, Feb. 27, 1926
Dial, 86:349-50, April, 1929
Drama, 19:201, April, 1929
Literary Digest, 100:21-2, March 2, 1929
Nation, 128:264-6, Feb. 27, 1929
New Republic, 58:43-4, Feb. 27, 1929
Outlook, 151:331, Feb. 27, 1929
Review of Reviews, 79:158-60, April, 1929

"The Emperor Jones", 1920

Cargill, Oscar; Fagin, Nathan, and Fisher, William J.,
eds., O'Neill and His Plays; Four Decades of Criticism,
New York Univ. Pr., 1961, p. 144-46 and 197-99
Cole, Toby, Playwrights on Playwriting; the Meaning and
Making of Modern Drama from Ibsen to Ionesco, Hill and
Wang, 1960, p. 234-35
Galinsky, Hans and Lang, Hans-Joachim, eds., "Kleine
Beitrage zur Amerikanischen Literaturgeschichte:
Arbeitsproben aus Deutschen Seminaren und Instituten,
Heidelberg, 1960, p. 95-113
Mais, Stuart Petre Brodie, Some Modern Authors,
Richards, 1923, p. 296-302
Moses, Montrose Jonas, "O'Neill and 'The Emperor Jones'",
Independent, 105:158-9, Feb. 12, 1921
Theatre Arts Anthology; a Record and a Prophecy, ed. by
Rosamond Gilder and others, Theatre Arts Books, 1950,
p. 592-94

Drama, 14:132, Jan., 1924
Literary Digest, 79:24-5, Dec. 29, 1923

London Mercury, 12:651, Oct., 1925
New Statesman, 25:628-9, Sept. 19, 1925
Outlook (Lond), 56:229, Oct. 3, 1925
Outlook, 126:710-11, Dec. 22, 1920
Review of Reviews, 3:567-8, Dec. 8, 1920
Saturday Review, 140:308-9, Sept. 19, 1925

"Exorcism", n. d.

Cargill, Oscar; Fagin, Nathan, and Fisher, William J.,
eds., O'Neill and His Plays; Four Decades of Criticism,
New York Univ. Pr., 1961, p. 142-43

"The First Man", n. d.

Cargill, Oscar; Fagin, Nathan and Fisher, William J.,
eds., O'Neill and His Plays; Four Decades of Criticism,
New York Univ. Pr., 1961, p. 157-59
Gay, Robert Malcolm, ed., Fact, Fancy and Opinion;
Examples of Present Day Writing, Little, 1923, p. 344-45

"The Fountain", 1925

Cargill, Oscar; Fagin, Nathan and Fisher, William J., eds.,
O'Neill and His Plays; Four Decades of Criticism, New
York Univ. Pr., p. 172-74
Downer, Alan S., ed., American Drama and Its Critics,
Univ. Chicago Pr., 1965, p. 85-88

Arts and Decoration, 24:84-6, Feb., 1926
Drama, 16:175-6, Feb., 1926
New Republic, 45:160-1, Dec. 30, 1925

"Gold", 1926

Cargill, Oscar; Fagin, Nathan and Fisher, William J., eds.,
O'Neill and His Plays; Four Decades of Criticism, New York
Univ. Pr., 1961, p. 150-51

Review of Reviews, 4:584-5, June 18, 1921
Saturday Review, 142:613-14, Nov. 20, 1926

"The Great God Brown", 1926

Cargill, Oscar; Fagin, Nathan and Fisher, William J., eds.,
O'Neill and His Plays; Four Decades of Criticism, New
York Univ. Pr., 1961, p. 175-77

Cole, Toby, Playwrights on Playwriting; the Meaning and
  Making of Modern Drama from Ibsen to Ionesco, Hill and
  Wang, 1960, p. 237-39
Day, Cyrus, ' "Amor Fati'; O'Neill's Lazarus as Superman
  and Savior", Modern Drama, 3:297-305, 1960
Dusenbury, Winifred Loesch, The Theme of Loneliness in
  Modern American Drama, Univ. of Florida, Press, 1960,
  p. 155-78
Metzger, D. P., "Variations on a Theme: a Study of
  'Exiles' by James Joyce and 'The Great God Brown' by
  Eugene O'Neill", Modern Drama, 8:174-84, Sept., 1965
Tynan, Kenneth, Curtains; Selections from the Drama
  Criticism and Related Writings, Atheneum, 1961, p. 322-24
Young, Stark, Immortal Shadows; a Book of Dramatic
  Criticism, Scribner, 1948, p. 61-66
America, 102:139-40, Oct. 31, 1959
Catholic World, 122:805-7, March, 1926
Independent, 116:275, March 6, 1926
London Mercury, 16:308-9, July, 1927
Nation, 189:259-60, Oct. 24, 1959 and 122:164-5, Feb. 10,
  1926
New Republic, 45:329-30, Feb. 10, 1926
New Republic, 141:29, Oct. 19, 1959
New Statesman, 29:342-3, June 25, 1927
New Yorker, 35:131-3, Oct. 17, 1959
Newsweek, 54:80, Oct. 19, 1959
Theatre Arts, 43:88, Dec., 1959
Time, 74:56, Oct. 19, 1959

"The Hairy Ape", 1922

Baum, Bernard, ' "Tempest' and 'Hairy Ape' ", Modern
  Language Quarterly, 14:258-73, 1953
Cargill, Oscar; Fagin, Nathan, and Fisher, William J., eds.,
  O'Neill and His Plays; Four Decades of Criticism, New
  York Univ. Pr., 1961, p. 160-62
Cole, Toby, Playwrights on Playwriting; the Meaning and
  Making of Modern Drama from Ibsen to Ionesco, Hill and
  Wang, 1960, p. 235-37
Dusenbury, Winifred Loesch, The Theme of Loneliness in
  Modern American Drama, Univ. of Florida Press, 1960,
  p. 113-34

"France Choses 'The Hairy Ape'", Drama, 13:110, Dec., 1922
Gay, Robert Malcolm, ed., Fact, Fancy and Opinion;
  Examples of Present-day Writing, Little, 1923, p. 344-45
Gump, Margaret, "From Ape to Man and Man to Ape",
  Kentucky Foreign Language Quarterly, 4:177-85, 1957

Independent, 110:282-4, April 28, 1923
Literary Digest, 77:35, April 7, 1923
New Republic, 30:112-13, March 22, 1922
New Statesman and Nation, 1:461-2, May 23, 1931

"Hughie", 1958

Cargill, Oscar; Fagin, Nathan, and Fisher, William J., eds.,
  O'Neill and His Plays; Four Decades of Criticism, New York
  Univ. Pr., 1961, p. 224-26

Commonweal, 70:187-8, May 15, 1959
Commonweal, 81:518, Jan. 15, 1965
Nation, 200:65, Jan. 18, 1965
New Yorker, 40:58, Jan. 2, 1965
Newsweek, 65:52, Jan. 4, 1965
Saturday Review, 41:27, Oct. 4, 1958
Saturday Review, 48:40, Jan. 16, 1965
Theatre Arts, 43:14-15, Aug., 1959
Time, 85:53, Jan. 1, 1965

"The Iceman Cometh", 1946

Arested, Sverre, "'The Iceman Cometh' and 'The Wild
  Duck'", Scandinavian Studies, 20:1-11, 1948
Bentley, Eric Russell, In Search of Theatre, Knopf, 1953,
  p. 233-47
Brashear, William R., "The Wisdom of Silenus in O'Neill's
  'Iceman'", American Literature, 36:180-88, 1964
Brown, John Mason, Dramatis Personae; a Retrospective
  Show, Viking, 1963, p. 57-62
Brown, John Mason, Seeing More Things, McGraw, 1948,
  p. 257-65
Brustein, Robert Sanford, The Theatre of Revolt; an
  Approach to the Modern Drama, Little, 1964, p. 319-59
Cargill, Oscar; Fagin, Nathan and Fisher, William J., eds.,
  O'Neill and His Plays; Four Decades of Criticism, New York
  Univ. Press, 1961, p. 203-08, 212-13, 431-32, and 459-61
Chabrowe, Leonard, "Dionysus in 'The Iceman Cometh'",
  Modern Drama, 4:377-88, 1962

Day, Cyrus, "The Iceman and the Bridegroom", Modern
    Drama, 1:3-9, 1958
Dusenbury, Winifred Loesch, The Theme of Loneliness in
    Modern American Drama, Univ. of Florida Pr., 1960,
    p. 8-37
Gassner, John, ed., O'Neill; A Collection of Critical Essays,
    Prentice-Hall, 1964, p. 99-109
McCarthy, Mary Therese, Sights and Spectacles, 1937-1956,
    Farrar, Straus, 1956, p. 81-88
Myers, Henry Alonzo, Tragedy; A View of Life, Cornell
    Univ. Pr., 1956, p. 98-109
Nathan, George Jean, Theatre Book of the Year, 1946-47,
    Knopf, p. 93-111
Stamm, Rudolf, "A New Play by Eugene O'Neill", English
    Studies, 29:138-145, 1948
Theatre Arts Anthology; A Record and A Prophecy; ed. by
    Rosamond Gilder and others, Theatre Arts Books, 1950,
    p. 662-65
Tynan, Kenneth, Curtains; Selections from the Drama
    Criticism and Related Writings, Atheneum, 1961,
    p. 198-200
Young, Stark, Immortal Shadows; A Book of Dramatic
    Criticism, Scribner, 1948, p. 271-74

America, 95:251, June 2, 1956
Atlantic Monthly, 178:64-6, Nov., 1946
Catholic World, 164:168-9, Nov., 1946
Catholic World, 183:310, July, 1956
Commonweal, 45:44-6, Oct. 25, 1946
Commonweal, 64:515, Aug. 24, 1956
English (Oxford), 12:58, 1958
Illustrated London News, 232:276, Feb. 15, 1958
Life, 21:109-11, Oct. 28, 1946
Nation, 163:481, Oct. 26, 1946
Nation, 182:458, May 26, 1956
New Republic, 115:517-18, Oct. 21, 1946
New Yorker, 32:72, May 26, 1956
New Yorker, 22:53-7, Oct. 19, 1946
N.Y. Times Mag., p. 22-3, Oct. 13, 1946
Newsweek, 28:92, Oct. 21, 1946
Saturday Review, 39:24, May 26, 1956
Sewanee Review, 55:344-6, April, 1947
Sewanee Review, 56:118-26, Jan., 1948
Spectator, 200:174, Feb. 7, 1958

Theatre Arts, 30:635-6, Nov., 1946
Theatre Arts, 30:684, Dec., 1946
Theatre Arts, 31:31, Dec., 1947
Theatre Arts, 40:72-3, Oct., 1956
Time, 48:71-2, Oct. 21, 1946

"Ile", 1916

Cargill, Oscar; Fagin, Nathan and Fisher, William J., eds.,
O'Neill and His Plays; Four Decades of Criticism, New
York Univ. Pr., 1961, p. 132-33

"In the Zone", 1917

Goldhurst, William, "A Literary Source for O'Neill's 'In the
Zone'", American Literature, 35:530-34, 1964
Nathan, George Jean, Theatre Book of the Year, 1948-1949,
Knopf, p. 32-35

"Lazarus Laughed", 1926

Alexander, Doris M., "'Lazarus Laughed' and Buddha",
Modern Language Quarterly, 17:357-365, 1956
Cargill, Oscar; Fagin, Nathan and Fisher, William J., eds.,
O'Neill and His Plays; Four Decades of Criticism, New
York Univ. Pr., 1961, p. 178-80
Dahlstrom, Carl E. W. L., "'Dynamo' and 'Lazarus
Laughed'; Some Limitations", Modern Drama, 3:224-30,
1960
Day, Cyrus, "'Amor Fati'; O'Neil's Lazarus as Superman
and Savior", Modern Drama, 3:297-305, 1960
Gassner, John, ed., O'Neill; A Collection of Critical
Essays, Prentice-Hall, 1964, p. 72-81

Arts and Decoration, 27:68-9, Sept., 1927
Catholic World, 167:264, June, 1948
Commonweal, 48:674, April 30, 1948
Drama, 18:244-6, May, 1928
Review of Reviews, 78:439-40, Oct., 1928
Theatre Arts, 12:447-8, June, 1928

"Long Day's Journey Into Night", 1956

Brustein, Robert Sanford, The Theatre of Revolt; An
Approach to the Modern Drama, Little, 1964, p. 319-59
Cargill, Oscar; Fagin, Nathan and Fisher, William J., eds.,
O'Neill and His Plays; Four Decades of Criticism, New

York Univ. Pr., 1961, p. 214-20

Cerf, Walter, "Psycho-analysis and the Realistic Drama",
  Journal of Aesthetics and Art Criticism, 16:328-36, 1958

Engel, Edwin A., "Eugene O'Neill's 'Long Day's Journey
  Into Night'", Michigan Alumnus Quarterly Review,
  63:348-54, 1957

Finkelstein, Sidney, "O'Neill's 'Long Day's Journey'",
  Mainstream, 16:47-51, 1963

Lokhorst, Emmy van, "Toneelkroniek; Een Nocturne",
  DeGids, 120:276-79, 1957

"O'Neill's drama of the Psyche", Catholic World, 193:120-25,
  1963

Oppenheimer, George, ed., Passionate Playgoer, A
  Personal Scrapbook, Viking, 1958, p. 281-88

Raleigh, John Henry, "O'Neill's 'Long Day's Journey Into
  Night' and New England Irish-Catholicism", Partisan Review,
  26:573-92, 1959

Redford, Grant H., "Dramatic Art vs. Autobiography; A Look
  at "Long Day's Journey Into Night'", College English,
  25:527-35, 1964

Roig, Rosendo, "Despues de 'Viaje de un Largo Dia Hacia la
  Noche' de O'Neill", Razon y fe (Madrid), 158:367-370, 1958

Shawcross, John T., "The road to ruin; the beginning of
  O'Neill's 'Long days journey'", Modern Drama, 3:289-96,
  1960

Tynan, Kenneth, Curtains; selections from the drama
  criticism and related writings, Atheneum, 1961, p. 223-25

Winther, Sophus Kerth, "O'Neill's tragic themes; 'Long
  Day's Journey Into Night'", Arizona Quarterly, 13:295-307,
  1957

America, 95:141, May 5, 1956

Catholic World, 184:306, Jan., 1957

Christian Century, 74:235, Feb. 20, 1957

Commonweal, 63:614-15, March 16, 1956

Commonweal, 64:515, Aug. 24, 1956

Commonweal, 65:467-8, Feb. 1, 1957

English (Oxford), 12:140, 1959

Harper, 212:96, March, 1956

Life, 40:93-4, March 12, 1956

Life, 41:123-4, Nov. 19, 1956

Mademoiselle, 44:186, Feb., 1957

N. Y. Times Mag., p. 56, Feb. 19, 1956

N. Y. Times Mag., p. 74, Oct. 21, 1956

Nation, 183:466, Nov. 24, 1956

New Republic, 134:20, March 5, 1956
New Yorker, 32:120, Nov. 24, 1956
Newsweek, 47:92, Feb. 20, 1956
Newsweek, 48:117, Nov. 19, 1956
Reporter, 15:38-9, Dec. 13, 1956
Saturday Review, 39:15-16, Feb. 25, 1956
Saturday Review, 39:58, Oct. 20, 1956
Saturday Review, 39:30-1, Nov. 24, 1956
Spectator, 201:369, Sept. 19, 1958
Theatre Arts, 40:25, April, 1956
Theatre Arts, 40:65, May, 1956
Theatre Arts, 41:25-6, Jan., 1957
Time, 67:89, Feb. 20, 1956
Time, 68:57, Nov. 19, 1956
Vogue, 128:105, Nov. 15, 1956

"Long Voyage Home", 1919

"Local censors in Shanghai ban O'Neill's 'Long Voyage Home' ",
China Weekly Review, 97:264, Aug. 2, 1941
Nathan, George Jean, Theatre Book of the Year, 1948-1949,
Knopf, p. 32-35

"Marco Millions", 1928

Cargill, Oscar; Fagin, Nathan and Fisher, William J., eds.,
O'Neill and his plays; four decades of criticism, New York
Univ. Pr., 1961, p. 181-83

America, 110:656, May 9, 1964
American Mercury, 8:499-505, Aug., 1926
Commonweal, 80:89, April 10, 1964
Great Britain and the East, 52:43, Jan. 12, 1939
Literary Digest, 96:26-7, Feb. 4, 1928
Nation, 124:562-4, May 18, 1927 and 126:104-5, Jan. 25,
1928
Nation, 198:249-50, March 9, 1964
New Republic, 53:272-3, Jan. 25, 1928
New Statesman and Nation, 16:1124, Dec. 31, 1938
New Yorker, 40:106, Feb. 29, 1964
Newsweek, 63:56, March 2, 1964
Saturday Review of Literature, 4:590, Feb. 11, 1928
Saturday Review, 47:23, March 7, 1964
Theatre Arts, 23:175, March, 1939
Time, 83:61, Feb. 28, 1964
Vogue, 143:40, April 1, 1964

"A Moon for the Misbegotten", 1947

    Bentley, Eric Russell, Dramatic event; an American
    Chronicle, Horizon 1954, p. 30-33
    Cargill, Oscar; Fagin, Nathan and Fisher, William J., eds.,
    O'Neill and his plays; four decades of criticism, New York
    Univ. Pr., 1961, p. 209-11
    McCarthy, Mary Therese, Sights and spectacles, 1937-1956,
    Farrar, Straus, 1956, p. 81-88

    America, 97:270, May 25, 1957
    Catholic World, 185:308-9, July, 1957
    Christian Century, 74:657, May 22, 1957
    Commonweal, 66:541, Aug. 30, 1957
    Illustrated London News, 236:226, Feb. 6, 1960
    Life, 42:109-10, June 24, 1957
    Nation, 178:409, May 8, 1954
    Nation, 184:446, May 18, 1957
    New Statesman, 59:149, Jan. 30, 1960
    New Yorker, 33:84, May 11, 1957
    Newsweek, 49:70, May 13, 1957
    Saturday Review, 40:34, May 18, 1957
    Spectator, 204:137, Jan. 29, 1960
    Theatre Arts, 36:6-7, Sept., 1952
    Theatre Arts, 41:67-8, May, 1957
    Theatre Arts, 41:12-13, July, 1957
    Time, 49:47, March 3, 1947
    Time, 60:80, Aug. 4, 1952
    Time, 69:91, May 13, 1957

"The Moon of the Caribbees", 1918

    Cargill, Oscar; Fagin, Nathan and Fisher, William J., eds.,
    O'Neill and his plays; four decades of criticism, New York
    Univ. Pr., 1961, p. 230-33
    Nathan, George Jean, Theatre Book of the Year, 1948-1949,
    Knopf, p. 32-35
    Times, London; Literary Supplement, American writing
    today; its independence and vigor, ed. by Allan Angoff,
    New York Univ. Pr., 1957, p. 341-48

"More Stately Mansions", 1962

    Saturday Review, 45:26, Dec. 1, 1962
    Saturday Review, 47:46, May 30, 1964
    Spectator, 209:760, Nov. 16, 1962
    Spectator, 209:815-16, Nov. 23, 1962

"Mourning Becomes Electra", 1931

> Alexander, D.M., "Captain Brant and Captain Brassbound; the origin of an O'Neill character", Modern Language Notes, 74:306-10, 1959
>
> Alexander, D.M., "Psychological fate in 'Mourning becomes Electra' ", Modern Language Assn., Publications, 68:923-34, Dec., 1953
>
> Asselineau, Roger, " 'Mourning becomes Electra' as a tragedy", Modern Drama, 1:143-50, 1958
>
> Brown, John Mason, Dramatis personae; a retrospective show, Viking, 1963, p. 53-57
>
> Brown, John Mason, Two on the Aisle; Ten Years of the American Theatre in Performance, Norton, 1938, p. 136-42
>
> Cargill, Oscar; Fagin, Nathan and Fisher, William J., eds., O'Neill and his plays; four decades of criticism, New York Univ., Pr., 1961, p. 190-93
>
> Dusenbury, Winifred Loesch, The Theme of Loneliness in Modern American Drama, Univ. Florida, Pr., 1960, p. 57-85
>
> Gassner, John, ed., O'Neill; a collection of critical essays, Prentice-Hall, 1964, p. 82-88
>
> Hanzeli, Victor E., "The progeny of Atreus", Modern Drama, 3:75-81, 1960
>
> Moses, Montrose Jonas and Brown, John Mason, American Theatre as seen by its critics, 1752-1934, Norton, 1934, p. 262-65
>
> Nagarajan, S., "Eugene O'Neill's 'Mourning becomes Electra': the classical aspect", Literary Criterion (Univ. Mysore, India) 5:#3, 148-54, 1962
>
> Oppenheimer, George, ed., Passionate playgoer, a personal scrapbook, Viking, 1958, p. 580-84
>
> Theatre Arts Anthology; a record and a prophecy, ed., by Rosamond Gilder and others, Theatre Arts Books, 1950, p. 619-22
>
> Valente, Pier Luigi, "Il lutto s'addice ad Eletrra di E. G. O'Neill e la tragedia greca", Convivium 28:318-29, 1960
>
> Weissman, Philip, " 'Mourning becomes Electra' and 'The prodigal': Electra and Orestes", Modern Drama, 3:257-59, 1960
>
> Woollcott, Alexander, Portable Woollcott, Viking, 1946, p. 326-30
>
> Young, Stark, Immortal shadows; a book of dramatic criticism, Scribner, 1948, p. 132-39

Zabel, Morton Dauwen, ed., Literary opinion in America;
essays illustrating the status, methods and problems of
criticism in the United States since the war, Harper, 1937,
p. 278-87

Zabel, Morton Dauwen, ed., Literary opinion in America,
3rd edition, Harper, 1962, p. 522-29

Arts & Decoration, 36:52, Jan., 1932
Bookman, 74:440-5, Dec., 1931
Bookman, 75:290-1, June, 1932
Catholic World, 134:330-1, Dec., 1931
Commonweal, 15:46-7, Nov. 11, 1931 and 15:386, Feb. 3,
1932
Literary Digest, 111:18-19, Nov. 21, 1931
London Mercury, 37:330, Jan., 1938
Nation, 133:551-2, Nov. 18, 1931
Nation, 134:210-11, Feb. 17, 1932
New Republic, 68:352-5, Nov. 11, 1931
New Statesman and Nation, 14:875-7, Nov. 27, 1937
Outlook, 159:343, Nov. 11, 1931
Saturday Review of Literature, 8:257-8, Nov. 7, 1931
Theatre Arts, 16:13-16, Jan., 1932
Theatre Arts, 22:101-7, Feb., 1938

"S. S. Glencairn", 1948

Nathan, George Jean, Theatre Book of the Year, 1948-1949,
Knopf, p. 32-35

Rust, R. D., "Unity of O'Neill's 'S. S. Glencairn' ",
American Literature, 37:280-90, Nov., 1965

Commonweal, 48:185, June 4, 1948
New Republic, 118:27-9, June 7, 1948
New Yorker, 24:43, May 29, 1948
School and Society, 67:478, June 26, 1948

"Strange Interlude", 1927

Aiken, Conrad Potter, Reviewer's ABC; collected criticism
of Conrad Aiken, from 1916 to the present, Meridian Books,
1958, p. 315-18

Alexander, D. M., "Strange interlude' and Schopenhauer",
American Literature, 25:213-28, May, 1953

Cargill, Oscar; Fagin, Nathan and Fisher, William J., eds.,
O'Neill and his plays; four decades of criticism, New York
Univ. Pr., 1961, p. 184-86

Downer, Alan S. , ed. , <u>American drama and its critics,</u>
Univ. Chicago Pr. , 1965, p. 100-101

Dusenbury, Winifred Loesch, <u>The Theme of Loneliness in</u>
<u>Modern American Drama,</u> Univ. of Florida Pr. , 1960,
p. 86-112

Luten, C. J. , "'Strange Interlude' ", <u>American Record</u>
<u>Guide</u>, 30:578-80, March, 1964

Malone, K. , "Diction of 'Strange interlude' ", <u>American</u>
<u>Speech</u>, 6:19-28, Oct. , 1930

Phillips, A. E. , " 'Strange interlude' and the blah
brotherhood", <u>Drama</u>, 19:171, March, 1929

<u>America</u>, 108:594, April 20, 1963
<u>American Mercury</u>, 11:499-506, Aug. , 1927
<u>Arts & Decoration</u>, 28:65, April, 1928
<u>Catholic World</u>, 127:77-80, April, 1928
<u>Commonweal</u>, 78:72-3, April 12, 1963
<u>Dial</u>, 84:348-41, April, 1928
<u>Journal des Debats</u>, 35 pt. 2:572-4, Oct. 5, 1928
<u>Literary Digest</u>, 96:26-7, Feb. 25, 1928
<u>Nation</u>, 126:192, Feb. 15, 1928
<u>Nation</u>, 196:274-5, March 30, 1963
<u>New Republic</u>, 53:349-50, Feb. 15, 1928
<u>New Republic</u>, 148:28-9, March 30, 1963
<u>New Yorker</u>, 39:73, March 23, 1963
<u>Newsweek</u>, 61:97, March 25, 1963
<u>Outlook</u>, 148:304-5, Feb. 22, 1928
<u>Overland</u> ns. , 87:220, July, 1929
<u>Preussische Jahrbucher</u>, 218:405, Dec. , 1929
<u>Saturday Review of Literature</u>, 4:590, Feb. 11, 1928
<u>Saturday Review of Literature</u>, 4:641, March 3, 1928
<u>Saturday Review</u>, 46:36, March 30, 1963
<u>Theatre Arts</u>, 12:237-40, April, 1928
<u>Theatre Arts</u>, 15:286-9, April, 1931
<u>Theatre Arts</u>, 47:12-13, May, 1963
<u>Time</u>, 81:74, March 22, 1963
<u>Westermanns Monatshefte</u>, 147:523-4, Jan. , 1930

"The Straw", n. d.

Cargill, Oscar; Fagin, Nathan and Fisher, William J. , eds. ,
<u>O'Neill and his plays; four decades of criticism</u>, New York
Univ. Pr. , 1961, p. 155-56

<u>Drama</u>, 12:152, Feb. , 1922

"Thirst", n. d.
>Cargill, Oscar; Fagin, Nathan and Fisher, William, eds.,
>O'Neill and his plays; four decades of criticism, New York
>Univ. Pr., 1961, p. 229

"A Touch of the Poet", 1958
>Cargill, Oscar; Fagin, Nathan and Fisher, William J., eds.,
>O'Neill and his plays; four decades of criticism, New York
>Univ. Pr., 1961, p. 221-23
>Marcus, M., "Eugene O'Neill's debt to Thoreau in 'A touch
>of the poet' ", Journal of English and German Philology,
>62:270-9, April, 1963
>Tynan, Kenneth, Curtains; Selections from the drama
>criticism and related writings, Atheneum, 1961, p. 445-46

>America, 100:118, Oct. 25, 1958
>Catholic World, 188:243-4, Dec., 1958
>Christian Century, 75:252-4, Feb. 26, 1958
>Christian Century, 75:1401-2, Dec. 3, 1958
>Commonweal, 69:151-3, Nov. 7, 1958
>Life, 42:116, June 24, 1957
>Nation, 187:298-9, Oct. 25, 1958
>N. Y. Times Mag., p. 49, April 28, 1957
>New Republic, 136:21, June 3, 1957
>New Republic, 139:23, Oct. 20, 1958
>New Statesman, 66:420, Sept. 27, 1963
>New Yorker, 34:87, Oct. 11, 1958
>Newsweek, 49:66, April 8, 1957
>Newsweek, 52:112, Oct. 13, 1958
>Reporter, 19:37-8, Nov. 13, 1958
>Saturday Review, 40:24, April 13, 1957
>Saturday Review, 41:56, Oct. 18, 1958
>Saturday Review, 40:21, Sept. 21, 1957
>Theatre Arts, 42:9-10, Dec., 1958
>Theatre Arts, 42:16-17, Oct., 1958
>Time, 70:102, Sept. 30, 1957
>Time, 69:77, April 8, 1957
>Time, 72:89, Oct. 13, 1958
>Vogue, 132:105, Nov. 15, 1958

"Welded", 1924
>Cargill, Oscar; Fagin, Nathan and Fisher, William, eds.,
>O'Neill and his plays; four decades of criticism, New York
>Univ. Pr., 1961, p. 163-65

Downer, Alan S., ed., American drama and its critics,
Univ. Chicago Pr., 1965, p. 81-83

Nation, 118:376-7, April 2, 1924

"Where the Cross is Made", 1918

Pira, Gisela, "Eugene O'Neill, 'Where the cross is made';
versuch einer interpretation", Die Neueren Sprachen,
p. 179-82, 1960

BYRON ONGLEY

SEE

WINCHELL SMITH AND BYRON ONGLEY

PAUL OSBORN

"Bell for Adano", 1944

Brown, John Mason, Seeing things, McGraw, 1946, p. 282-86
Nathan, George Jean, Theatre Book of the Year, 1944-1945,
Knopf, p. 179-87

"Innocent Voyage", 1943

Nathan, George Jean, Theatre Book of the Year, 1943-1944,
Knopf, p. 128-30

"Morning's at Seven", 1939

Catholic World, 181:64, Oct., 1955
Commonweal, 62:469, Aug. 12, 1955
Theatre Arts, 39:80, Oct., 1955

"On Borrowed Time", (dramatization of novel by L. E. Watkins),
1938

Commonweal, 57:552, March 6, 1953
Nation, 176:192, Feb. 28, 1953
New Yorker, 29:61, Feb. 21, 1953
Newsweek, 41:62, Feb. 23, 1953
Saturday Review, 36:37, Feb. 28, 1953
Time, 61:86, Feb. 23, 1953

"Point of No Return", (dramatization of novel by J. P. Marquand),
1950

    Brown, John Mason, As they appear, McGraw, 1952,
       p. 213-17
    Gassner, John, Theatre at the crossroads; plays and play-
       wrights of the mid-century American stage, Holt, 1960,
       p. 146-49
    Nathan, George Jean, Theatre in the Fifties, Knopf, 1953,
       p. 52-55

    Catholic World, 174:391, Feb., 1952
    Commonweal, 55:325, Jan. 4, 1952
    Life, 32:59-60, Jan. 7, 1952
    Nation, 173:574, Dec. 29, 1951
    New Republic, 126:22-3, Jan. 7, 1952
    New Yorker, 27:47, Dec. 22, 1951
    Newsweek, 38:43, Dec. 24, 1951
    Saturday Review, 35:24-5, Jan. 5, 1952
    Saturday Review, 35:22, Jan. 26, 1952
    Theatre Arts, 36:73, Feb., 1952
    Theatre Arts, 37:31-3, March, 1953
    Time, 58:44, Dec. 24, 1951

"The World of Suzie Wong" (dramatization of novel by R. Mason),
1958

    Catholic World, 188:246, Dec., 1958
    Commonweal, 69:292, Dec. 12, 1958
    Illustrated London News, 235:818, Dec. 5, 1959
    Nation, 188:76, Jan. 24, 1959
    New Republic, 139:22, Oct. 27, 1958
    New Yorker, 34:88, Oct. 25, 1958
    Newsweek, 52:64, Oct. 27, 1958
    Reporter, 19:37-8, Nov. 13, 1958
    Saturday Review, 41:28, Nov. 1, 1958
    Theatre Arts, 42:10-11, Dec., 1958
    Time, 72:84, Oct. 27, 1958
    Vogue, 132:28, Nov. 15, 1958
    Spectator, 203:829, Dec. 4, 1959

LAWRENCE OSGOOD

"Pigeons", 1965

    New Yorker, 41:108, March 13, 1965

MARCO PAGE, PSEUD.
SEE
HARRY KURNITZ

JOHN PATRICK

"Curious Savage", 1950

Catholic World, 172:227, Dec., 1950
Christian Science Monitor Mag., p. 8, Oct. 28, 1950
Commonweal, 53:121, Nov. 10, 1950
Nation, 171:418, Nov. 4, 1950
New Republic, 123:21, Nov. 13, 1950
New Yorker, 26:76, Nov. 4, 1950
Newsweek, 36:88, Nov. 6, 1950
Theatre Arts, 34:17, Dec., 1950
Time, 56:57, Nov. 6, 1950

"Everybody Loves Opal", 1961

America, 106:132, Oct. 28, 1961
New Yorker, 37:131, Oct. 21, 1961
Theatre Arts, 45:70, Dec., 1961
Time, 78:64, Oct. 20, 1961

"Good as Gold" (dramatization of novel by A. Toombs), 1957

Nation, 184:262, March 23, 1957
New Yorker, 33:79, March 16, 1957
Saturday Review, 40:7-8, April 6, 1957
Saturday Review, 40:24, March 23, 1957
Theatre Arts, 41:19, May, 1957

"Hasty Heart", 1945

Catholic World, 160:452-3, Feb., 1945
Commonweal, 41:396, Feb. 2, 1945
Life, 18:103-4, Feb. 5, 1945
Nation, 160:81, Jan. 20, 1945
New Republic, 112:118, Jan. 22, 1945
New Yorker, 20:38, Jan. 13, 1945
Newsweek, 25:78, Jan. 15, 1945
Saturday Review, 28:26-7, March 3, 1945
Theatre Arts, 29:138, March, 1945
Time, 45:55, Jan. 15, 1945

"Lo and Behold! ", 1951

>   Catholic World, 174:392-3, Feb. , 1952
>   Commonweal, 55:300, Dec. 28, 1951
>   Nation, 173:574, Dec. 29, 1951
>   New Republic, 126:22, Jan. 7, 1952
>   New Yorker, 27:48-9, Dec. 22, 1951
>   Newsweek, 38:43, Dec. 24, 1951
>   Theatre Arts, 36:73, Feb. , 1952
>   Time, 58:44, Dec. 24, 1951

"Story of Mary Surratt", 1947

>   Catholic World, 164:551, March, 1947
>   Commonweal, 45:491, Feb. 28, 1947
>   Nation, 164:226-7, Feb. 22, 1947
>   New Republic, 116:40, Feb. 24, 1947
>   New Yorker, 22:50-1, Feb. 15, 1947
>   Newsweek, 29:88, Feb. 17, 1947
>   Theatre Arts, 31:20, April, 1947
>   Time, 49:53, Feb. 17, 1947

"Teahouse of the August Moon" (dramatization of novel by
V. Sneider), 1953

>   Bentley, Eric Russell, Dramatic event; an American
>   chronicle, Horizon Press, 1954, p. 222-25
>
>   America, 90:186, Nov. 14, 1953
>   Catholic World, 178:228-9, Dec. , 1953
>   Catholic World, 184:306, Jan. , 1957
>   Commonweal, 59:163, Nov. 20, 1953
>   Illustrated London News, 224:762, May 8, 1954
>   Life, 35:129-30, Nov. 2, 1953
>   Life, 36:101-2, June 14, 1954
>   Nation, 177:357-8, Oct. 31, 1953
>   Nation, 178:429-30, May 15, 1954
>   New Republic, 129:21, Oct. 26, 1953
>   New Republic, 130:28, May 17, 1954
>   New Statesman, 47:560, May 1, 1954
>   New Yorker, 29:66, Oct. 24, 1953
>   Newsweek, 42:60, Dec. 21, 1953
>   Newsweek, 42:92, Oct. 26, 1953
>   Saturday Review, 36:29, Oct. 31, 1953
>   Saturday Review, 36:45, Dec. 12, 1953

Spectator, 192:512, April 30, 1954
Theatre Arts, 37:22-4, Dec., 1953
Theatre Arts, 39:32-3, June, 1955
Theatre Arts, 41:31-2, Jan., 1957
Time, 62:72, Oct. 26, 1953

JAMES KIRKE PAULDING

"The Bucktails", 1847

Watkins, F.C., "James Kirke Paulding's early ring-tailed
roarer", Southern Folklore Quarterly, 15:183-7,
Sept., 1951

"The Lion of the West", n.d.

Adkins, N.F., "James K. Paulding's 'Lion of the west'",
American Literature, 3:249-58, Nov., 1931
Hodge, Francis, "Biography of a lost play, 'Lion of the
west'", Theatre Annual, 12:48-61, 1954

COLE PORTER

SEE

MOSS HART AND COLE PORTER

CLEMENCE RANDOLPH

SEE

JOHN COLTON AND CLEMENCE RANDOLPH

MICHAEL REDGRAVE

"Aspern Papers" (dramatization of novel by Henry James), 1959

Commonweal, 75:597, March 2, 1962
Educational Theatre Journal, 14:174, May, 1962
English, 13:20-1, Spring, 1960
Illustrated London News, 235:150, Aug. 29, 1959

Nation, 194:200, March 3, 1962
New Republic, 146:21, Feb. 19, 1962
New Yorker, 35:153-4, Sept. 12, 1959
Newsweek, 59:88, Feb. 19, 1962
Saturday Review, 45:36, Feb. 24, 1962
Spectator, 203:223-4, Aug. 21, 1959
Spectator, 203:907, Dec. 18, 1959
Theatre Arts, 46:58, April, 1962
Time, 79:60, Feb. 16, 1962

MARK WHITE REED

"Petticoat Fever", 1935

Catholic World, 141:90, April, 1935
Commonweal, 21:600, March 22, 1935
Literary Digest, 119:16, March 16, 1935
Newsweek, 5:29, March 16, 1935
Theatre Arts, 19:325, May, 1935

"Yes, My Darling Daughter", 1937

Block, Anita Cahn, Changing world in plays and theatre,
Little, 1939, p. 76-132
O'Hara, Frank Hurburt, Today in American drama, Univ. of
Chicago Press, 1939, p. 190-234

Catholic World, 144:730-1, March 1937
New Republic, 90:139, March 10, 1937
Theatre Arts, 21:262, April, 1937
Time, 29:46, Feb. 22, 1937

ELMER L. RICE

"Adding Machine", 1923

Bidou, H., "'La machine a calculer'; adaptee par L. Jean-
Proix", Journal des Debats 34 pt. 2:899-901, Nov. 25,
1927
Block, Anita Cahn, Changing world in plays and theatre,
Little, 1939, p. 194-250
Hogan, Robert, The independence of Elmer Rice, Sou. Ill.
Univ. Pr., 1965, p. 30-36

Moses, Montrose Jonas and Brown, John Mason, eds.,
American theatre as seen by its critics, 1752-1934, Norton,
p. 196-98

English Review, 46:236-8, Feb., 1928
The Freeman, 7:184-5, 231-2, 1923
The Independent, 110:270-2, April 14, 1923
Nation, 116:399, April 4, 1923
New Republic, 34:164-5, April 4, 1923
New Statesman and Nation, 22:699-700, March 22, 1924
New Statesman, 30:462-3, Jan. 21, 1928
Outlook (Lond), 53:203, March 22, 1924
Outlook (Lond), 61:84, Jan. 21, 1928
Saturday Review, 145:36-7, Jan. 14, 1928
Spectator, 140:42, Jan. 14, 1928

"American Landscape", 1938

Hogan, Robert, The independence of Elmer Rice, Sou. Ill.
Univ. Pr., 1965, p. 93-95

Catholic World, 148:472-3, Jan., 1939
Commonweal, 29:273, Dec. 30, 1928
Nation, 147:700, Dec. 24, 1938
New Republic, 97:230, Dec. 28, 1938
North American Review, 247 no. 1:155, March, 1939
Theatre Arts, 23:86-9, Feb., 1939
Time, 32:31, Dec. 12, 1938

"Between Two Worlds", 1934

Hogan, Robert, The independence of Elmer Rice, Sou. Ill.
Univ. Pr., 1965, p. 74-76

Catholic World, 140:342-3, Dec., 1934
Nation, 139:574, Nov. 14, 1934
Theatre Arts, 18:900-2, Dec., 1934

"Black Sheep", 1932

Theatre Arts, 16:961-2, Dec., 1932

"Counsellor-at-law", 1931

Nathan, George Jean, Theatre Book of the Year, 1942-1943,
Knopf, p. 145-47

Hogan, Robert, The independence of Elmer Rice, Sou. Ill.
    Univ. Pr., 1965, p. 60-63

Arts & Decoration, 36:68, Jan., 1932
Catholic World, 134:470-1, Jan., 1932
Catholic World, 156:601, Feb., 1943
Commonweal, 15:102, Nov. 25, 1931
Commonweal, 37:206, Dec. 11, 1942
Current History, 3:457, Jan., 1943
Independent Woman, 22:155, May, 1943
Nation, 133:621-2, Dec. 2, 1931
New Republic, 69:69, Dec. 2, 1931
Outlook, 159:407, Nov. 25, 1931
Spectator (Lond), 152:618, April 20, 1934
Theatre Arts, 16:21-2, Jan., 1932
Theatre Arts, 27:16, Jan., 1943

"Cue for Passion", 1958

Hogan, Robert, The Independence of Elmer Rice, Sou. Ill.
    Univ. Pr., 1965, p. 118-21

Catholic World, 188:418, Feb., 1959
New Yorker, 34:116-17, Dec. 6, 1958
Newsweek, 52:66, Dec. 8, 1958
Theatre Arts, 43:21-2, Feb., 1959
Time, 72:77, Dec. 8, 1958

"Dream Girl", 1945

Nathan, George Jean, Theatre Book of the Year, 1942-1943,
    Knopf, p. 225-33
Hogan, Robert, The Independence of Elmer Rice, Sou. Ill.
    Univ. Pr., 1965, p. 106-10

Catholic World, 162:454-5, Feb., 1946
Catholic World, 173:306, July, 1951
Commonweal, 43:456-7, Feb. 15, 1946
Commonweal, 54:165, May 25, 1951
Forum, 105:564, Feb., 1946
Life, 19:36-8, Dec. 31, 1945
Nation, 162:54, Jan. 12, 1946
New Republic, 113:903, Dec. 31, 1945
New Republic, 124:23, May 28, 1951
New Yorker, 21:36, Dec. 22, 1945

Newsweek, 26:88, Dec. 24, 1945
Theatre Arts, 30:72-9, Feb., 1946
Time, 46:77-8, Dec. 24, 1945

"Flight to the West", 1940

Hogan, Robert, The Independence of Elmer Rice, Sou. Ill.
Univ. Pr., 1965, p. 100-04

Catholic World, 152:595-6, Feb., 1941
Commonweal, 33:328, Jan. 17, 1941
Nation, 152:53, Jan. 11, 1941
New Republic, 104:84, Jan. 20, 1941
New Yorker, 16:33, Jan. 11, 1941
Newsweek, 17:52, Jan. 13, 1941
Theatre Arts, 25:112, Feb., 1941
Theatre Arts, 25:112, Feb., 1941
Time, 37:57, Jan. 13, 1941

"Grand Tour", 1951

Nathan, George Jean, Theatre in the Fifties, Knopf, 1953,
p. 42-44
Hogan, Robert, The Independence of Elmer Rice, Sou. Ill.
Univ. Pr., 1965, p. 111-15

Commonweal, 55:299, Dec. 28, 1951
New Yorker, 27:49, Dec. 22, 1951
Newsweek, 38:43, Dec. 24, 1951
Theatre Arts, 36:73, Feb., 1952

"Judgment Day", 1934

Hogan, Robert, The independence of Elmer Rice, Sou. Ill.
Univ. Pr., 1965, p. 70-74

Catholic World, 140:89-90, Oct., 1934
Commonweal, 20:509, Sept. 28, 1934
Golden Book, 20:506, Nov., 1934
Literary Digest, 118:20, Sept. 29, 1934
London Mercury, 36:277, Jan., 1937
Nation, 139:392, Oct. 3, 1934
Newsweek, 4:28, Sept. 22, 1934
Spectator (Lond), 158:987-8, May 28, 1937
Theatre Arts, 18:814-15, Nov., 1934

"Left Bank", 1931

>   Arts and Decoration, 36:68, Dec., 1931
>   Catholic World, 134:210, Nov., 1931
>   Nation, 133:440-1, Oct. 21, 1931
>   New Republic, 68:264, Oct. 21, 1931
>   Outlook, 159:248, Oct. 21, 1931
>   Theatre Arts, 15:983-4, Dec., 1931

"Love Among the Ruins", 1963

>   Hogan, Robert, The independence of Elmer Rice, Sou. Ill.
>   Univ. Pr., 1965, p. 122-37

"New Life", 1943

>   Nathan, George Jean, Theatre Book of the Year, 1943-1944,
>   Knopf, p. 63-66

>   Catholic World, 158:187, Nov., 1943
>   Commonweal, 38:585, Oct. 1, 1943
>   New Republic, 109:426, Sept. 27, 1943
>   Newsweek, 22:90, Sept. 27, 1943
>   Theatre Arts, 27:640-4, Nov., 1943

"Not for Children", 1951

>   Nathan, George Jean, Theatre Book of the Year, 1950-1951,
>   Knopf, p. 222-24
>   Hogan, Robert, The independence of Elmer Rice, Sou. Ill.
>   Univ. Pr., 1965, p. 81-86

>   Commonweal, 53:541, March 9, 1951
>   New Yorker, 27:66, Feb. 24, 1951
>   Newsweek, 37:49, Feb. 26, 1951
>   Spectator (Lond), 155:900, Nov. 29, 1935
>   Theatre Arts, 35:19, April, 1951
>   Time, 57:50, Feb. 26, 1951

"On Trial", 1914

>   Hogan, Robert, The independence of Elmer Rice, Sou. Ill.
>   Univ. Pr., 1965, p. 17-21

>   American Heritage, 16:46-9, April 1965

"See Naples and Die", 1929

> Nation, 129:409, Oct. 16, 1929
> New Republic, 60:243-4, Oct. 16, 1929
> Spectator (Lond), 148:476, April 2, 1932

"Sidewalks of New York", n. d.

> Hogan, Robert, The independence of Elmer Rice, Sou. Ill. Univ. Pr., 1965, p. 44-45

"Street Scene", 1929

> Dusenbury, Winifred Loesch, The theme of loneliness in modern American drama, Univ. of Florida Press, 1960, p. 113-34
> Hogan, Robert, The independence of Elmer Rice, Sou. Ill. Univ. Pr., 1965, p. 46-54
> Moses, Montrose Jonas and Brown, John Mason, eds., American Theatre as seen by its critics, 1752-1934, Norton, 1934, p. 281-83
> Nathan, George Jean, Theatre Book of the Year, 1943-1944, Knopf, p. 275-78
> Oppenheimer, George, ed., Passionate playgoer, a personal scrapbook, Viking, 1958, p. 564-67

> "Organized Charity Turns Censor", Nation, 132:628-30, June 10, 1031

> Rice, Elmer, L., Living Theatre, Harper, 1959, p. 208-23.
> Young, Start, Immortal Shadows; a Book of Dramatic Criticism, Scribner, 1948, p. 106-09
> Zabel, Morton Dauwen, ed., Literary Opinion in America; Essays Illustrating the Status, Methods and Problems of Criticism in the United States since the War, Harper, 1937, p. 287-91
> Zabel, Morton Dauwen, ed., Literary Opinion in America; Essays Illustrating the Status, Methods and Problems of Criticism in the United States in the 20th Century, 3rd ed., Harper, 1962, p. 529-32, vol. 2.

> Catholic World, 128: 720-2, March, 1929
> Commonweal, 9:348-9, Jan. 23, 1929
> Drama, 19:170, March, 1929
> London Mercury, 23:176, December, 1930

Nation, 128:142, Jan. 30, 1929
New Republic, 57:296-8, Jan. 30, 1929
New Statesman, 35:733, Sept. 20, 1930
Outlook, 151:140, Jan. 23, 1929
Preussische Jahrbucher, 219:322-3, March, 1930
Saturday Review, 150:339, Sept. 20, 1930
Saturday Review of Literature, 30:24-6, Feb. 1, 1947
Spectator (Lond), 145:407, Sept. 27, 1930
Theatre Arts, 13:164-6; March, 1929
Theatre Arts, 14:164-6, February, 1930
Theatre Arts, 43:59-64, November, 1959

"The Subway", 1929

Hogan, Robert, The independence of Elmer Rice, Sou. Ill.
Univ. Pr., 1965, p. 36-41

"Two on an Island", 1940

Hogan, Robert, The independence of Elmer Rice, Sou. Ill.
Univ. Pr., 1965, p. 95-100

Catholic World, 150:729-30, March, 1940
Commonweal, 31:348, Feb. 9, 1940
Life, 8:42-4, Feb. 19, 1940
Nation, 150-136, Feb. 3, 1940
Newsweek, 15:34, Feb. 5, 1940
Theatre Arts, 24:167-8, March, 1940
Time, 35:41, Feb. 5, 1940

"We, the People", 1933

Brown, John Mason, Two on the aisle; ten years of the
American theatre in performance, Norton, 1938, p. 204-08
Hogan, Robert, The independance of Elmer Rice, Sou. Ill.
Univ. Pr., 1965, p. 66-70

Arts and Decoration, 38:58, March, 1933
Catholic World, 136:717-18, March, 1933
Christian Century, 50:231, Feb. 15, 1933
Commonweal, 17:411, Feb. 8, 1933
Literary Digest, 115:15, Feb. 11, 1933
Literary Digest, 115:19, March 4, 1933
Nation, 136:158-60, 172, Aug. 15, 1933
New Republic, 74:18-19, Feb. 15, 1933

New Outlook, 161:10, March, 1933
Theatre Arts, 17:258-60, April, 1933
World Tomorrow, 16:176, Feb. 22, 1933

"The Winner", 1954

Hogan, Robert, The independence of Elmer Rice, Sou. Ill.
Univ. Pr., 1965, p. 115-18

America, 90:664, March 20, 1954
New Yorker, 30:78-80, Feb. 27, 1954
Newsweek, 43:71, March 1, 1954
Saturday Review, 37:25, March 6, 1954
Theatre Arts, 38:16, April, 1954
Time, 63:76, March 1, 1954

SEE ALSO

HATCHER HUGHES AND ELMER L. RICE

AND

PHILIP BARRY AND ELMER RICE

JACK RICHARDSON

"Christmas in Las Vegas", 1965

Commonweal, 83:243, 11-26-65
New Yorker, 41:154, Nov. 13, 1965

"Gallows Humor", 1961

Nation, 192:399, May 6, 1961
New Yorker, 37:93, April 29, 1961
Newsweek, 57:62, May 1, 1961
Saturday Review, 44:39, May 6, 1961
Theatre Arts, 45:32, June, 1961

"Lorenzo", 1963

New Republic, 148:29, March 9, 1963
New Yorker, 39:112, Feb. 23, 1963
Newsweek, 61:60, Feb. 25, 1963

Saturday Review, 46:24, March 9, 1963
Theatre Arts, 47:13, April, 1963
Time, 81:75, Feb. 22, 1963

"The Prodigal", 1960

Esquire, 55:47-8, April, 1961
Nation, 190:214, March 5, 1960
New Yorker, 36:104, Feb. 20, 1960
Time, 75:54, April 18, 1960

HOWARD RIGSBY
SEE
DOROTHY H. HEYWARD AND HOWARD RIGSBY

ANNA CORA MOWATT RITCHIE

"Fashion", 1845

Moses, Montrose Jonas and Brown, John Mason, eds.,
American theatre as Seen by Its Critics, 1752-1934,
Norton, 1934, p. 59-66
America, 100:613, Feb. 21, 1959
Catholic World, 189:60, April, 1959
London Mercury, 19:534, March, 1929
New Statesman, 32:440-1, 632, 1929
New Yorker, 34:64, Jan. 31, 1959
Saturday Review, 147:43, Jan. 12, 1929
Spectator (Lond), 142:80, Jan. 19, 1929
Time, 73:66, Feb. 16, 1959

BERTRAND ROBINSON
SEE
HOWARD LINDSAY AND BERTRAND ROBINSON

RICHARD ROGERS
SEE
OSCAR HAMMERSTEIN AND RICHARD ROGERS

MAJOR ROBERT ROGERS

"Ponteach; or The savages of America", 1766

<u>Dial</u>, 59:60-2, July 15, 1915

SIGMUND ROMBERG

SEE

OSCAR HAMMERSTEIN AND SIGMUND ROMBERG

DAMON RUNYON

SEE

HOWARD LINDSAY AND DAMON RUNYON

MORRIS RYSKIND

SEE

GEORGE S. KAUFMAN AND MORRIS RYSKIND

WILLIAM SAROYAN

"Across the Board on Tomorrow Morning", 1942

Nathan, George Jean, <u>Theatre Book of the Year, 1942-1943</u>, Knopf, p. 40-43

"Adventures of Wesley Jackson", 1946

Wilson, Edmund, <u>Classics and Commercials; a Literary Chronicle of the Forties</u>, Farrar, Straus, 1952, p. 327-30

"Beautiful People", 1941

<u>Catholic World</u>, 153:342-3, June, 1941
<u>Commonweal</u>, 34:38, May 2, 1941
<u>Life</u>, 10:128-31, May 19, 1941
<u>Nation</u>, 152:537, May 3, 1941
<u>New Republic</u>, 104:632, 664, May 12, 1941

New Yorker, 17:30, May 3, 1941
Newsweek, 17:67, May 5, 1941
Theatre Arts, 25:411-13, June, 1941
Time, 37:66, May 5, 1951

"The Cave Dwellers", 1957

Gassner, John, Theatre at the Crossroads; Plays and Play-
    Wrights of the Mid-century American Stage, Holt, 1960,
    p. 151-53

America, 98:299, Nov. 30, 1957
Catholic World, 186:305, January, 1958
Christian Century, 74:1425, Nov. 27, 1957
Commonweal, 67:289, Dec. 13, 1957
Nation, 185:330-1, Nov. 9, 1957
New Republic, 137-20, Nov. 4, 1957
New Yorker, 33:85-7, Nov. 2, 1957
New Yorker, 37:138, Oct. 28, 1961
Saturday Review, 40:22, Nov. 2, 1957
Theatre Arts, 41:20-1, Dec. , 1957
Time, 70:92, Oct. 28, 1957

"Get Away, Old Man", 1943

Nathan, George Jean, Theatre Book of the Year, 1943-1944,
    Knopf, p. 143-46

Commonweal, 39:205, Dec. 10, 1943
New Republic, 109:851, Dec. 13, 1943
Theatre Arts, 28:77-8, Feb. , 1944
Time, 42:42, Dec. 6, 1943

"Hello, Out There", 1942

Nathan, George Jean, Theatre Book of the Year, 1942-1943,
    Knopf, p. 79-82
Catholic World, 156:214, Nov. 1942
Commonweal, 36:615, Oct. 16, 1942
Nation, 155:357, Oct. 10, 1942
New Republic, 107:466, Oct. 12, 1942
New Yorker, 18:30, Oct. 10, 1942

"Jim Dandy", 1941

Library Journal, 67:299, March 1, 1942
Time, 38:68, Nov. 17, 1941

"London Comedy or, Sam the Highest Jumper of Them All", 1960

> Spectator (Lond), 204:573, April 22, 1960
> Time, 75:47, March 28, 1960

"Love's Old Sweet Song", 1940
> Brown, John Mason, Broadway in Review, Norton, 1940,
>   p. 187-97
> Young, Stark, Immortal Shadows, a Book of Dramatic
>   Criticism, Scribner, 1948, p. 215-17
>
> Catholic World, 151:344-5, June, 1940
> Commonweal, 32:82, May 17, 1940
> Nation, 150:634-5, May 18, 1940
> New Republic, 102:760, June 3, 1940
> New Yorker, 16:28, May 11, 1940
> Newsweek, 15:44-5, April 29, 1940
> Time, 35:52, May 13, 1940

"My Heart's in the Highlands", 1939
> Brown, John Mason, Broadway in Review, Norton, 1940,
>   p. 184-97
> McCarthy, Mary Therese, Sights and Spectacles, 1937-1956,
>   Farrar, Straus, 1956, p. 46-56
>
> Catholic World, 149:343-4, June, 1939
> Commonweal, 30:22, April 28, 1939
> Nation, 148:538, May 6, 1939
> New Republic, 98:379, May 3, 1939
> Newsweek, 13:45, May 1, 1939
> North American Review, 247 no. 2:365, June, 1939
> Theatre Arts, 23:396, June, 1939
> Time, 33:64, April 24, 1939

"Sunset Sonata", 1939

> Newsweek, 13:35, June 12, 1939

"Talking to You", 1942

> Nathan, George Jean, Theatre Book of the Year, 1942-1943,
>   Knopf, p. 40-43

"The Time of Your Life", 1939

> Brown, John Mason, Broadway in Review, Norton, 1940,
>   p. 187-97

Dusenbury, Winifred Loesch, The Theme of Loneliness in
  Modern American Drama, Univ. of Florida Press, 1960,
  p. 155-78
McCarthy, Mary Therese, Sights and Spectacles, 1937-1956,
  Farrar, Straus, 1956, p. 46-52
Schulberg, Budd, "Saroyan; Ease and Unease on the Flying
  Trapeze", Esquire, 54:#4:85-91, 1960

America, 92:518, Feb. 12, 1955
Catholic World, 150:335, Dec., 1939
Catholic World, 180:467, March, 1955
Commonweal, 31:78, Nov. 10, 1939
Commonweal, 32:512, Oct. 11, 1940
Nation, 149:505-6, Nov. 4, 1939
Nation, 180:124-5, Feb. 5, 1955
New Republic, 101:169, Nov. 29, 1939
New Yorker, 30:44, Jan. 29, 1955
Newsweek, 14:30, Oct. 23, 1939
Newsweek, 45:80-1, Jan. 31, 1955
North American Review, 248 no. 2:403-4, Dec., 1939
Theatre Arts, 24:11-13, Jan., 1940
Theatre Arts, 30:351, June, 1946
Theatre Arts, 39:22-4, Jan., 1955
Theatre Arts, 39:22, 25, April, 1955
Time, 34:32, Nov. 6, 1939
Time, 65:71, Jan. 31, 1955

WILLIAM SAROYAN AND HENRY CECIL

"Settled Out of Court", 1960

Illustrated London News, 237:818, Nov. 5, 1960

DORE SCHARY

"Devil's Advocate" (dramatization of novel by M. L. West), 1961

America, 105:161-3, April 15, 1961
Catholic World, 193:8-12, April, 1961
Christian Century, 78:458, April 12, 1961
Commonweal, 74:278, June 9, 1961
Nation, 192:312, April 8, 1961
New Yorker, 37:126, March 18, 1961

Newsweek, 57:88, March 20, 1961
Reporter, 24:44, April 13, 1961
Saturday Review, 44:35, March 25, 1961
Theatre Arts, 45:54-5, May, 1961
Time, 77:42, March 17, 1961

"The Highest Tree", 1959

America, 102:253, Nov. 21, 1959
New Yorker, 35:117-18, Nov. 14, 1959
Reporter, 21:39, Dec. 10, 1959
Saturday Review, 42:34, Nov. 21, 1959
Time, 74:57, Nov. 16, 1959

"Sunrise at Campobello", 1959

America, 98:735, March 22, 1958
Catholic World, 187:67, April, 1958
Christian Century, 75:622-3, May 21, 1958
Commonweal, 67:592, March 7, 1958
Life, 44:91-4, Feb. 10, 1958
Look, 22:98-101, April 1, 1958
N. Y. Times Mag., p. 42, Jan. 19, 1958
Nation, 186:146, Feb. 15, 1958
National Review, 138:20, Feb. 10, 1958
New Yorker, 33:93-6, Feb. 8, 1958
Newsweek, 51:69, Feb. 10, 1958
Reporter, 18:35, March 6, 1958
Saturday Review, 41:28, Feb. 15, 1958
Theatre Arts, 42:15-16, April, 1958
Time, 71:57, Feb. 10, 1958

MURRAY SCHISGAL

"Ducks and Lovers", 1961

New Statesman, 62:624, Oct. 27, 1961
Spectator, 205:577, Oct. 27, 1961

"Luv", 1963

America, 112:232-3, Feb. 13, 1965
Catholic World, 200:383, March, 1965
Commonweal, 81:389, Dec. 11, 1964
Drama, #69:22-3, Summer, 1963

Hudson Review, 18:84-6, Spring, 1965
Life, 58:79-81, Jan. 8, 1965
Nation, 199:415, Nov. 30, 1964
New Republic, 151:20, Dec. 12, 1964
New Statesman, 65:689, May 3, 1963
New Yorker, 40:143, Nov. 21, 1964
Newsweek, 64:102, Nov. 23, 1964
Saturday Review, 47:29, Nov. 28, 1964
Time, 84:81, Nov. 20, 1964
Vogue, 145:68, Jan. 1, 1965

"Schrecks", 1960

New Statesman, 60:969, Dec. 17, 1960

"Tiger", 1963

Commonweal, 77:665, March 22, 1963
Nation, 196:166-7, Feb. 23, 1963
New Yorker, 38:116, Feb. 16, 1963
Newsweek, 61:56, Feb. 18, 1963
Time, 81:63, Feb. 15, 1963

"Typists", 1961

Commonweal, 77:665, March 22, 1963
Nation, 196:166-7, Feb. 23, 1963
New Yorker, 38:114, Feb. 16, 1963
Newsweek, 61:56, Feb. 18, 1963
Time, 81:63, Feb. 15, 1963

JOSEPH SCHRANK

SEE

PHILIP DUNNING AND JOSEPH SCHRANK

JEROME LAURENCE SCHWARTZ

SEE

JEROME LAURENCE

ROD SERLING

"Patterns", 1955

> Wakefield, Dan, "From the Dark Towers", Nation,
> 185:210-12, Oct. 5, 1957

"The Rank and File", 1959

> Time, 73:52, June 8, 1959

IRWIN SHAW

"Assassin", 1945

> Commonweal, 43:69, Nov. 2, 1945
> Free World, 10:85-6, Dec., 1945
> New Republic, 113:573, Oct. 29, 1945
> New Republic, 114:479-80, April 8, 1946
> New Yorker, 21:42, Oct. 27, 1945
> Newsweek, 26:90, Oct. 29, 1945
> Theatre Arts, 29:679, 684-5, Dec., 1945

"Bury the Dead", 1936

> Catholic World, 143:338-40, June, 1936
> Commonweal, 24:48, May 8, 1936
> Literary Digest, 121:19, May 2, 1936
> Nation, 142:592-3, May 6, 1936
> New Republic, 87:21, May 13, 1936
> New Statesman and Nation, 15:834, May 14, 1938
> Newsweek, 7:29, April 25, 1936
> Theatre Arts, 20:417-19, June, 1936
> Time, 27:56, April 27, 1936

"Children From Their Games", 1963

> New Yorker, 39:96, April 20, 1963
> Newsweek, 61:90, April 22, 1963
> Saturday Review, 46:27, April 27, 1963
> Theatre Arts, 47:65, June, 1963

"Gentle People", 1939

> Catholic World, 148:598, Feb., 1939
> Commonweal, 29:358, Jan. 20, 1939

New Republic, 97:343, Jan. 25, 1939
New Statesman and Nation, 18:83-4, July 15, 1939
Newsweek, 13:26, Jan. 16, 1939
North American Review, 247 no. 2:368-9, June, 1939
Theatre Arts, 23:170, March, 1939
Time, 33:41, Jan. 16, 1939

"Retreat to Pleasure", 1941

New Yorker, 16:29, Dec. 28, 1940
Newsweek, 16:38, Dec. 30, 1940
Theatre Arts, 25:96, Feb., 1941

"Sons and Soldiers", 1943

McCarthy, Mary Therese, Sights and Spectacles, 1937-
1956, Farrar, Straus, 1956, p. 63-66

EDWARD SHELDON

"The Boss", 1911

Hamilton, C., "Natural Plays", Bookman, 33:32,
March, 1911
"'The Boss' staged", Everybody's Magazine, 24:670-3,
May, 1911

"The Garden of Paradise", 1914

American Magazine, 79:42-6, April, 1915
New Republic, 1:23, Dec. 5, 1914

"High Road", n. d.

Cather, W. S., "Play of Real Life", McClure, 40:66-9,
March, 1913

"Romance", 1913

Moses, Montrose Jonas and Brown, John Mason, ed. s,
American Theatre as Seen by Its Critics, 1752-1934,
Norton, 1934, p. 169-71
Hamilton, C., "Impressive Theme", Bookman, 37:306-8,
May, 1913

"Salvation Nell", 1908

> Cohn, A., "'Salvation Nell', an overlooked milestone in American theatre", Educational Theatre Journal, 9:11-22, March, 1957

EDWARD SHELDON AND MARGARET AYER BARNES

"Dishonored Lady", 1930

> Commonweal, 11:453, Feb. 19, 1930
> New Republic, 62:20-1, Feb. 19, 1930
> Saturday Review, 149:615, May 17, 1929

"Jenny", 1929

> Catholic World, 130:332-3, Dec., 1929

EDWARD SHELDON AND SIDNEY HOWARD

"Bewitched", 1924

> The Independent, 113:403, Nov. 15, 1924

EDWARD SHELDON AND H. SUDERMANN

"Song of Songs", 1914

> Bookman, 40:637-8, Feb., 1915
> Nation, 100:87, Jan. 21, 1915
> New Republic, 1:25, Jan. 2, 1915

ELSA SHELLEY

"Foxhole in the Parlor", 1945

> Commonweal, 42:191, June 8, 1945
> New Republic, 112:815, June 11, 1945
> New Yorker, 21:38, June 2, 1945
> Theatre Arts, 29:389, July, 1945

"Pick-up Girl", 1944

>Catholic World, 159:264-6, June, 1944
>Commonweal, 40:110-11, May 19, 1944
>Life, 16:68-70, June 12, 1944
>New Yorker, 20:44, May 13, 1944
>Theatre Arts, 28:572, Oct., 1944
>Theatre Arts, 30:591, Oct. 1946

"With a Silk Thread", 1950

>Nathan, George Jean, Theatre Book of the Year, 1949-1950, Knopf, p. 266-69

>New Yorker, 26:60, April 22, 1950
>Newsweek, 35:95, April 24, 1950
>Theatre Arts, 34:17, June, 1950

ROBERT EMMET SHERWOOD

"Abe Lincoln in Illinois", 1938

>Dusenbury, Winifred Loesch, The Theme of Loneliness in Modern American Drama, Univ. of Florida Press, 1960, p. 179-98
>Gates, Theodore J. and Wright, Austin, eds., College Prose, Heath, 1942, p. 400-04
>King, William Lyon Mackenzie, Canada and the Fight for Freedom, Duell, 1944, p. 13-29
>Lerner, Max, Ideas are Weapons; the History of the Use of Ideas, Viking, 1939, p. 48-53
>O'Hara, Frank Hurburt, Today in American Drama, Univ. of Chicago Press, 1939, p. 53-141
>Oppenheimer, George, ed., Passionate Playgoer; a Personal Scrapbook, Viking, 1958, p. 537-40

>Canadian Forum, 19:355-6, Feb., 1940
>Catholic World, 148:340-1, Dec., 1938
>Commonweal, 29:20, Oct. 28, 1938
>Commonweal, 77:543, Feb. 15, 1963
>Forum, 101:72, Feb., 1939
>Independent Woman, 17:348, Nov., 1938
>Nation, 147:487-88, Nov. 5, 1938
>Nation, 196:125-6, Feb. 9, 1963

New Republic, 97:18, Nov. 9, 1938
New Yorker, 38:69-70, Feb. 2, 1963
Newsweek, 12:29, Oct. 31, 1938
North American Review, 246:373-4, Dec., 1938
Saturday Review, 46:20, Feb. 9, 1963
Southern Review (L.S.U.), 5 no. 3:560-2, 1940
Theatre Arts, 22:853-5, Dec., 1938
Theatre Arts, 47:58-9, March, 1963
Time, 32:53, Oct. 24, 1938

"Acropolis", 1933

Saturday Review, 156:587, Dec. 2, 1933
Spectator, 151:801, Dec. 1, 1933

"Idiot's Delight", 1936

Brown, John Mason, Two on the Aisle; Ten Years of the
American Theatre in Performance, Norton, 1938, p. 163-68

Catholic World, 143:212, May, 1936
Catholic World, 173:306-7, July, 1951
Commonweal, 23:664, April 10, 1936
Commonweal, 54:213, June 8, 1951
Commonweal, 24:104, May 22, 1936
Forum, 95:348-9, June, 1936
Literary Digest, 121:20, March 28, 1936
Nation, 142:490-2, April 15, 1936
New Republic, 86:253, April 8, 1936
New Statesman and Nation, 15:568, April 2, 1938
Newsweek, 7:32, April 4, 1936
Pictorial Review, 37:65, July, 1936
Spectator, 160-583, April 1, 1938
Theatre Arts, 20:340-1, May, 1936
Theatre Arts, 20:466-7, June, 1936
Theatre Arts, 22:410-11, June, 1938
Time, 27:38, April 6, 1936

"Love Nest", 1927

Saturday Review of Literature, 4:499-500, Jan. 7, 1928

"The Petrified Forest", 1935

Brown, John Mason, Dramatis Personae; a Retrospective
Shown, Viking, 1963, p. 77-79

Brown, John Mason, Two on the Aisle; Ten Years of the
American Theatre in Performance, Norton, 1938,
p. 163-68
Nathan, George Jean, Theatre Book of the Year, 1943-1944,
Knopf, p. 112-14

Canadian Forum, 15:194, Feb., 1935
Catholic World, 140:601-2, Feb., 1935
Commonweal, 21:375, Jan. 25, 1935
Literary Digest, 119:19, Jan. 19, 1935
Nation, 140:111, Jan. 23, 1935
New Republic, 82:21, Feb. 13, 1935
New Statesman and Nation, 24:424, Dec. 26, 1942
Spectator, 169:598, Dec. 25, 1942
Theatre Arts, 19:169-70, March, 1935

"The Queen's Husband", 1928

Saturday Review, 152:498, Oct. 17, 1931

"Reunion in Vienna", 1931

Les Annales Politiques et Litteraires, 105:137, Feb. 10,
1935
Arts & Decoration, 36:68, Jan., 1932
Bookman, 74:564, Jan., 1932
Catholic World, 134:467-8, Jan., 1932
Commonweal, 15:160, Dec. 9, 1931
Nation, 133:650, Dec. 9, 1931
New Republic, 69:70, Dec. 2, 1931
New Statesman and Nation, 7:41, Jan. 13, 1934
North American Review, 234:174, Aug., 1932
Outlook, 159:438, Dec. 2, 1931
Spectator, 152:46, Jan. 12, 1934
Theatre Arts, 16:96-7, Feb., 1932

"Road to Rome", 1927

English Review, 64:480-1, April, 1937
Journal des Debats, 36 pt. 2:892-4, Nov. 29, 1929
Nation, (Lond), 43:251-2, May 26, 1928
New Republic, 50:70-1, March 9, 1927
New Statesman and Nation, 13:368, March 6, 1937
Outlook, (Lond), 61:657, May 26, 1928
Outlook, 146:546-7, Aug. 24, 1927

Saturday Review, 145:660, May 26, 1928
Spectator, 140:826-7, June 2, 1928
Spectator, 158:516, March 19, 1937

"Rugged Path", 1945

Nathan, George Jean, Theatre Book of the Year, 1945-1946, Knopf, p. 167-75

Catholic World, 162:264, Dec., 1945
Commonweal, 43:168, Nov. 30, 1945
Free World, 11:71-2, Jan., 1946
Forum, 105:468, Jan., 1946
Life, 19:88-90, Dec. 3, 1945
Nation, 161:562, Nov. 24, 1945
New Republic, 113:711, Nov. 26, 1945
New Yorker, 21:47, Nov. 17, 1945
Newsweek, 26:84, Nov. 1, 1945
Saturday Review of Literature, 28:18-20, Nov. 24, 1945
Theatre Arts, 30:6, 8-10, Jan., 1946
Time, 46:63, Nov. 19, 1945

"Small War on Murray Hill", 1957
Catholic World, 184:470-1, March, 1957
Christian Century, 74:201, Feb. 13, 1957
Theatre Arts, 41:19, March, 1957

"There Shall Be No Night", 1940

Brown, John Mason, Broadway in Review, Norton, 1940, p. 154-59
Healey, R. C., "Anderson, Saroyan, Sherwood: new directions; 'Key Largo', 'The Time of Your Life' and 'There Shall Be No Night' ", Catholic World, 152:174-80, November, 1940
Theatre Arts Anthology; a Record and a Prophecy, ed. by Rosamond Gilder and others, Theatre Arts Books, 1950, p. 649-51

Catholic World, 151:343-4, June, 1940
Commonweal, 32:62, May 10, 1940
Life, 8:48, May 13, 1940
Nation, 150:605-6, May 11, 1940
New Republic, 102:641, May 13, 1940
New Statesman and Nation, 26:415, Dec. 25, 1943

New Yorker, 16:28, May 11, 1940
Newsweek, 15:34, May 13, 1940
Sociology and Social Research, 25:295, Jan., 1941
Spectator, 171:598, Dec. 24, 1943
Survey Graphic, 29:408, July, 1940
Theatre Arts, 24:398-401, June, 1940 and 25:788, Nov., 1941
Theatre Arts, 24:548, Aug., 1940
Time, 35:52, May 13, 1940

"This is New York", 1930

Bookman, 72:516, Jan., 1931
Catholic World, 132:464, Jan., 1931
Drama, 21:13, Jan., 1931
Outlook, 156:629, Dec. 17, 1930

"Waterloo Bridge", 1930

Nation, 130:106, Jan. 22, 1930
New Republic, 61:251, Jan. 22, 1930

SEE ALSO

PHILIP BARRY AND ROBERT E. SHERWOOD

NEIL SIMON

"Barefoot in the Park", 1963

America, 109:753, Dec. 7, 1963
Commonweal, 79:226, Nov. 15, 1963
New Yorker, 39:93, Nov. 2, 1963
Newsweek, 62:62, Nov. 4, 1963
Saturday Review, 46:32, Nov. 9, 1963
Theatre Arts, 48:68, Jan., 1964
Time, 82:74, Nov. 1, 1963

"Come Blow Your Horn", 1961

America, 105:355, May 20, 1961
Nation, 192:222, March 11, 1961
New Yorker, 37:93, March 4, 1961
Saturday Review, 44:38, March 11, 1961
Time, 77:60, March 3, 1961

"The Odd Couple", 1965

> America, 112:810-11, May 29, 1965
> Catholic World, 201:343-4, Aug., 1965
> Commonweal, 82:51-2, April 2, 1965
> Life, 58:35-6, April 9, 1965
> Nation, 200:373-4, April 5, 1965
> New Yorker, 41:83, March 20, 1965
> Newsweek, 65:90-1, March 22, 1965
> Saturday Review, 48:44, March 27, 1965
> Time, 85:66, March 19, 1962
> Vogue, 145:142, May, 1962

BETTY SMITH

SEE

GEORGE ABBOTT AND BETTY SMITH

WILLIAM H. SMITH

"The Drunkard or the Fallen Saved", 1933

American Mercury, 81:140-2, Dec., 1955

WINCHELL SMITH

"Only Son", 1911

> Bookman, 34:367-8, Dec., 1911
> Everybody's, 26:88-90, Jan., 1912

WINCHELL SMITH AND FRANK BACON

"Lightnin' ", 1918

> French, W. F., "Lightnin' Bill Jones, himself", Worlds
>   Work, 38:502-4, Dec., 1922
> Schmidt, K., "There were liars in those days", Everybody's
>   40:43, Jan., 1919
>
> Catholic World, 148:212, Nov., 1938
> Commonweal, 28:589, Sept. 30, 1938

Literary Digest, 84:31, March 14, 1925
Outlook (Lond), 55:89, Feb. 7, 1925
Theatre Arts, 22:774, Nov., 1938
Time, 32:39, Sept. 26, 1938

WINCHELL SMITH AND V. MAPES

"Boomerang", 1915

Harper's Weekly, 61:206-7, Aug. 28, 1915
Nation, 101:240, Aug. 19, 1915
New Republic, 4:76, Aug. 21, 1915

WINCHELL SMITH AND BYRON ONGLEY

"Brewster's Millions", 1902

Outlook, (Lond), 53:267, April 19, 1924

BELLA AND SAMUEL SPEWACK

"Boy Meets Girl", 1935

O'Hara, Frank Hurburt, Today in American Drama, Univ.
of Chicago Pr., 1939, p. 190-234

Catholic World, 142:471, Jan., 1936
Commonweal, 23:188, Dec. 13, 1935
Literary Digest, 120:19, Dec. 14, 1935
New Republic, 85:175, Dec. 18, 1935
Newsweek, 6:42, Dec. 7, 1935
Theatre Arts, 20:19, Jan., 1936
Time, 26:53, Dec. 9, 1935

"Clear All Wires", 1932

Arts and Decoration, 38:44-5, Nov., 1932
Catholic World, 136:209-10, Nov., 1932
Commonweal, 16:512, Sept. 28, 1932
Literary Digest, 114:21, Oct. 15, 1932
Nation, 135:290-1, Sept. 28, 1932
Theatre Arts, 16:865-6, Nov., 1932

"Festival", 1955

>America, 92:545, Feb. 19, 1955
>New Republic, 132:22, Feb. 7, 1955
>New Yorker, 30:46-7, Jan. 29, 1955
>Saturday Review, 38:24, Feb. 12, 1955
>Theatre Arts, 39:15, 89, April, 1955
>Time, 65:71, Jan. 31, 1955

"Golden State", 1950

>Commonweal, 53:253, Dec. 15, 1950
>New Yorker, 26:82, Dec. 2, 1950
>Newsweek, 36:74, Dec. 4, 1940
>Theatre Arts, 35:14, Feb., 1951
>Time, 56:65, Dec. 4, 1950

"Leave It To Me", 1938

>Brown, John Mason, Broadway in Review, Norton, 1940,
>   p. 254-56
>Theatre Arts Anthology; a Record and a Prophecy; ed. by
>   Rosamond Gilder and others, Theatre Arts Books, 1950,
>   p. 646-49

>Catholic World, 148:477, Jan., 1939
>Commonweal, 29:132, Nov. 25, 1938
>Nation, 147:572-3, Nov. 26, 1938
>New Republic, 97:100, Nov. 30, 1938
>Newsweek, 12:24, Nov. 21, 1938
>North American Review, 247 no. 2:369, June, 1939
>Theatre Arts, 23:6, Jan., 1939
>Time, 32:66, Nov. 21, 1938

"My Three Angels" (adaptation of La cuisine des angels by A.
Husson), 1953

>America, 88:716-17, March 28, 1953
>Catholic World, 177:149, May, 1953

>Illustrated London News, 226:982, May 28, 1955
>Life, 34:101-2, May 11, 1953
>Nation, 176:273, March 28, 1953
>New Yorker, 29:64, March 21, 1953
>Newsweek, 41:98, March 23, 1953

Saturday Review, 36:27, March 28, 1953
Theatre Arts, 38:32-3, June, 1954
Time, 61:80, March 23, 1953

"Spring Song", 1934

Catholic World, 140:214, Nov., 1934
Theatre Arts, 18:817, Nov., 1934

"Two Blind Mice", 1949

Catholic World, 169-64, April, 1949
Commonweal, 49:592, March 25, 1949
Life, 26:141-2, April 4, 1949
New Yorker, 25:48, March 12, 1949
Newsweek, 33:8k, March 14, 1949
School and Society, 69:338, May 7, 1949
Theatre Arts, 33:23, 26, May, 1949
Time, 53:58, March 14, 1949

"Under the Sycamore Tree", 1952

Life, 33:169, Oct. 13, 1952
New Yorker, 36:121-2, March 19, 1960

"Woman Bites Dog", 1946

Nathan, George Jean, Theatre Book of the Year, 1945-1946,
Knopf, p. 358-61

Commonweal, 44:72, May 3, 1946
Forum, 105:940-1, June, 1946
New Yorker, 22:44, April 27, 1946

LEONARD SPIGELGASS

"Dear Me, The Sky is Falling", 1963

Commonweal, 78:47, April 5, 1963
Nation, 196:254, March 23, 1963
New Yorker, 39:132, March 9, 1963
Newsweek, 61:69, March 18, 1963
Saturday Review, 46:28, March 23, 1963
Theatre Arts, 47:10-12, April, 1963
Time, 81:70, March 15, 1963

"Majority of One", 1958

> America, 100:671, March 7, 1959
> Catholic World, 189:158, May, 1959
> Commonweal, 69:625, March 13, 1959
> Illustrated London News, 236:522, March 26, 1960
> Life, 46:50, March 9, 1959
> Nation, 188:215, March 7, 1959
> New Yorker, 35:66, Feb. 28, 1959
> Newsweek, 53:82, March 2, 1959
> Reporter, 20:40, March 19, 1959
> Saturday Review, 42:29, March 7, 1959
> Theatre Arts, 43:11, April, 1959
> Time, 73:49, March 2, 1959

JOHN CALLING SQUIRE

SEE

JOHN LLOYD BALDERSTON AND JOHN CALLING SQUIRE

LAURENCE STALLINGS

"Farewell to Arms" (dramatization of story by Ernest Hemingway),
1930

> Bookman, 72:296, Nov., 1930
> New Republic, 64:208-9, Oct. 8, 1930

"Streets Are Guarded", 1944

> Nathan, George Jean, Theatre Book of the Year, 1944-1945,
> Knopf, p. 156-60

> Commonweal, 41:205, Dec. 8, 1944
> New Republic, 111:746, Dec. 4, 1944
> New Yorker, 20:44, Dec. 2, 1944
> Theatre Arts, 29:11-13, January, 1945
> Time, 44:48, Dec. 4, 1944

SEE ALSO

MAXWELL ANDERSON AND LAURENCE STALLINGS

JOSEPH STEIN

"Enter Laughing) (dramatization of novel by C. Reiner), 1963

> Commonweal, 78:47, April 5, 1963
> Nation, 196:333, April 20, 1963
> New Yorker, 39:74, March 23, 1963
> Newsweek, 61:98, March 25, 1963
> Saturday Review, 46:40, April 6, 1963
> Theatre Arts, 47:72, May, 1963
> Time, 81:77, March 22, 1963

HARRIET BEECHER STOWE

"Uncle Tom's Cabin", 1852

> Corbett, E. F., "Footnote to the drama; America's one folk
>   play, 'Uncle Tom's Cabin'", Drama, 16:285-6, May, 1926
> Hewitt, Barnard, "Uncle Tom and Uncle Same; new light
>   from an old play", Quarterly Journal of Speech, 37:63-70,
>   1951
> Moses, Montrose Jonas and Brown, John Mason, eds.,
>   American Theatre as Seen by Its Critics, 1752-1934,
>   Norton, 1934, p. 72-75
> Roppolo, J. P., "Uncle Tom in New Orleans; three lost
>   plays", New England Quarterly, 27:213-26, June, 1954
> Ryerson, F. and Clements, C. C., "Harriet; drama;
>   scene from act number covering writing of 'Uncle Tom's
>   Cabin'", Scholastic, 44:13-16, April 24, 1944
>
> Theatre Arts, 36:18-24, Oct., 1952

PRESTON STURGES

"Child of Manhattan", 1932

> Arts & Decoration, 37:56, May, 1932
> Nation, 134:351-2, March 23, 1932
> New Republic, 70:127, March 16, 1932
> Theatre Arts, 16:362, May, 1932

"Make a Wish", n.d.

> Nathan, George Jean, Theatre Book of the Year, 1950-1951,
>   Knopf, p. 269-73

"Strictly Dishonorable", 1929

>Commonweal, 10-592, Oct. 9, 1929
>Drama, 20:40, Nov., 1929
>English Review, 52:510-11, April, 1931
>Nation, 129:392-3, Oct. 9, 1929
>New Republic, 60:270, Oct. 23, 1929
>Outlook, 153:232, Oct. 9, 1929
>Saturday Review, 151:413, March 21, 1931
>Spectator (Lond), 146:452-3, March 21, 1931

H. SUDERMANN

SEE

EDWARD SHELDON AND H. SUDERMANN

ARNOLD SUNDGAARD

"First Crocus", 1942

>Commonweal, 35:320, Jan. 16, 1942
>Theatre Arts, 26:156, March, 1942

"Great Campaign", 1947

>New Republic, 116:37, April 21, 1947
>Theatre Arts, 30:53, Jan., 1946

ARNOLD SUNDGAARD AND MARC CONNELLY

"Everywhere I Roam", 1938

>Catholic World, 148:597, Feb., 1939
>Commonweal, 29:330, Jan. 13, 1939
>Nation, 148:73-4, Jan. 14, 1939
>Theatre Arts, 23:164, March, 1939
>Time, 33:25, Jan. 9, 1939

BOOTH TARKINGTON

"Clarence", 1919

>Hamilton, Clayton Meeker, Seven on the Stage, Holt, 1920, p. 192-203

"Colonel Satan", 1931

> Commonweal, 13:385, Feb. 4, 1931
> Nation, 132:134, Feb. 4, 1931
> Saturday Review, 151:119, Jan. 24, 1931

"Gentle Julia", n. d.

> Woollcott, Alexander, Portable Woollcott, Viking, 1946,
>   p. 343-47

"How's Your Health", 1930

> Catholic World, 130:469-70, Jan., 1930

"Seventeen", 1918

> Current Opinion, 64:251-4, April, 1918
> Everybody's, 38:84, April, 1918

AUGUSTUS THOMAS

"Alabama", 1891

> Athenaeum,106:331, Sept. 7, 1895
> Dial, 26:402, June 16, 1899

"As a Man Thinks", 1911

> Bookman, 33:354-7, June, 1911
> Outlook, 97:714, April 1, 1911

"Capital", 1895

> Critic, 27(ns24):172, Sept. 14, 1895

"Copperhead", 1918

> Art World, 3:460, March, 1918
> New Republic, 14:267, March 30, 1918

"Harvest Moon", 1909

> Forum, 42:575-6, Dec. 1909

"Hoosier Doctor", 1899

> Critic, 32 (ns29):286, April 23, 1898

"The Meddler", 1898

> Critic, 33:297, Oct., 1898

"Nemesis", n.d.

> Lewishon, Ludwig, Drama on the Stage, Harcourt, 1922,
> p. 89-93

"New Blood", 1894

> Critic, 25(ns22):194, Sept. 22, 1894

"Rio Grande", 1916

> Bookman, 43:343, May, 1916
> Nation, 102:420, April 13, 1916
> New Republic, 6:353-4, April 29, 1916

"Still Water", 1926

> Catholic World, 123:92-3, April, 1926

BRANDON THOMAS

"Charley's Aunt", 1893

> Catholic World, 152:334, Dec., 1940
> Catholic World, 178:387, Feb., 1954
> Commonweal, 33:80, Nov. 8, 1940
> Life, 9:47-50, Nov. 18, 1940
> Nation, 151:431, Nov. 2, 1940
> New Republic, 103:629, Nov. 4, 1940
> Theatre Arts, 24:848, Dec., 1940
> Theatre Arts, 38:18, March, 1954

JAMES THURBER

"The Beast in Me", 1949

> New Statesman and Nation, 37:279, March 19, 1949

SEE ALSO

ELLIOTT NUGENT AND JAMES THURBER

SOPHIE TREADWELL

"Hope for A Harvest", 1941

>Catholic World, 154:472-3, Jan. , 1942
>Nation, 153:621, Dec. 13, 1941
>New Republic, 105:762, Dec. 8, 1941
>Theatre Arts, 26:12, Jan. , 1942
>Time, 38:39, Dec. 8, 1941

"Ladies Leave", 1929

>Outlook, 153:272, Oct. 16, 1929

"Machinal", 1928

>America, 103:203, April 30, 1960
>American Mercury, 15:376-7, Nov. , 1928
>Commonweal, 72:306, June 17, 1960
>New Republic, 56:299-300, Oct. 31, 1928
>New Republic, 142:21-2, April 25, 1960
>New Yorker, 36:134-6, April 16, 1960
>Theatre Arts, 12:774-80, Nov. , 1928

"Plumes in the Dust", 1936

>Catholic World, 144:336-7, Dec., 1936
>Commonweal, 25:104, Nov. 20, 1936
>New Republic, 89:116, Nov. 25, 1936
>Newsweek, 8:58, Nov. 14, 1936
>Time, 28:89, Nov. 16, 1936

EDMUND TRZCINSKI

SEE

DONALD JOSEPTH BEVAN AND EDMUND TRZCINSKI

ROYALL TYLER

"The Contrast", 1787

>Balch, M. , "Jonathan the First; The Origin of the Stage Yankee",
>Modern Language Notes, 46:281-88, May, 1931

Bishop, W. , "First American comedy: 'The Contrast' ",
The Mentor, 15:39, January, 1928

Moses, Montrose Jonas and Brown, John Mason, eds. ,
American Theatre as Seen by Its Critics, 1752-1934, Norton,
1934, p. 24-25

Nethercot, A. H. , "Dramatic Background of Royall Tyler's
'The Contrast' " American Literature, 12:435-46,
January, 1941

"Our first truly national play: 'The Contrast' ", Delineator,
85:7, July, 1914

JOHN VAN DRUTEN

"After All", 1929

Arts and Decoration, 36:56, Feb. , 1932
Catholic World, 134:468-9, Jan. , 1932
Commonweal, 15:187, Dec. 16, 1931
Nation, 133:706, Dec. 23, 1931
Outlook, 159:502, Dec. 16, 1931
Theatre Arts, 16:101, Feb. , 1932
New Statesman, 33:212-13, May 25, 1929
Saturday Review, 147:640, May 11, 1929
Saturday Review, 151:227, Feb. 14, 1931

"Behold We Live", 1932

English Review, 55:430-2, Oct. , 1932
Saturday Review, 154:220, Aug. 27, 1932
Spectator, 149:259, Aug. 27, 1932

"Bell, Book and Candle", 1950

Nathan, George Jean, Theatre Book of the Year, 1950-1951,
Knopf, p. 101-07

Catholic World, 172:307, Jan. , 1957
Christian Science Monitor Mag. , p. 10, Nov. 25, 1950
Commonweal, 53:197, Dec. 1, 1950
Illustrated London News, 225:712, Oct. 23, 1954
Life, 29:111-12, Dec. 11, 1950
Nation, 171:493, Nov. 25, 1950
New Republic, 123:22, Dec. 25, 1950
New Yorker, 26:62, Nov. 25, 1950

Newsweek, 36:76, Nov. 27, 1950
Saturday Review of Literature, 33:24, Dec. 16, 1950
School and Society, 73:104, Feb. 17, 1951
Theatre Arts, 35:15, Jan., 1951
Time, 56:76, Nov. 27, 1950

"Distaff Side", 1933

Catholic World, 140:212, Nov., 1934
Commonweal, 20:563, Oct. 12, 1934
Golden Book, 20:510, Nov., 1934
Nation, 139:418-19, Oct. 10, 1934
New Republic, 80:273, Oct. 17, 1934
Newsweek, 4:22-3, Oct. 6, 1934
Spectator, 151:309, Sept. 8, 1933
Theatre Arts, 18:818, Nov., 1934

"Diversion", n.d.

English Review, 47:726-8, Dec., 1928
Saturday Review, 146:422, Oct. 6, 1928
Spectator, 141:481-2, Oct. 13, 1928

"Druid Circle", 1947

McCarthy, Mary Therese, Sights and Spectacles, 1937-1956,
    Farrar, Straus, 1956, p. 121-30
Nathan, George Jean, Theatre Book of the Year, 1947-1948,
    Knopf, p. 116-18

Catholic World, 166:265, Dec., 1947
Commonweal, 47:95, Nov. 7, 1947
New Republic, 117:36, Nov. 3, 1947
New Yorker, 23:44, Nov. 1, 1947
Newsweek, 30:76, Nov. 3, 1947
School and Society, 66:507-8, Dec. 27, 1947
Theatre Arts, 32:11, Jan., 1948
Time, 50:68, Nov. 3, 1947

"Flowers of the Forest", 1934

Catholic World, 141:216-18, May, 1935
Commonweal, 21:740, April 26, 1935
Nation, 140:490-1, April 24, 1935
New Republic, 82:316, April 24, 1935
Newsweek, 5:17, April 20, 1935

Saturday Review, 158:475, Dec. 1, 1934
Spectator, 153:836, Nov. 30, 1934
Theatre Arts, 19:3, 400-1, Jan., June, 1935

"Gertie Maude", 1937

New Statesman and Nation, 14:282, Aug. 21, 1937
Spectator, 159:347, Aug. 27, 1937
Theatre Arts, 21:847, Nov., 1937

"I Am a Camera" (dramatization of Berlin stories by C. Isherwood), 1951

Brown, John Mason, As They Appear, McGraw, 1952,
    p. 207-12
Gassner, John, Theatre at the Crossroads, Plays and
    Playwrights of the Mid-century American Stage, Holt, 1960,
    p. 144-57
Tynan, Kenneth, Curtains, Selections from the Drama
    Criticism and Related Writings, Atheneum, 1961, p. 247-48

Catholic World, 174:309, Jan., 1952
Commonweal, 55:277, Dec. 21, 1951
Nation, 173:554, Dec. 22, 1951
New Republic, 125:22, Dec. 24, 1951
New Statesman, 47:355, March 20, 1954
Newsweek, 38:50, Dec. 10, 1951
Saturday Review of Literature, 34:26, Dec. 22, 1951
Saturday Review of Literature, 35:27, July 5, 1952
School and Society, 75:41, Jan. 19, 1952
Spectator, 192:321, March 19, 1954
Theatre Arts, 36:20-2, 30, Feb., 1952
Time, 58:63, Dec. 10, 1951

"I Remember Mamma" (dramatization of Mamma's Bank Account by
    K. Forbes), 1944

Brown, John Mason, Seeing Things, McGraw, 1946,
    p. 217-23
Nathan, George Jean, Theatre Book of the Year, 1944-1945,
    Knopf, p. 109-12

Catholic World, 160:259, Dec., 1944
Commonweal, 41:72, Nov. 3, 1944
Life, 17:104-6, Nov. 20, 1944
Nation, 159:568, Nov. 4, 1944

New Republic, 111:836, Dec. 18, 1944
New Statesman and Nation, 35:214, March 13, 1948
N.Y. Times Mag., p. 16, Dec. 3, 1944
N.Y. Times Mag., p. 24-5, Oct. 14, 1945
New Yorker, 20:39, Oct. 28, 1944
Newsweek, 24:86, Oct. 30, 1944
Saturday Review of Literature, 27:18, Dec. 16, 1944
Spectator, 180:313, March 12, 1948
Theatre Arts, 28:692, Dec., 1944
Theatre Arts, 29:81-2, 87, Feb., 1945
Theatre Arts, 29:215-17, April, 1945
Time, 44:68, Oct. 30, 1944

"I've Got Sixpence", 1952

Commonweal, 57:306, Dec. 26, 1952
New Yorker, 28:86, Dec. 13, 1952
Newsweek, 40:62, Dec. 15, 1952
Saturday Review, 35:25, Dec. 20, 1952
Theatre Arts, 36:15, Dec., 1952
Theatre Arts, 37:26, Feb., 1953
Time, 60:73, Dec. 15, 1952

"Leave Her to Heaven", 1940

Commonweal, 31:455, March 15, 1940
Newsweek, 15:35, March 11, 1940
Theatre Arts, 24:317, May, 1940
Time, 35:32, March 11, 1940

"London Wall", 1931

Saturday Review, 151:680, May 9, 1931
Spectator, 146:734, May 9, 1931

"Make Way for Lucia", 1949

Nathan, George Jean, Theatre Book of the Year, 1948-1949,
    Knopf, p. 212-15

Commonweal, 49:352, Jan. 14, 1949
Nation, 168:81, Jan. 15, 1949
New Yorker, 24:34, Jan. 1, 1949
Newsweek, 33:54, Jan. 3, 1949
Time, 53:49, Jan. 3, 1949

"Mermaids Singing", 1945

> Nathan, George Jean, Theatre Book of the Year, 1945-1946, Knopf, p. 204-11

> Catholic World, 162:358, Jan., 1946
> Commonweal, 43:263, Dec. 21, 1945
> New Republic, 113:839, Dec. 17, 1945
> New Yorker, 21:56-8, Dec. 8, 1945
> Newsweek, 26:93, Dec. 10, 1945
> Saturday Review of Literature, 28:14-16, Dec. 15, 1945
> Theatre Arts, 30:7, Jan., 1946
> Theatre Arts, 30:78, Feb., 1946
> Time, 46:76, Dec. 10, 1945

"Most of the Game", n.d.

> Theatre Arts, 19:823, Nov., 1935

"Old Acquaintance", 1941

> Catholic World, 152:597, Feb., 1941
> Commonweal, 33:303, Jan. 10, 1941
> Nation, 152:137, Feb. 1, 1941
> New Statesman and Nation, 22:524, Dec. 27, 1941
> Spectator, 167, 598, Dec. 26, 1941
> Theatre Arts, 25:93-4, Feb., 1941
> Time, 37:41, Jan. 6, 1941

"Solitaire" (dramatization of novel by E. Carle), 1942

> Catholic World, 154:730, March, 1942
> Commonweal, 35:418, Feb. 13, 1942
> Nation, 154:201-2, Feb. 14, 1942
> New Republic, 106:204, Feb. 9, 1942
> Newsweek, 19:63, Feb. 9, 1942
> Theatre Arts, 26:224-5, April, 1942

"Somebody Knows", 1932

> Saturday Review, 153:539, May 28, 1932
> Spectator, 148:726, May 21, 1932

"There's Always Juliet", 1932

> Catholic World, 135:73, April, 1932
> Bookman, 74:667, March, 1932

Commonweal, 15:495, March 2, 1932
Nation, 134:266, March 2, 1932
New Republic, 70:97, March 9, 1932
North American Review, 237:174-5, Aug., 1932
Theatre Arts, 16:270-1, April, 1932

"Voice of the Turtle", 1943

Nathan, George Jean, Theatre Book of the Year, 1943-1944,
  Knopf, p. 158-66
Isaacs, H.R., "Featuring 'The Voice of the Turtle'",
  Theatre Arts, 28:280-4, 1944

American Mercury, 58:464-8, April, 1944
Catholic World, 158:487-8, Feb., 1944
Commonweal, 39:253, Dec. 24, 1943
Life, 15:45-6, Dec. 27, 1943
Nation, 157:767, Dec. 25, 1943
New Republic, 109:915, Dec. 27, 1943
New Yorker, 19:44, Dec. 18, 1943
Newsweek, 22:86, Dec. 20, 1943
Theatre Arts, 28:73-5, Feb., 1944
Time, 42:36, Dec. 20, 1943

"Young Woodley", 1925

New Republic, 45:133-4, Dec. 23, 1925

JOHN VAN DRUTEN AND LLOYD R. MORRIS

"Damask Cheek", 1942

Nathan, George Jean, Theatre Book of the Year, 1942-1943,
  Knopf, p. 110-12
Catholic World, 156:335-6, Dec., 1942
Commonweal, 37:71-2, Nov. 6, 1942
Illustrated London News, 214:280, Feb. 26, 1949
Independent Woman, 21:368, Dec., 1942
Life, 13:68, Nov. 23, 1942
New Republic, 107:609-10, Nov. 9, 1942
New Yorker, 18:30, Oct. 31, 1942
Newsweek, 20:86, Nov. 2, 1942
Theatre Arts, 26:740-1, Dec., 1942
Time, 40:57, Nov. 2, 1942

JOHN VAN DRUTEN AND REBECCA WEST

"Return of the Soldier" (adapted from story of R. West), 1918

    English Review, 47:114, July, 1928
    London Mercury, 18:421-2, Aug., 1928
    Outlook, (Lond), 61:792, June 23, 1928
    Saturday Review, 145:801, June 23, 1928
    Spectator, 141:47, July 14, 1928

ALFRED VAN RONKEL

SEE

ANNE NICHOLS AND ALFRED VAN RONKEL

JOHN PHILIP VARLEY (PSEUD)

SEE

LANGDON ELWYN MITCHELL

GORE VIDAL

"The Best Man", 1960

    America, 103:422, July 2, 1960
    Commonweal, 72:128-9, April 29, 1960
    Life, 48:55, April 25, 1960
    Nation, 190:343, April 16, 1960
    New Republic, 142:21-2, April 18, 1960
    New Yorker, 36:88, April 9, 1960
    Newsweek, 55:86, April 11, 1960
    Reporter, 22:38-9, April 28, 1960
    Saturday Review, 43:33, April 16, 1960
    Time, 75:85, April 11, 1960

"Romulus" (adaptation of Romulus the Great by Durrenmatt), 1962

    America, 106:772-3, March 10, 1962
    Christian Century, 79:233, Feb. 21, 1962
    National Review, 12:173-4, March 13, 1962

Nation, 194:106-7, Feb. 3, 1962
New Republic, 146:20, Jan. 29, 1962
New Yorker, 37:63, Jan. 20, 1962
Newsweek, 59:50, Jan. 22, 1962
Saturday Review, 45:29, Jan. 27, 1962
Theatre Arts, 46:62-3, March, 1962
Time, 79:68, Jan. 19, 1962

"Visit to a Small Planet", 1957

America, 96:629, March 2, 1957
Catholic World, 185:68, April, 1957
Christian Century, 74:918, July 31, 1957
Commonweal, 65:662-3, March 29, 1957
Life, 42:87-8, March 4, 1957
Nation, 184:174, Feb. 23, 1957
New Yorker, 32:78, Feb. 16, 1957
Newsweek, 49:95, Feb. 18, 1957
Reporter, 16:40, March 7, 1957
Reporter, 17:35-6, July 11, 1957
Saturday Review, 40:29, Feb. 23, 1957
Theatre Arts, 41:17, April, 1957
Time, 69:60, Feb. 18, 1957

EUGENE WALTER

"The Easiest Way", 1908

Moses, Montrose Jonas and Brown, John Mason, eds.,
American Theatre as Seen by Its Critics, 1752-1934,
Norton, 1934, p. 184-87

New Republic, 28:138-9, Sept. 28, 1921

"Paid in Full", 1907

Current Literature, 44:654-9, June, 1908
Harper's Weekly, 52:28, March 14, 1908

DERIC WASHBURN

"Love Nest", 1963

New Yorker, 38:70, Feb. 2, 1963
Theatre Arts, 47:65, March, 1963

KURT WEILL

<u>SEE</u>

MAXWELL ANDERSON AND KURT WEILL

REBECCA WEST

<u>SEE</u>

JOHN VAN DRUTEN AND REBECCA WEST

THORNTON WILDER

"The Bridge of San Luis Rey", 1927

> Davidson, Donald, The Spyglass; <u>Views and Reviews,</u>
> <u>1924-1930</u>, Vanderbilt Univ. Press, 1963, p. 167-69
> Fischer, W., "Thornton Wilder's 'The Bridge of San Luis
> Rey' und Prosper Merimees 'La Carosse du Saint-
> Sacrement'", <u>Anglia</u>, 60 no. 1-2:234-40, 1936

"The Ides of March", 1948

> Times, London; Literary Supplement, <u>American Writing</u>
> <u>Today; its Independence and Vigor</u>, ed. by Allan
> Angoff, New York Univ. Press, 1957, p. 402-03

"Life in the Sun", 1955

> <u>Saturday Review</u>, 38:42, Sept. 10, 1955
> <u>Spectator</u>, 195:305, Sept. 2, 1955

"The Matchmaker", 1955

> <u>America</u>, 94:363, Dec. 24, 1955
> <u>Catholic World</u>, 182:386, Feb., 1956
> <u>Colliers</u>, 137,6, March 2, 1956
> <u>Commonweal</u>, 63:379-80, Jan. 13, 1956
> <u>Holiday</u>, 19:85, May, 1956
> <u>Life</u>, 40:131-2, Jan. 23, 1956
> <u>Illustrated London News</u>, 225:370, Sept. 4, 1954
> <u>Nation</u>, 181:562-3, Dec. 24, 1955
> <u>New Republic</u>, 134:21, Jan. 2, 1956

New Yorker, 31:78-80, Dec. 17, 1955
Saturday Review, 38:26, Dec. 24, 1955
Theatre Arts, 40:14-5, Feb., 1956
Time, 66:80, Dec. 19, 1955

"The Merchant of Yonkers", 1938

Catholic World, 148:599-600, Feb., 1939
Commonweal, 29:330, Jan. 13, 1939
Nation, 148:74, Jan. 14, 1939
Newsweek, 13:32, Jan. 9, 1939
Theatre Arts, 23:173-74, March, 1939
Time, 33:25, Jan. 9, 1939

"Our Town", 1938

Ballet, Arthur H., "In Our Living and in Our Dying",
English Journal, 45:243-49, 1956
Brown, John Mason, Dramatis Personae; a Retrospective
Show, Viking, 1963, p. 79-84
Brown, John Mason, "'Our Town'; Reappraisal",
Saturday Review of Literature, 32:33-4, Aug. 6, 1949
Brown, John Mason, Two on the Aisle; Ten Years of the
American Theatre in Performance, Norton, 1938, p. 187-93
Corrigan, Robert W. "Thornton Wilder and the Tragic
Sense of Life", Educational Theatre Journal, 13:167-73,
1961
Fergusson, Francis, "Three Allegorists; Brecht, Wilder,
and Eliot", Sewanee Review, 64:544-73, 1956
Fussell, Paul, Jr., "Thornton Wilder and the German
Psyche", Nation, 186:394-5, 1958
McCarthy, Mary Therese, Sights and Spectacles, 1937-1956,
Farrar, Straus, 1956, p. 21-29
Nathan, George Jean, Theatre Book of the Year, 1943-1944,
Knopf, p. 205-06
Oppenheimer, George, ed., Passionate Playgoer,
a Personal Scrapbook, Viking, 1958, p. 541-44
Sawyer, J., "Wilder and Stein: kinship between 'Our Town'
and 'The Making of Americans'", Saturday Review of
Literature, 26:27, April 17, 1943
Scott, Winfield Townley, "'Our Town' and the Golden Veil",
Virginia Quarterly Review, 29:103-17, 1953
Wise, Jacob Hooper and others, eds., Essays for Better
Reading, Harcourt, 1940, p. 468-72

America, 101:231, April 18, 1959
Canadian Forum, 19:355-6, Feb. , 1940
Catholic World, 146:729, March, 1938
Catholic World, 189:242-3, June, 1959
Christian Century, 55:943-4, Aug. 3, 1938
Commonweal, 27:496, Feb. 25, 1938
Commonweal, 28:161, June 3, 1938
Commonweal, 39:373, Jan. 28, 1944
Commonweal, 70:128-30, May 1, 1959
Independent Woman, 17:147, May, 1938
Nation, 146:224-5, Feb. 19, 1938
Nation, 188:324, April 11, 1959
New Republic, 94:74, Feb. 23, 1938
New Yorker, 35:80, April 11, 1959
Saturday Review, 42:35, April 11, 1959
Scribners Magazine, 103:65, May, 1938
Theatre Arts, 22:172-3, March, 1938
Theatre Arts, 24:815-24, Nov. , 1940
Theatre Arts, 28:137, March, 1944
Time, 31:36-7, Feb. 14, 1938

"Plays for Bleecker Street", 1962

Simon, John, "Theatre Chronicle", Hudson Review,
15:268-70, 1962-63

Commonweal, 75:516-7, Feb. 9, 1962
Nation, 194:86-7, Jan. 27, 1962
New Republic, 146:30, Feb. 5, 1962
New Yroker, 37:64, Jan. 20, 1962
Newsweek, 59:50, Jan. 22, 1962
Reporter, 26:48, March 1, 1962
Saturday Review, 45:26, Feb. 3, 1962
Theatre Arts, 46:63, March, 1962
Time, 79:68, Jan. 19, 1962

"Pullman Car Hiawatha", 1962

New Yorker, 38:130, Dec. 15, 1962

"Skin of our Teeth", 1942

Campbell, J. and Robinson, H. M. , "Skin of Whose Teeth?
Strange Case of Mr. Wilder's New Play and 'Finnegan's
Wake'", Saturday Review of Literature 25:3-4, Dec. 19, 1942
and 26:16, Feb. 13, 1943

Corrigan, Robert W. , "Thornton Wilder and the Tragic
  Sense of Life", Educational Theatre Journal, 13:167-73, 1961
Fergusson, Francis, "Three Allegorists: Brecht, Wilder
  and Eliot", Sewanee Review, 64:544-73, 1956
McCarthy, Mary Therese, Sights and Spectacles, 1937-1956,
  Farrar, Straus, 1956, p. 53-56
Nathan, George Jean, Theatre Book of the Year, 1942-1943,
  Knopf, p. 132-36
Robinson, Henry Morton, "The Curious Case of Thornton Wilder",
  Esquire, 47:70-71, 124-26, 1957
Theatre Arts Anthology; a Record and a Prophecy, ed. by
  Rosamond Gilder and others, Theatre Arts Books, 1950,
  p. 652-55
Wilson, Edmund, Classics and Commercials; a Literary
  Chronicle of the Forties. Farrar, Straus, 1952, p. 81-86
Woollcott, Alexander, Long, Long Ago, Viking, 1943,
  p. 244-47
Woollcott, Alexander, Portable Woollcott, Viking, 1946,
  p. 693-96

America, 93:574, Sept. 10, 1955
Atlantic Monthly, 171:121, March, 1943
Catholic World, 156:473-4, Jan. , 1943
Catholic World, 166:73-4, Oct. , 1947
Catholic World, 181:62-3, Oct. , 1955
Commonweal, 37:175-6, Dec. 4, 1942
Commonweal, 37:229, Dec. 18, 1942
Commonweal, 63:13, Oct. 7, 1955
Current History, ns 3:458-9, Jan. , 1943
Independent Woman, 21:368, Dec. , 1942
Life, 13:93-4, Nov. 30, 1942
Life, 39:71-2, Aug. 29, 1955
Nation, 155:629, Dec. 5, 1942
Nation, 181:210, Sept. 3, 1955
New Republic, 107:714, Nov. 30, 1942
N.Y. Times Mag. , p. 20-1, Nov. 1, 1942
N.Y. Times Mag. , p. 26-7, Aug. 7, 1955
New Statesman and Nation, 29:335, May 26, 1945
New Yorker, 18:35, Nov. 28, 1942
New Yorker, 19:32, May 8, 1943
New Yorker, 19:34, March, 1944
New Yorker, 31:72, Aug. 27, 1955
Newsweek, 20:86-7, Nov. 30, 1942
Newsweek, 46:67, Aug. 29, 1955

Saturday Review, 38:22, Aug. 27, 1955
Spectator, (Lond), 174:474, May 25, 1945
Spectator, (Lond), 177:287, Sept. 20, 1946
Theatre Arts, 27:9-11, Jan. , 1943
Theatre Arts, 27:334, June, 1943
Theatre Arts, 30:704-5, Dec. , 1946
Theatre Arts, 39:66-9, Sept. , 1955
Time, 40:57, Nov. 30, 1942
Time, 66:32, Aug. 29, 1955

ALAN WILLIAMS

SEE

ALAN WILLIAMS AND HATCHER HUGHES

MARGARET WILLIAMS AND HUGH WILLIAMS

"The Grass is Greener", 1958

Saturday Review, 42:25, July 4, 1959
Spectator, 201:853, Dec. 12, 1958

"Irregular Verb To Love", 1963

America, 109:396, Oct. 5, 1963
Hudson Review, 16:582, Winter 1963-64
New Yorker, 39:94, Sept. 28, 1963
Newsweek, 62:60, Sept. 30, 1963
Theatre Arts, 47:10-11, Dec. , 1963
Time, 82:66, Sept. 27, 1963

"Plaintiff in a Pretty Hat", 1956

Illustrated London News, 229:720, Oct. 27, 1956
Theatre Arts, 41:31, May, 1957

JESSE LYNCH WILLIAMS

"And So They Were Married", 1914

Nation, 99:755, Dec. 24, 1914
New Republic, 1:28, Dec. 5, 1914

"Why Marry?", 1917

>   Hamilton, Clayton Meeker, Seen on the Stage, Holt, 1920,
>   p. 63-69

TENNESSEE WILLIAMS

"Baby Doll", 1956

>   Brooks, Charles, "The comic Tennessee Williams",
>   Quarterly Journal of Speech, 44:275-81, 1958
>   Dusenbury, Winifred Loesch, " 'Baby Doll' and 'The Ponder
>   Heart' ", Modern Drama, 3:393-95, 1961
>   Scott, M.A., Jr., "Baby doll furor", Christian Century,
>   74:110-12, Jan. 23, 1957

"Camino Real", 1953

>   Bentley, Eric Russell, Dramatic Event; an American
>   Chronicle, Horizon Press, 1954, P. 105-10
>   Cole, Toby, ed., Playwrights on Playwriting; the Meaning
>   and Making of Modern Drama from Ibsen to Ionesco, Hill
>   and Wang, 1960, p. 277-81
>   Ganz, Arthur, "The desperate morality of the plays of
>   Tennessee Williams", American Scholar, 31:278-94, 1962
>   Hawkins, W., " 'Camino real' reaches the printed page",
>   Theatre Arts, 37:26-7, October, 1953
>   Hewes, H., "Tennessee Williams, last of our solid gold
>   Bohemians; analysis of 'Camino Real' ", Saturday Review,
>   36:25-7, March 28, 1953
>   Nathan, George Jean, Theatre in the 50's, Knopf, 1953,
>   p. 109-12
>   Tynan, Kenneth, Curtains; Selections from the Drama
>   Criticism and Related Writings, Atheneum, 1961,
>   p. 173-76
>
>   America, 89:25, April 4, 1953
>   America, 89:59, April 11, 1953
>   America, 103:422-4, July 2, 1960
>   Catholic World, 177:148, May, 1953
>   Commonweal, 58:51-2, April 17, 1953
>   English, (Oxford)11:186, 1957
>   Illustrated London News, 230:702, April 27, 1957

Look, 17:17, May 5, 1953
Nation, 176:293-4, April 4, 1953
New Republic, 128:30-1, March 30, 1953
New Yorker, 29:69, March 28, 1953
New Yorker, 36: 92, May 28, 1960
Newsweek,41:63, March 30, 1953
Saturday Review, 36:28-30, April 18, 1953
Spectator, (Lond) 198:488, April 12, 1957
Theatre Arts, 37:88, June, 1953
Time, 61:46, March 30, 1953

"Cat on a Hot Tin Roof", 1955

Brooks, Charles, "The comic Tennessee Williams",
  Quarterly Journal of Speech, 44:275-81, 1958
Dukore, Bernard F. , "The cat has nine lives", Tulane
  Drama Review, 8, i:95-100, 1963
Ganz, Arthur, "The desperate morality of the plays of
  Tennessee Williams," American Scholar, 31:278-94, 1962
Theatre Annual, 1956; a publication of Information and
  Research in the Arts and History of the Theatre, ed. by
  Blanche A. Corin and others, Theatre Library Assn. ,
  1956, p. 46-50
Tynan, Kenneth, Curtains; Selections from the Drama
  Criticism and Related Writings, Atheneum, 1961,
  p. 202-04

Catholic World, 181:147-8, May, 1955
Colliers, 137:6, March 2, 1956
Commonweal, 62:230-1, June 3, 1955
Hudson Review, 8:633-5, and 268-72, 1956
Kenyon Review, 18:125-6, 1956
Life, 38:137-8, April 18, 1955
Nation, 180:314, April 9, 1955
New Republic, 132:38, April 11, 1955
New Yorker, 31:68, April 11, 1955
Newsweek, 45:54, April 4, 1955
Saturday Review, 38:32-3, April 9, 1955
Saturday Review, 38:26, April 30, 1955
Spectator, (Lond) 200:174, Feb. 7, 1958
Theatre Arts, 39:18-19, 22-3, June, 1955
Time, 65:98, April 4, 1955

"Garden District", 1958

> Tynan, Kenneth, Curtains; Selections from the Drama
> Criticism and Related Writings, Atheneum, 1961,
> p. 278-80
>
> Catholic World, 186:469-70, March, 1958
> Christian Century, 75:136, Jan. 29, 1958
> Commonweal, 68:232-3, May 30, 1958
> Nation, 186:86-7, Jan. 25, 1958
> New Republic, 138:20, Jan. 27, 1958
> New Yorker, 33:66, Jan. 18, 1958
> Newsweek, 51:84, Jan. 20, 1958
> Reporter, 18:42-3, Feb. 6, 1958
> Saturday Review, 41:26, Jan. 25, 1958
> Spectator, (Lond), 201:401, Sept. 26, 1958
> Theatre Arts, 42:13, March, 1958
> Time, 71:42, Jan. 20, 1958
> Twentieth Century, 164:461-3, Nov., 1958

"Glass Menagerie", 1944

> —Beaurline, L. A.," 'Glass Menagerie': from story to play",
> Modern Drama, 8:142-9, Sept., 1965
> — Bluefarb, Sam," 'The glass menagerie'; three visions of
> time", College English, 24:513-18, 1963
> Brown, John Mason, Seeing Things, McGraw, 1946,
> p. 224-30
> —Ganz, Arthur, "The desperate morality of the plays of
> Tennessee Williams", American Scholar, 31:278-294, 1962
> Nathan, George Jean, Theatre Book of the Year, 1944-1945,
> Knopf, p. 324-27
> Oppenheimer, George, ed., Passionate Playgoer, a
> Personal Scrapbook, Viking, 1958, p. 588-91
> — Stein, Roger B., "'The glass menagerie' revisited;
> catastrophe without violence", Western Humanities
> Review, 18:141-53, 1964
> Theatre Arts Anthology; a Record and a Prophecy, ed., by
> Rosamond Gilder and others, Theatre Arts Books, 1950,
> p. 657-61
> Young, Stark, Immortal Shadows; a Book of Dramatic
> Criticism, Scribner, 1948, p. 249-53
>
> America, 112:888, June 19, 1965
> Catholic World, 161:166-7, May, 1945

Catholic World, 161:263-4, June, 1945
Catholic World, 184:307, Jan., 1957
Christian Science Monitor Mag., p. 8, April 15, 1950
Commonweal, 42:16-17, April 20, 1945
Commonweal, 82:356-7, June 4, 1965
Illustrated London News, 213:250, Aug. 28, 1948
Life, 18:81-3, April 30, 1945
Life, 18:12-14, June 11, 1945
Life, 58:16, May 28, 1965
Nation, 160:424, April 14, 1945
Nation, 199:60, Aug. 10, 1964
New Republic, 112:505, April 16, 1945
New Statesman and Nation, 36:113, Aug. 7, 1948
New York Times Mag., p. 28-9, March 4, 1945
New Yorker, 21:40, April 7, 1945
New Yorker, 41:158, May 15, 1965
Newsweek, 25:86, April 9, 1945
Newsweek, 65:92, May 17, 1965
Saturday Review of Literature, 28:34-6, April 14, 1945
Saturday Review, 39:29, Dec. 8, 1956
Spectator, (Lond) 181:173, Aug. 6, 1948
Spectator, (Lond) 200:389, March 28, 1958
Theatre Arts, 29:263, May, 1945
Theatre Arts, 29:325-7, June, 1945
Theatre Arts, 29:554, Oct. 1945
Theatre Arts, 31:38-9, Aug. 1947
Theatre Arts, 41:24, Feb. 1957
Time, 45:86, April 9, 1945
Time, 85:64, May 14, 1965

"The Milktrain Doesn't Stop Here Any More", 1963

America, 108:449, March 30, 1963
Commonweal, 77:515-17, Feb. 8, 1963
Educational Theatre Journal, 15:186-7, 1963
Hudson Review, 16:87-9, 1963
Nation, 196:106, Feb. 2, 1963
National Review, 14:29, April 9, 1963
New Republic, 148:27, Feb. 2, 1963
New Yorker, 38:72, Jan. 26, 1963
Newsweek, 61:79, Jan. 28, 1963
Newsweek, 63:70, Jan. 12, 1964
Reporter, 28:48, April 25, 1963
Saturday Review, 46:20-1, Feb. 2, 1963

Saturday Review, 47:22, Jan. 18, 1964
Theatre Arts, 47:66, Feb. , 1963
Time, 80:40, July 20, 1962
Time, 81:53, Jan. 25, 1963
Time, 83:52, Jan. 10, 1964

"The Night of the Iguana", 1961

Kerr, Walter, The Theatre in Spite of Itself, Simon and
Schuster, 1963, p. 247-55

America, 106:604, Feb. 3, 1962
Catholic World, 194:380-1, March, 1962
Christian Century, 79:169, Feb. 7, 1962
Commonweal, 75:460, Jan. 26, 1962
Educational Theatre Journal, 14:69, 1962
Hudson Review, 15:120-21, 1962
Life, 52:67, April 13, 1962
Nation, 194:86, Jan. 27, 1962
New Republic, 146:20, Jan. 22, 1962
New Yorker, 37:61, Jan. 13, 1962
Newsweek, 59:44, Jan. 8, 1962
Reporter, 26:45, Feb. 1, 1962
Saturday Review, 45:36, Jan. 20, 1962 and 42:30, Aug. 1,
1959
Theatre Arts, 46:57, March, 1962
Time, 79:53, Jan. 5, 1962

"Orpheus Descending", 1957

Gassner, John, Theatre at the Crossroads; Plays and
Playwrights of the Mid-century American Stage, Holt,
1960, p. 223-26

America, 97:148-50, April 27, 1957
Catholic World, 185:226-7, June, 1957
Catholic World, 189:192-3, June, 1959
Christian Century, 74:455, April 10, 1957
Commonweal, 66:94-7, April 26, 1957
Harper, 214:76-7, May, 1957
Illustrated London News, 234:942, May 30, 1959
Nation, 184:301-2, April 6, 1957
New Republic, 136:21, April 8, 1957
New Statesman, 57:721-2, May 23, 1959
New Yorker, 33:84, March 30, 1957

Newsweek, 49:81, April 1, 1957
Reporter, 16:43, April 18, 1957
Saturday Review, 40:26, March 30, 1957
Spectator, (Lond) 202:725-6, May 22, 1959
Theatre Arts, 41:20, May, 1957
Theatre Arts, 42:25-6, Sept., 1958
Time, 69:61, April 1, 1957

"Period of Adjustment", 1960

Ganz, Arthur, "The desperate morality of the plays of
Tennessee Williams", American Scholar, 31:278-94, 1962

America, 104:410-11, Dec. 17, 1960
Catholic World, 192:255-6, Jan., 1961
Christian Century, 77:1536, Dec. 28, 1960
Commonweal, 74:255, June 2, 1961
Educational Theatre Journal, 13:51-3, March, 1961
Horizon, 3:102-3, March, 1961
Hudson Review, 14:83-5, 1961
Nation, 191:443-4, Dec. 3, 1960
Nation, 195:59, Aug. 11, 1962
New Republic, 143:38-9, Nov. 28, 1960
New Yorker, 36:93, Nov. 19, 1960
Newsweek, 56:79, Nov. 21, 1960
Reporter, 23:35, Dec. 22, 1960
Saturday Review, 43:28, Nov. 26, 1960
Spectator, (Lond) 208:823, June 22, 1962
Theatre Arts, 45:57-8, Jan., 1961
Time, 73:54, Jan. 12., 1959
Time, 76:75, Nov. 21, 1960

"Portrait of a Madonna", 1957

Theatre Arts, 43:9, June, 1959

"The Rose Tattoo", 1951

Brooks, Charles, "The comic Tennessee Williams",
Quarterly Journal of Speech, 44:275-81, 1958
Brown, John Mason, As They Appear, McGraw, 1952,
p. 161-66
Ganz, Arthur, "The desperate morality of the plays of
Tennessee Williams", American Scholar, 31:278-94, 1962
Nathan, George Jean, Theatre Book of the Year, 1950-51,
Knopf, p. 209-12

Catholic World, 172:467-8, March, 1951
Commonweal, 53:492-4, Feb. 23, 1951
English, (Oxford) 12:184, 1959
Illustrated London News, 234:180, Jan. 31, 1959
Life, 30:80, Feb. 26, 1951
Nation, 172:161, Feb. 17, 1951
New Republic, 124:22, Feb. 19, 1951
New Yorker, 26:58, Feb. 10, 1951
Newsweek, 37:72, Feb. 12, 1951
Partisan Review, 18:333-4, May, 1951
Saturday Review of Literature, 34:22-4, March 10, 1951
School and Society, 73:181-3, March 24, 1951
Spectator, (Lond) 202:103, Jan. 23, 1959
Theatre Arts, 35:16, April, 1951
Time, 57:53-4, Feb. 12, 1951

"Something Unspoken", 1953

Gassner, John, Theatre at the Crossroads; Plays and
Playwrights of the Mid-century American Stage, Holt,
1960, p. 226-28

"Streetcar Named Desire", 1947

Brown, John Mason, Dramatis Personae; a Retrospective
Show, Viking, 1963, p. 89-94
Brown, John Mason, Seeing More Things, McGraw, 1948,
p. 266-72
Cole, Toby and Chinoy, Helen Krich, eds., Directing the
Play; a Sourcebook of Stagecraft, Bobbs, 1953, p. 296-310
Cole, Toby and Chinoy, Helen Krich, eds., Directors and
Directing; a Source Book of the Modern Theatre, Bobbs,
1963, p. 364-79
Funatsu, Tatsumi, "Blanche's loneliness in 'A streetcar
named Desire'", Kyusha American Literature, (Fukuoka,
Japan) 5:36-41
Ganz, Arthur, "The desperate morality of the plays of
Tennessee Williams", American Scholar, 31:278-94, 1962
Gassner, John, Theatre in our Time; a Survey of the Men,
Materials and Movements in the Modern Theatre, Crown,
1954, p. 355-63
Hurrell, John D., Two Modern American Tragedies;
Reviews and Criticisms of "Death of a Salesman" and
"A Streetcar Named Desire", Scribner, 1961, p. 89-130

Lewis, Allan, The Contemporary Theatre; the Significant
Playwrights of Our Time, Crown, 1962, p. 282-303
McCarthy, Mary Therese, Sights and Spectacles, 1937-1956,
Farrar, Straus, 1956, p. 131-35
Nathan, George Jean, Theatre Book of the Year, 1947-1948,
Knopf, p. 163-66
Oppenheimer, George, ed. , Passionate Playgoer, A
Personal Scrapbook, Viking, 1958, p. 342-56

Riddel, Joseph, " 'A streetcar named Desire' - Nietzsche
descending", Modern Drama, 5:421-30, 1963
Theatre Annual, 1950; a Publication of Information and
Research in the Arts and History of the Theatre, ed. by
William Van Lennep and others, The Theatre Library
Assn. , 1950, p. 25-33

Atlantic Monthly, 186:94-5, July, 1950
Catholic World, 166:358, Jan. , 1948
Catholic World, 183:67, April, 1956
Commonweal, 47:254, Dec. 19, 1947
Esquire, 29:46, 1948
Forum, 109:86-8, Feb. , 1948
France Illustrated Supplement, 5:545, Nov. 12, 1949
Illustrated London News, 215:712, Nov. 5, 1949
Life, 23:101-2, Dec. 15, 1947
Life, 27:66, Dec. 19, 1949
Nation, 165:686, Dec. 20, 1947
New Republic, 117:34-5, Dec. 22, 1947
New Statesman and Nation, 38:451, Oct. 22, 1949
New Statesman and Nation, 38:723, Dec. 17, 1949
N. Y. Times Mag. , p. 14, Nov. 23, 1947
New Yorker, 23:50, Dec. 13, 1947
New Yorker, 32:90, Feb. 25, 1956
Newsweek, 30:82-3, Dec. 15, 1947
Saturday Review of Literature, 30:22-4, Dec. 27, 1947
Saturday Review, 39:22, March 3, 1956
School and Society, 67:241-3, March 27, 1948
Spectator, (Lond) 183:533, Oct. 21, 1949
Theatre Arts, 32:10-1, Jan. , 1948
Theatre Arts, 32:35, Feb. , 1948
Theatre Arts, 32:30, April, 1948
Theatre Arts, 32:21, Oct. , 1948
Theatre Arts, 33:44, June, 1949
Theatre Arts, 33:14, Nov. , 1949

Theatre Arts, 40:24, April, 1956
Time, 50:85, Dec. 15, 1947
Time, 54:54, Oct. 31, 1949
Time, 67:61, Feb. 27, 1956

"Suddenly Last Summer", 1958

Ganz, Arthur, "The desperate morality of the plays of
Tennessee Williams", American Scholar, 31:278-94, 1962
Gassner, John, Theatre at the Crossroads; Plays and
Playwrights of the Mid-century American Stage, Holt,
1960, p. 226-28
Hurt, James R. , " 'Suddenly last summer'; Williams and
Melville", Modern Drama, 3:396-400, 1961
Johnson, Mary Lynn, "Williams' 'Suddenly last summer',
scene one", Explicator, 21:item 66, 1963
Oppenheimer, George, ed. , Passionate Playgoer, a
Personal Scrapbook, Viking, 1958, p. 250-54

"Summer and Smoke", 1948

Gassner, John, Theatre at the Crossroads; Plays and
Playwrights of the Mid-century American Stage, Holt,
1960, p. 218-23
Nathan, George Jean, Theatre Book of the Year, 1948-1949,
Knopf, p. 114-21

Catholic World, 168:161, Nov. , 1948
Catholic World, 176:148-9, Nov. , 1952
Commonweal, 49:68-9, Oct. 29, 1948
Forum, 110:352-3, Dec. , 1948
Nation, 167:473-4, Oct. 23, 1948
New Republic, 119:25-6, Oct. 25, 1948
New Republic, 119:27-8, Nov. 15, 1948
N.Y. Times Mag. , p. 66-7, Sept. 26, 1948
New Yorker, 24:51, Oct. 16, 1948
Newsweek, 32:88, Oct. 18, 1948
Saturday Review of Literature, 31:31-3, Oct. 30, 1948
Saturday Review, 35:28, May 10, 1952
School and Society, 68:303-4, Oct. 30, 1948
Spectator, (Lond) 187:772, Dec. 7, 1951
Theatre Arts, 31:11, Sept. , 1947
Theatre Arts, 33:10-11, Jan. , 1949
Time, 52:82-3, Oct. 18, 1948

"Sweet Bird of Youth", 1959

> Gassner, John, Theatre at the Crossroads; Plays and
>   Playwrights of the Mid-Century American Stage, Holt,
>   1960, p. 228-31
> Kerr, Walter, The Theatre in Spite of Itself, Simon and
>   Schuster, 1963, p. 247-55
> Roulet, William M. , " 'Sweet bird of youth': Williams' re-
>   demptive epic", Cithara, 3:31-36, 1964
> Tynan, Kenneth, Curtains; Selections from the Drama
>   Criticism and Related Writings, Atheneum, 1961,
>   p. 306-09
>
> America, 101:55-6, April 4, 1959
> Catholic World, 189:158-9, May, 1959
> Catholic World, 189:191-4, June, 1959
> Christian Century, 76:726, June 17, 1959 and 76:854,
>   July 22, 1959
> Hudson Review, 12:255-60, 1959
> Life, 46:71-3, April 20, 1959
> Nation, 188:281-3, March 28, 1959
> New Republic, 140:21-2, April 20, 1959
> New Yorker, 35:98-100, March 21, 1959
> Newsweek, 53:75, March 23, 1959
> Reporter, 20:34, April 16, 1959
> Saturday Review, 42:26, March 28, 1959
> Saturday Review, 42:29, April 18, 1959
> Theatre Arts, 40:66-7, August, 1956
> Theatre Arts, 43:21-2, May, 1959
> Time, 73:58, March 23, 1959

"Twenty-seven Wagons Full of Cotton", 1956

> America, 93:193, May 14, 1955
> Catholic World, 181:227, June, 1955
> Commonweal, 62:255, June 10, 1955
> New Republic, 132:22, May 2, 1955
> New Yorker, 31:69-71, April 30, 1955
> Saturday Review, 38:26, May 14, 1955
> Theatre Arts, 39:17, 23, July, 1955
> Time, 65:78, May 2, 1955

TENNESSEE WILLIAMS AND DONALD WINDHAM

"You Touched Me", 1945

> Catholic World, 162:166, Nov., 1945
> Commonweal, 42:623, Oct. 12, 1945
> Free World, 10:87-8, Nov., 1945
> Nation, 161:349, Oct. 6, 1945
> New Republic, 113:469, Oct. 8, 1945
> N.Y. Times Mag., p. 28-9, Sept. 23, 1945
> New Yorker, 21:48, Oct. 6, 1945
> Theatre Arts, 29:618-21, Nov., 1945
> Theatre Arts, 29:680, Dec., 1945
> Time, 46:77, Oct. 8, 1945

WILLIAM CARLOS WILLIAMS

"Many Loves", 1959

> Nation, 188:125, Feb. 7, 1959
> New Yorker, 34:74, Jan. 24, 1959
> Saturday Review, 42:24, Jan. 31, 1959

CALDER WILLINGHAM

"End as a Man", 1953

> Bentley, Eric Russell, Dramatic Event; an American Chronicle, Horizon Press, 1954, p. 171-75

> America, 90:158, Nov. 7, 1953
> Catholic World, 178:147, Nov., 1953
> Commonweal, 59:119, Nov. 6, 1953
> Nation, 177:277-8, Oct. 3, 1953
> New Republic, 130:20-1, Jan. 4, 1954
> New Yorker, 29:68, Oct. 24, 1953
> Newsweek, 42:92, Oct. 26, 1953
> Newsweek, 42:60, Dec. 21, 1953
> Saturday Review, 36:42, Oct. 3, 1953
> Saturday Review, 36:47, Dec. 12, 1953
> Theatre Arts, 37:21, Nov., 1953
> Time, 62:47, Sept. 28, 1953

HARRY LEON WILSON

SEE

BOOTH TARKINGTON AND HARRY LEON WILSON

DONALD WINDHAM

SEE

TENNESSEE WILLIAMS AND DONALD WINDHAM

JOHN P. WINTERGREEN (PSEUD)

SEE

MORRIS RYSKIND

VICTOR WOLFSON

"American Gothic", 1953

Bentley, Eric Russell, Dramatic Event; an American Chronicle, Horizon Press, 1954, p. 163-66

America, 90:251, Nov. 28, 1953
Catholic World, 178:309, Jan., 1954
New Republic, 129:21, Nov. 30, 1953
New Yorker, 29:85-6, Nov. 21, 1953
Saturday Review, 36:30, Nov. 28, 1953

"Pride's Crossing", 1950

Christian Science Monitor Mag., p. 10, Nov. 25, 1950
Commonweal, 53:231, Dec. 8, 1950
New Yorker, 26:83, Dec. 2, 1950
Theatre Arts, 35:17, Jan., 1951
Time, 56:65, Dec. 4, 1950

SAMUEL WOODWORTH

"The Cannibals; or Massacre Island", 1833

 Coad, Oral Sumner, "The Plays of Samuel Woodworth",
 Sewanee Review, 27:163-75, 1919

"The Deed of Gift", 1822

 Coad, Oral Sumner, "The Plays of Samuel Woodworth,
 Sewanee Review, 27:163-75, 1919

"The Forest Rose; or American Farmers", 1825

 Coad, Oral Sumner, "The Plays of Samuel Woodworth",
 Sewanee Review, 27:163-75, 1919

"LaFayette; or The Castle of Olmutz", 1824

 Coad, Oral Sumner, "The Plays of Samuel Woodworth",
 Sewanee Review, 27:163-75, 1919

"The Widow's Son; or Which is the Traitor?", 1825

 Coad, Oral Sumner, "The Plays of Samuel Woodworth",
 Sewanee Review, 27:163-75, 1919

ALEXANDER WOOLLCOTT

SEE

GEORGE S. KAUFMAN AND ALEXANDER WOOLLCOTT

HERMAN WOUK

"The Caine Mutiny Court Martial", 1953

 Bentley, Eric Russell, Dramatic Event; an American
 Chronicle, Horizon Press, 1954, p. 191-94
 McClean, L., "Incredible Voyage of the 'Caine' ", Vogue,
 121:194-5, Feb. 1, 1953
 Tynan, Kenneth, Curtains; Selections from the Drama
 Criticism and Related Writings, Atheneum, 1961,
 p. 272-74

 America, 90:516, Feb. 13, 1954
 Catholic World, 178:466, March, 1954

Colliers, 132:50-3, Nov. 13, 1953
Commonweal, 59:523, Feb. 26, 1954
Illustrated London News, 228:836, June 30, 1956
Life, 35:75-6, Dec. 14, 1953
Nation, 178:138, Feb. 13, 1954
Nation, 178:260-1, March 27, 1954
New Republic, 130:21, Feb. 15, 1954
N. Y. Times Mag., p. 12-13, March 21, 1954
N. Y. Times Mag., p. 6, April 4, 1954
New Yorker, 29:66, Jan. 30, 1954
Newsweek, 43:73, Feb. 1, 1954
Saturday Review, 37:24, Feb. 6, 1954
Theatre Arts, 39:58-61, Jan., 1955
Theatre Arts, 38:18-19, April, 1954
Time, 63:36, Feb. 1, 1954

"Nature's Way", 1957

Christian Century, 74:1384, Nov. 20, 1957
Nation, 185:310, Nov. 2, 1957
New Yorker, 33:96-8, Oct. 26, 1957
Theatre Arts, 41:25-6, Dec., 1957
Time, 70:92, Oct. 28, 1957

"The Traitor", 1949

Nathan, George Jean, Theatre Book of the Year, 1948-1949, Knopf, p. 336-39

Catholic World, 169:145, May, 1949
Commonweal, 50:45-6, April 22, 1949
New Republic, 120:30, April 18, 1949
New Yorker, 25:55, April 9, 1949
Newsweek, 33:79, April 11, 1949
Saturday Review of Literature, 32:34-6, May 21, 1949
School and Society, 69:339, May 7, 1949
Theatre Arts, 33:13, June, 1949
Time, 53:87, April 11, 1949

RICHARD WRIGHT AND PAUL GREEN

"Native Son", 1940

Nathan, George Jean, Theatre Book of the Year, 1942-1943, Knopf, p. 113-15

Catholic World, 153:217, May, 1941
Commonweal, 33:622, April 11, 1941
Independent Woman, 21:378, Dec., 1942
Life, 10:94-6, April 7, 1941
Nation, 152:417, April 5, 1941
New Republic, 104:468-9, April 7, 1941
Theatre Arts, 25:329-32, May, 1941
Theatre Arts, 25:467-70, June, 1941
Theatre Arts, 26:744, Dec., 1942
Time, 37:76, April 7, 1941

LOREES YERBY

"The Last Minstrel", 1963

New Yorker, 39:82, May 18, 1963
Theatre Arts, 47:12, July, 1963

"Save Me A Place At Forest Lawn", 1963

Kostelanetz, Richard, ed., The New American Arts,
N.Y., Horizon Press, 1965, p. 72

America, 108:892, June 22, 1963
Theatre Arts, 47:12, July, 1963

STANLEY PRESTON YOUNG

"Ask My Friend Sandy", 1943

Nathan, George Jean, Theatre Book of the Year, 1942-1943,
Knopf, p. 236-37

Commonweal, 37:444, Feb. 19, 1943
Theatre Arts, 27:211, April, 1943

"Bright Rebel", 1938

Commonweal, 29:330, Jan. 13, 1939
Newsweek, 13:32, Jan. 9, 1939

"Mr. Pickwick" (dramatization of <u>Pickwick Papers</u> by Charles Dickens), 1952

> Bentley, Eric Russell, <u>Dramatic Event; an American Chronicle</u>, Horizon Press, 1954, p. 38-41
> Nathan, George Jean, <u>Theatre in the Fifties</u>, Knopf, 1953, p. 89-91
>
> <u>Catholic World,</u> 176:146-7, Nov., 1952
> <u>Commonweal,</u> 57:13-14, Oct. 10, 1952
> <u>New Republic,</u> 127:30-1, Oct. 6, 1952
> <u>New Yorker,</u> 28:64, Sept. 27, 1952
> <u>Newsweek,</u> 40:88, Sept. 29, 1952
> <u>Saturday Review,</u> 35:32-3, Sept. 20, 1952
> <u>Theatre Arts,</u> 36:14-15, Sept., 1952
> <u>Time,</u> 60:72, Sept. 29, 1952

"Robin Landing", 1937

> <u>Time,</u> 30:36, Nov. 29, 1937

"List of Books Indexed
<u>American Drama Criticism</u>,(c. 1967) (this book)

See:

Suppl. I (c, 1970), pp. 91-95
Palmer, Helen H., comp.
    American Drama Criticism,
Suppl. I. Shoe String Press,
c. 1970,

Ref.
Z
5781
P2
Suppl.
V. I
pp. 91-95

"List of Books Indexed, American Drama Criticism, 1967", See: pp. 9-15 of Suppl. I

230

INDEX